Kurt,

I hope this will inspire you to ... notes so you someday will share your story with your children and ... extended family ... you are well on your way to sculpting a life worth recording

Ralph

Running Scared

RALPH R. DiSIBIO

THE PALADIN GROUP LLC
Aiken, South Carolina USA

Published by The Paladin Group LLC
123 Summer Squall Lane
Aiken, South Carolina 29803
email: publishpaladin@aol.com

Cover design and layout by Stephen Muller

Printed in the United States of America

ISBN 0-9779273-2-6

061205

This book is dedicated
to my grandchildren

Anthony • Kayla • Andrew • Mary Frances

Remember who you are,

where you're from and

what you represent.

Table of Contents

Foreword

IN APRIL OF 2004, I RETIRED as the President of Washington Group International's Energy and Environment business unit. I chose to retire even though I was in good health and enjoying my most productive and successful career years. The reasons for and structure of that retirement were essentially known only to me; of course, the rationale I presented to the public had a somewhat different tenor. I explained that I had wanted to "pull the plug" at the top of my game, but the business unit profit forecast for 2005 and beyond exceeded even the success of 2004, so that was not totally forthcoming. I also allowed as to how the chances for a normal life expectancy were problematic due to a dismal family heart history and my own sextuple bypass in 1999; but, in truth, my own health was excellent when I left full-time work.

While I had no pension awaiting me because I had changed career paths and positions as often as opportunities presented themselves, I had succeeded, along with my wife's contributions, to have enough in IRA's and savings to live fairly comfortably. Of course, to do so I would have to supplement those savings with consulting and board positions. One or two additional years of productive service, and I could more fully have been able to rest assured of financial security, even if I lived beyond my self-predicted early demise. So why did I call it a career? Well—FEAR.

Things aren't always as they seem. I am sure most people who have known or observed me over the years have described me variously as confident, ambitious, tough or cocky, but never as fearful or scared. I am reminded of the insight offered by the tale of the lion and the gazelle. Each and every day is the same for both, and from the moment they awake, they both begin to run with focus and determination. The lion runs because he is the beast who must chase and kill enough food to continue to exist, while the gazelle runs to ensure that the ultimate failure—of being dinner for the lion—is avoided. Despite the strength of the lion and the speed of the gazelle, they are equally fragile beings, each in search of success. Success for both is defined as survival. Failure for either is defined as death. They both live in fear of failure.

Like the lion and the gazelle, fear has been my main driving force. I finally came to the realization that if I retired, I would no longer have to fight the fear of impending failure. In my career, failure was always just around the corner, and the fear of failure was omnipresent. I had always looked at life as challenge, as a contest, perhaps not one with life and death consequences, but all serious business to me nonetheless. I hasten to add that I have also had more than my share of laughter and joy.

My favorite comedian, Mel Brooks, looked at the lion differently. In his character as the 2000-year-old man, Brooks was asked what the mode of transportation in cave man days was. His response was, "It was fear. You would hear a lion roar, and you would run a mile in a minute." Fear is serious but often funny as well. In declaring retirement, I had managed for many reasons, and with the contributions of many, to be in a position to be declared the winner in this life battle. In retirement, I could be certain that whatever happened, from that point forward, I could always focus on the success I had achieved, and I would never have to fear failure again. It is hard to fail at retirement.

Of course, it is no great leap to conclude that I was also interested in having others perceive me as successful. I have been impelled by that desire since I was growing up in Camden, New Jersey. I wanted to be liked, respected and perceived as a success. Perhaps more than anything, I wanted to avoid, at all costs, having people feel sorry for me. My early life was profoundly driven by my need to avoid invoking sympathy. Those factors, fear of failure and the aversion to sympathy, were great drivers for me throughout my entire personal and professional life.

My traditional "career" is now over. In retirement, I managed to contract with my corporation under a consulting agreement that has supplemented my "income." I get paid for my opinions and the advice I give, which is based on my forty-plus years of leadership experience. There are no profit and loss responsibilities, no work force to lead and be responsible for, no contract to win, essentially no tangible work product and, most importantly, no real possibility of failure. Avoidance of failure has become a truism: I can no longer fail—unless, of course, I run out of opinions and advice, which seems unlikely. In fact, those who know me best will certainly have no fear of that happenstance. I have often said, only half in jest, that I may often be wrong, but I am never in doubt. With that as my watchword, I have continued this fearless consulting endeavor now for more than two years since formal retirement.

I have further supplemented my mental challenges and my income by serving on a couple of corporate boards as a director. One is PaR Systems, a private company located in Minnesota that specializes in robotic materials handling. The other is Quanta Services, a NYSE-listed company specializing in providing services to the commercial power and telecommunications industries. These companies provide me mental stimulation and a diversion of sorts from more purely leisure activities such as golf. My directorships also allow me to travel and have thought-provoking discussions with other like-minded former executives, as well as providing me with opportunities to make some contribution to the success of the companies I serve.

My most engrossing activity since my retirement has been my ongoing consulting with Washington Group young executives. I have done this by developing and regularly presenting a leadership program based on films that lend themselves to the demonstration of leadership traits. The work has also inspired me to write a book, an effort that took almost two years. As a consequence of sales of the book, I have been invited to give additional presentations to the U.S. Navy and the Board of Directors of the International Boy Scouts, among others.

From a financial perspective and from a mental perspective, I am content in that I continue to carve out a life in retirement that is free from the fear of failure. In that regard, I have reached Nirvana. This pleasant state of affairs has given me additional time to contemplate my past. My book, "Reel Lessons in Leadership," gave me a chance to thank many of the people who have contributed to my contentment and, indeed, made the book a reality. That endeavor made me start to reflect on exactly how I got to be where I am. This work, "Running Scared," is a memoir that attempts to answer that question. It surely also answers the question I have been asked on countless occasions, "How did you go from the streets of Camden to being a teacher and then to being a corporate executive?"

"Running Scared" chronicles my life as my memory permits. It is primarily intended for my grandchildren, for they are the ones who will have the least first-hand knowledge of their heritage and the flavor and sense of the bygone era inhabited by the generations before them. The descriptions of homes and aunts and uncles are intended to allow those places and people to be envisioned and remembered. I also believe this will help my children better understand the rich tapestry of my upbringing and the ancestors whose blood pulses through my veins and theirs. My family members and friends who are recalled here may be stimulated to reflect on our experiences together as they read about my perspective on those experiences, and perhaps they will give some more thought to the people and events from their own histories that have brought them to where they are today.

Many readers will likely challenge some of my memories as inaccurate; they may be stimulated to examine their own recollections or add to my stories with tales of their own. This is a good thing. I am sure I have also left out, unintentionally, important incidents and people who, I hope, will recognize that I did the best I could to stay true to the facts, although I have taken occasional literary license to consolidate or abbreviate some events. My apologies, of course, if I've misspelled or have a name wrong.

My overall intention in all of this is to share incidents that I believe are indicative of particular phases of my life. If I have strayed into personal accomplishments, it has only been for the purpose of adding context to the descriptions. If you react emotionally to certain characters or events that appear in those descriptions, I have achieved one of my goals. If you are forced to reflect on your own life, I have achieved another. If you gain insight into what motivated and left an imprint on me, I have achieved a third. Most of all, you will know that all of you who appear in these pages have had a profound impact on me and the course of my life.

* * *

Once again, as in "Reel Lessons in Leadership," I was aided
enormously by the talents of Stephen Muller. This work
is professional in appearance because of him.
One day Steve will tell his own story and it will be
more compelling than mine, but it will not be
more professional in layout and design.

The Monarcas

Patriarch Mario and Matriarch Teresa blended warmth, courage and wisdom to produce a family to be envied.

The picture placement is apropos, in that their offspring appear to be emanating from their hearts. From left to right, the Monarca's are: Louise, Lydia, Pat, Phil, Mike, Lola, Anna, Marie, Dora.

Only Jim is missing from the beautiful group photograph.

The Monarcas

"He was small of stature,
but most of his 155 pounds was heart."

His citizenship papers could measure him and give all the statistics about dates and the certifications of authenticity, but it didn't show his grit, his heart or his dreams. Mario Monarca was small of stature, 5 feet 2 inches and 155 pounds, but most of the 155 pounds was heart.

Like the hundreds of thousands of immigrants who made their way to the welcoming arms of the grand lady in New York harbor, he had dreams, and he had a wife, Teresa, with ambitions greater than his. Somehow they made their way to Jamesville, Pennsylvania. There they literally chipped their way through the black gold of the anthracite coal fields of south central Pennsylvania. The precise reason they traveled to Jamesville has to be left to the memories of those who are no longer with us. More than likely, it was as a result of following a paisano or distant relative who would help them get started or offer the promise of a job. Finding what prompted this decision is an investigative job of great proportion that is helped by a recording of the eldest female child, Louise. Her grandson, Jesse Vitagliano, had the foresight to record some of her earliest memories, which are included in Appendix C at the back of the book.

The extended family has carried tales of Jamesville and the various adventures that each family member recalls. The remembrances are likely romanticized, but hearing them repeated over the years and handed down, as in Louisa's account, there is little doubt that it was a hard life, made bearable by a loving family that would grow with regularity. Mario and Teresa had arrived from their homeland with Louisa and Domenica, and later they blessed this land with the addition of Phillipo, Mario, Lola, Giacomo, Dora, Milena, Lydia, and Maria. It is miraculous that, at that time of the crudest of medical facilities and conditions less than sanitary, none of these Monarcas was born with congenital maladies, save for Giacomo who would have a heart condition that would claim his life at age 32. Teresa's practice of midwifery and, I am sure, the home-grown vegetables, lovingly prepared, seemed to have been worth more than the then nonexistent Dr. Spock.

By all accounts life was hard. This was early in the twentieth century, sometime in the 20's. The air was not conditioned indoors, and outdoors it was full of soot from the expectoration of the numerous coal mines giving up their black gold to the belly of the voracious industrial beast in the Northeast. It is hard to imagine the inconveniences and harshness of life without heated water, without electricity and without central heat.

A typical day, indeed every day, began at the first hint of a sun peaking over the horizon. The light signaled the rooster's call and ultimately the stirring of the clan. While Teresa began the strong espresso, in between gathering the eggs from the chickens who shared the area with the mule and the goat, Mario would be preparing for another day of hard labor in the mines. Louisa, as soon as she was four or five, would be helping care for Anna and, later, for Father Mario and taking clothes from the lines where they had hung during the night. Nighttime was best for this, because there was less belching from the mines and stirring from the animals, so the clothes had only a bit of the soot still clinging to them. Fillipo might be culling the weeds from the garden and washing up in the barrel used for gathering rainwater. A nearby stream provided water for cooking, washing the clothes and, of course, for drinking. A short walk away were the "toilet facilities," essentially a large hole in the ground, atop of which sat a crudely built shack to provide privacy and, later, seats with holes cut in for sitting down.

Days were spent in toil. Mario was all one could ask for with respect to work ethic, a trait he passed directly on to all of his offspring. One need only track the history of the family to know that the lesson was well learned. The patriarch would don his work clothes that Teresa had made or bought for him and take his meager lunch, consisting of salted meat, cheese and home-made bread. Then he would dutifully trek the well-worn paths to the mule-drawn wagons that would take him and the other, mostly Italian and Irish, immigrants into the bowels of the mine.

As soon as they cleared the entrance, the term "black as coal" became their reality. Outside, even though the sun had not fully exposed itself to extinguish the darkness, there was at least a little dawn appearing. But once past the entrance, excepting for the candles, there was no light. The men, armed with pickaxes and shovels, hacked their way through the veins of coal. The mines were so rich with coal that striking out in any direction brought the crunch of coal clattering to the floor of the mine. More of-ten than not, the men had to stoop when shoveling and always when picking up the fruits of their labor to put it into the carts that transported them. There was no OSHA, no gloves and no masks to protect them from the heavy and constant dust which caused black lung disease as commonly as the flu. This was the same dust that spewed forth with every swing of the ax and throw of the shovel. By the time they exited the mouth of the mine, the sun was already hiding behind the darkness of the night.

With the same resoluteness, Mario would retrace his steps to his tiny hovel and prepare for a dutifully and lovingly prepared dinner of a soup or pasta with warm bread and a glass of home-made wine. The only pleasure was an Italian stogie, each puff of which would ensure that the coal dust would be more efficiently attached to his lungs. It is hard to imagine a life that, month after month, yielded only a rare glimpse of sunshine or any semblance of leisure time. Even then there were unrelenting chores required to keep life and family alive: tending to the garden patch, milking the goat for cheese and nutrients, patching the roof and the unin-sulated walls to stave off the unending heat or cold, salting and storing the little meat they were able to hoard and catching and slaughtering the occasional rabbit and the homegrown chickens. Indeed, it was a hard life.

If Mario was the brawn, Teresa was the brains of the Monar-cas. By all accounts, she was a handsome woman of robust stature. Both she and Mario were born in Canale Monterano, a small vil-lage just fifty kilometers from the capital of Italy. They married at a traditionally young age, and it has often been surmised that it was an arranged marriage. The genesis of that notion was the clear difference in interest and intellectual levels of the two young vil-lagers. She was as delicate as he was calloused from hard labor; she was a reader and writer of stories, while he may have been illiterate; she had many interests and was a storyteller and unof-ficial mentor, while he was a man of few words and unexpressed thoughts. In a tiny world of an Italian village where everyone knew everything about everyone else, they were worlds apart. Some-how this unlikely pair, Mario Monarca and Teresa Rabbi, joined to produce a family of great contributors, a unit to be envied and admired by all who have been touched by their legacy.

Teresa was not spared from the toil and hard work required for mere existence early in the 20th century. In fact, her job may have been more difficult than Mario's. It was not by happenstance that this branch of the Monarca tree was a true matriarchy. Teresa made the decisions for the household almost without exception and, therefore, in addition to the constant challenge of providing sustenance for one and all she had the additional burdens of insuring that the bills were paid to the company store, that the meager paycheck could be stretched from month to month and that the parade of children would not only be clothed and fed but also nourished mentally.

Her day often commenced before the crowing of the family rooster. She would fetch the water for the coffee and get the kids started on their chores or wash and clothe them for the day ahead. She would make sure that Mario was tended to with work clothes to wear and his lunch in his pail, before seeing him out the door before sunrise. Her day would continue with unremitting challenges. While Mario's day was of dull sameness, Teresa's day was filled with a variety of tasks; even for her, the difficulty of the work to be done was relentless.

The gathering of the various elements that would make up lunch and dinner was no small undertaking. In addition to pulling the peppers, lettuce, potatoes and carrots from the garden, she had to gather the eggs and begin the daily baking of bread. And if sugar was available and butter had been churned, she might prepare a rare dessert cake or cookie. These baked goods were to become a legacy in themselves, one that continued through several generations with each of the girls baking some of their mother's favorites for her husband. With the original recipes only in Teresa's head, some of them have been kept alive through use and love.

She would also have to mend or make clothing, since each family member had only the sparsest wardrobe with one or two items of clothing.

Teresa would occasionally make her way to the company store, a monopoly that often was used to control the workers by providing the sole source of necessities, such as flour, sugar and coffee. The prices were exorbitant, but the store would allow credit against future paychecks, thereby ensuring that, regardless of the horrible working conditions, the workforce had little recourse but to succumb to a master-slave relationship. They may not actually have been indentured servants but, indeed, they were just that, for all intents and purposes. Historians are accurate when they opine that the industrial revolution in this country was built on the backs of immigrants from Europe and China.

From the soot, the hard labor and the relentless challenges grew a clan toughened by adversity. As the family grew, first by Phillipo, followed in close order by Mario, Lola, Giacomo, Dora and Milena, Pennsylvania became a real home. In some ways, life became both more bearable, because of shared duties, and more difficult, because of the expanded needs of the family. The chores were shared, but the youngsters could not yet earn money and were still a net liability. Still, the growing "workforce" of the Monarcas did make it possible for Teresa to spend more time working as a midwife. Services of this kind were paid for by barter, or in-kind services. Helping birth babies at the turn of the century enabled Teresa to get foodstuffs or cobbler services and the like. The eight hungry mouths required ingenuity and strength to feed. As they grew older, the boys would help tend neighbors' gardens or provide a trapped rabbit for Teresa's waiting pot, thus making a contribution to the needs of the family. Life began to take on a routine, albeit a rigorous one.

Nearly a decade had passed since the hearty Monarcas had become Pennsylvanians. The mines had continued to be productive at a blazing pace, and the immigrant population grew proportionally. While Mario was a solitary man, save for his interaction with his family, Teresa got about the town due to her part-time vocation, along with her other normal duties. The oldest children had begun school, and she was finding time to share stories of the homeland, beginning to impart her wisdom through parables or stories meant to supplement their education. Her interest was as much in building character as building knowledge.

My mother, Dora Monarca, was particularly struck by a story that she remembers as a child. As she recalls it, her mother learned that one of the siblings (Lydia admits to being the offender and has recounted the story numerous times) had surreptitiously taken some small item from the shelf of a local store. Lydia's transgression was discovered by her mother when they arrived home. Of course, she admonished the child, but she also immediately marched back to the store with the offending child holding the item, prayer-like , in front of her as they entered. The child was mortified to have to perform an act of contrition publicly, admitting to all those present that she had stolen the item. Together, mother and child marched back home and gathered the clan together for Teresa's lesson.

It seems that a criminal was awaiting execution in prison for murder committed during a robbery. As the hours until his approaching death ticked by, he was allowed a last visit with his mother. When the mother was admitted, sobbing, into the presence of her soon-to-die son, she held her arms out to him for a final, lingering embrace. When the mother pulled back to kiss her son for the last time, they looked into each other's eyes. He moved forward, but instead of planting a tender kiss on her cheek, he

---

opened his mouth and brutally bit the mother's nose with such force as to draw blood. With a cry of shock the mother choked out, "Why do you do this violence to me?" With tears streaming down his face, he explained, "When I was just a small boy, I came to you with a needle I had stolen from the company store, and you took it and used it to mend clothes without a word of rebuke." He hesitated for a moment and continued, "Had you taught me the lesson of the sin of stealing, I would not be here today. I hope, when you look at that wound and scar, you will remember the scar that you inflicted on me."

This was but one small example of the wisdom of Teresa Monarca, who gathered the clan to indelibly imprint this lesson that lasted a lifetime and endured through several generations. Teresa never failed to take the opportunity to teach a lesson. She was thoughtful and deliberate in delivering her messages. While she was a stern taskmaster, she never delivered punishment without an accompanying lesson. She was intelligent beyond formal education. Lydia is forever reminding the family that her mother would often enter contests that appeared on the back of commercial goods and, in fact, won a washing machine for her efforts. She was a teller and writer of stories, but, most importantly, she was universally respected and admired by all with whom she came into contact.

The time came when the Monarcas decided to uproot the eight youngsters and join other extended family members in neighboring New Jersey. The southern part of that state was following the lead of northern New Jersey in expanding its industrial base. While New Jersey in the north was feeding off of the booming New York, the southern part of the state took advantage of the expanding Philadelphia. The rich soils of southern New Jersey provided the additional option of seeking employment in the agricultural arena. The Morroni family, kin to the Monarcas via the same Canale Monterano roots, headed farther south of Philadelphia to the rich soils of Bridgeton, where their progeny remain to this day. They carved out a living among the agricultural giants of the day, like the forerunners of Birdseye.

The Monarcas did not follow suit. No one recalls the exact date, but it was circa 1920 that Camden beckoned. Rather then an agrarian life, the Monarcas chose to seek stability by working in the Camden factories that were beginning to blossom. From Camden's western boundary at the Delaware River, a strong arm could heave a stone and hit Philadelphia on the other side. The chemical plants and shipyards were always looking for strong men such as Mario to shovel coal or tend furnaces, and Mario was a willing participant in the burgeoning industrial revolution. Today, Camden, in addition to being among the highest-rated cities in major crime, has the dubious distinction of having the highest percentage of population—44 percent—that falls below the poverty line. But in the mid-thirties, Camden held the promise of a place where the dreams of this hard-working and loving clan could be fulfilled.

They settled on 3rd Street for the first few years. The children by now were in school and/or engaged in earning additional rewards, either money or bartered goods and services, by doing odd jobs. The girls often shared the family chores and the child-caring chores just as they had in Jamesville. And all of this change did not interrupt the continuing expansion of the family. Lydia was the first to be born in New Jersey, and she was followed by the last child, Maria. Once again, life began to take on a routine.

In the early years of their Camden tenure, the Monarcas were struck by a tragedy that would test their resiliency. Mario was working in a chemical plant, likely slinging coal to stoke the plant's boiler, when a huge explosion tore the plant into pieces. Scores of workers were killed and many more severely injured. Mario was to escape with his life but required a long convalescence from the injuries he sustained before he was able to again provide for his family. He likely broke his back in the massive collapse of the building, and he would be plagued by vestiges of the injury for the rest of his life. None of the family member can ever recall him once complaining of the pain he endured. This was another lesson that the Monarcas learned well.

Mario was the consistent breadwinner, Teresa the administrator and decision-maker, and the children all had assigned tasks. As with most immigrant families, there was a hierarchical flavor to the structure of the Monarca family. Age counted for much in that hierarchy, and gender often trumped age. The boys did most of the physical work, but never in the kitchen, unless it was to fetch water or wood for the wood-burning cooking stove. Men rarely assisted with childcare, except to tote one of the young ones upstairs. The older ones were "in charge" of their younger ones and were trusted to bestow admonishments and punishment when necessary. Of course, once the boys reached puberty, they wore the mantle of superiority solely by virtue of their gender and irrespective of age. While these roles were played out throughout the lives of the siblings, it did not necessarily carry over into the respective marriages, as will later be chronicled.

The family was now complete and required more expansive, but still modest, quarters. The 3rd Street address was comfortable for many reasons. Since it was their first residence in New Jersey, they had grown accustomed to their surroundings and acquaintances. Friendships had been formed, and relationships with merchants were comfortable. The neighborhood was dominated by Italians. There were radio stations that were broadcast completely in the native tongue; there was a weekly newspaper

in Italian; the local grocery store carried familiar Italian specialties. It was a neighborhood that fit like an old shoe and offered no
additional challenges in an already hard life. Still, one more move
remained, and they struck out for a completely new and unfamiliar
locale.

There is little doubt that there existed in the Monarcas an
adventuresome spirit. The trip from Italy, with two small children
and only hope as a tether, took great courage. The life in Pennsylvania may have often had them questioning the wisdom of that
journey, but, ever undaunted, they made progress, slow though it
might have been, toward assimilating into this American culture.

Why the family moved from the comfort of the South Camden neighborhood is unclear, but move they did. The 734 Vine
Street house, in the very heart of a diversified North Camden, became the place they would call home. Each move had presented a
new challenge, which they took up with optimism and resolve, and
each had proved to be an improvement in conditions. The Vine
Street home, the last move that Mario and Teresa would make together, was the one that all of the children would associate with
their formative years. The house at 734 would see marriages and
romances; 734 would see sibling rivalries flourish and subside; 734
would be the nest that grown men and women left, to seek a fuller
life with spouses and families of their own; 734 would be the address used in the obituary of Teresa in 1941.

Mario became lost without Teresa. Eventually, he would
be invited and accept a room in Domenica's home, which was,
very much like her mother's, a matriarchal home, and Mario was
comforted by the notion that she continued to make most of the
decisions for him. The ten children were all married by then,
and most were in easy walking distance of one another, save for
Phillipo and Giacomo. In fact, Domenica's home was less than 60

yards from 734 Vine Street, practically backing up against the meager backyard of the former family residence.

The lessons and experiences of the clan would play out in different ways, as each carved out a future founded upon their family experiences. Times were changing: Phillipo became Phil, Mario became Mike, Giacomo became Jim, Louisa became Louise, Domenica became Anna, Milena became Pat, Maria became Marie, and only Lola, Dora and Lydia remained the same by name. Unions caused the Monarcas to become the Vitaglianos, the Iannettas, the DiSibios, the Jamisons, the Mathews/Cinis, and the Marianis. In succeeding chapters, more will be told of this wonderful family of individuals.

Mario and Teresa did a remarkable job by any standard. *Molto gracia.* We salute you!

2
Camden Roots

The author at the door of 523 N. 8th. Mom and Dad had the place looking like a quality neighborhood shoe repair shop. I had already decided I would have to fight my way out of North Camden.

The inset picture is the truck that reflected Dad's enterprise as he developed a delivery business.

Camden Roots

"To the present generation and those future generations who may read this, it must be difficult to imagine such a close-knit family."

T HE KENNEDY'S HAD THE COMPOUND AT HYANNIS PORT, Massachusetts; the Monarcas had North Camden and claimed it as a compound of their own. Once Mario and Teresa made the decision to leave the Italian enclave of South Camden and establish a beachhead in North Camden, at 734 Vine Street, the die had been cast. Eventually seven of the 10 offspring would purchase homes within several hundred yards of the heads of the family. The propinquity of the family was the only thing that the Monarcas had in common with the Kennedys to this day, unless, of course you count enjoying a fine bottle of wine on regular occasions.

The last couple of generations of the family have enjoyed the benefits and frustrations of living in suburbia. Little can be learned from this account by describing traffic jams on Route 70 or I-295. Still less can be learned from detailed descriptions of strip malls, major malls, multi-screen cinema complexes or housing developments with cul-de-sacs. The latest generations know little of mass transportation or, indeed, of walking to the homes of several relatives in the same afternoon without thinking twice—or calling ahead. Who among us can contemplate life without an automobile?

I hope much will be learned by today's and future Monarcas, from the description of the times and rhythms of the early generations of your ancestors. The changes experienced by the generations that broke away from urban America to populate suburbia were vastly different from the experiences of the next several generations. For the last forty years or more, little contrast has colored the lives of the extended Monarca family. There is a sameness about modern life in suburbia that does not lend itself to rich description. How much can a description of the Cherry Hill Mall differ from a description of the Valley Forge Mall built almost a generation later? But North Camden has the ability to enrich your imagination. The suburbs, Cherry Hill or Marlton or even Haddon Heights, are the Berber carpet to the handmade Persian masterpiece that is the inner city. If the suburbs are eggshell white, North Camden was a rainbow.

Camden was a city made up of several distinctive informal neighborhoods which bled into one another at the edges. South and North Camden had the Delaware River as their boundary, separating them from Philadelphia to the west. East Camden, commencing when one crossed over a tributary creek at the 10th Street Bridge, made up the largest and least amalgamated section of the city.

South Camden also had some informal boundaries which included Kaigns Avenue and Haddon Avenue to the south and Federal Street to the north. From the river eastward beginning with Front Street, succeeding streets started with 2nd Street and continued, in order, to 10th Street, followed by various street names until meeting up with East Camden around Baird Boulevard. The perpendicular streets in South Camden had a variety of names, including Line, Mechanic, Berkley and Spruce. The main commercial streets of the city were ostensibly in South Camden, with Broadway running the same direction as the numbered streets and Market running perpendicular to Broadway. Broadway ended at Linden Street, and Market ran in the same direction as Linden two blocks short of North Camden. The first Monarca home was at 3rd and Line.

The 734 Vine Street address was in the heart of North Camden. The neighborhood started on Front Street at the river and, like in the South, began with 2nd Street and continued through to 10th. The perpendicular streets began with Linden on the south and then Pearl and Birch, Elm, Vine, State and others such as Cedar, Willard, Grant and Point. The house at 734 was practically at the hub of North Camden and was literally at the hub of what would become the spokes of the Monarca wheel.

To the present generation and those future generations who may read this, it will no doubt be difficult to imagine such a close-knit family. Some years ago, a first lady wrote a book entitled "It Takes a Village." The essence of the work was that it takes more than parents to raise a child. She opines that it takes the combined efforts of everyone engaged with a child, including teachers, relatives and friends, to nurture and produce a productive and balanced adult. In the context of that message, North Camden was the Monarca Village. Within some five square blocks, there were eyes and ears in every direction observing you and listening for you, none shy about scolding or punishing one of the nephews or nieces in addition to their own.

We Monarca children would find it difficult to "get away" with any indiscretion large or small. Some of us still managed to cross the line from time to time and go unpunished. But, unlike the present day when parents are rebuked for laying hands on their own children, in the '50s, it was not unusual for one of the aunts or uncles to swat your behind and send you off crying. If your mother ever found out, she wouldn't confront the spanker, nor would she report it to child welfare; rather you were likely to get "a good beating" at the hands of your mother when you got home.

The neighborhood configuration also lent itself to ease of transport and collaboration among family and neighbors. Like many cities on the East Coast, Camden was a poor rendition of the cities in the United Kingdom. Perhaps this is why Cousin John is such an Anglophile. Camden was unlike the villages in Italy, where houses were erected along paths spreading out from the town piazza and water well. The Italian properties often had attached vacant land for a garden and always access to a larger plot shared by other family members. English cities, by contrast, were laid out more or less in squares.

Unlike the variety of creative construction styles employed by the stonemasons and woodworkers of Italy, British houses tended to have a townhouse orientation, often done in cookie-cutter fashion with identical facades. They shared walls on both sides, one house against the other, and there would be no ostensible land beyond the entry and rear exit steps. Such also was the architecture of many Eastern cities, including Camden.

A square block in one section was very similar to a square block in another, although, even in Camden, there were sections, such as those on State Street or the upper ends of Vine Street, which had upscale homes. Here, one might even see a small patch of lawn both in the front of the house and in the back yard. These were the precursors of the lavish sod of today's suburbia. Most of the houses, however, had no lawns, and the backyard might have a patch set aside for herbs or tomatoes, but little else.

Imagine a rectangular block bounded by Birch Street and Elm Street at opposite ends and 7th and 8th at the perpendicular opposites. Each of the four corners of the rectangle had a house-like structure similar to all of the others, excepting the lower front of each that would be designed for a small store or such. The rest of the houses bounded by these stores would be exact duplicates of the others, without separation, house after house after house, similar to today's townhomes, only much smaller. You can visualize it by looking at a monopoly board and setting the little green houses along the four lines making up each of the properties; this is what a "block" looked like.

The row houses in Camden were between 10 and 12 feet wide and 25 to 30 feet long, always consisting of two floors. In today's world, that would translate into 500 to 650 square feet of living space. Today a master bath could approach that size, which in that time and place often housed a family of four or more. The houses in between the storefronts often, but not always, had a front porch. Block after block of the same configuration of these red brick houses was only broken by the various colors the owners would paint the cornices, window frames and doorways of each structure. Depending on the meticulousness and wherewithal of the owner, each house was in some state of disrepair or well kept.

Behind each row (in the spaces in the middle of the monopoly model at the center of the green houses) were small patches of backyard. The yards were separated from the other yards by a narrow alley, three feet or less across. These alleys were the turnpikes of all of the youngsters as we took the shortcut to every neighborhood through the alleyways, virtual cities within a city.

In addition to their value as shortcuts, the alleyways were used for games and as hideouts for stealing away from the prying eyes of friends, foes and relatives. More often then not, they were also used, mostly by the boys, as outdoor lavatories. Maybe that is why some men still use the woods on golf courses. The alleys were one of the few places where we would be unseen by the ubiquitous spies. Here we experimented with dreaded tobacco and demon beverages of the alcoholic variety. Some of us even had a dalliance or two, the kissing and groping kind, with the opposite sex.

While South Camden was a comfortable haven for the Italian immigrants, East Camden was the comfort zone for the Anglo-Saxon descendants, often referred to as "whitebreads" or "merigans" (Americans), and the Jews around Baird Boulevard. It was North Camden that was the most eclectic, with all manner of immigrants residing there. Almost every European country was represented; in addition, there were Puerto Ricans, an occasional South American or even the rare Asian. There was no dominant ethnic culture, and since none of us could feel superior, we all tolerated one another. Strikingly missing were the African-Americans, known then as "coloreds" or Negroes.

The black population, which was about equal to the Italian population in Camden in the 1940's, settled almost exclusively in South Camden. South Camden had most of the local industry and commercial sections and afforded easy access to jobs. The sometimes self-imposed segregation did not allow for easy assimilation later when the North Camden Schools were opened to South Camden residents in the mid-50s. We macho types would defend our neighborhoods from these interlopers which, of course, further imbued us with an unwarranted prejudice.

In contrast to recent headlines that have declared Camden the murder capital of America, the Camden of the 1940s and 1950s was safer then today's suburbs. It was not unusual to leave doors unlocked around the clock, nor was it uncommon to see the keys of unlocked cars dangling from the ignition. The same eyes and ears that looked out for the youngsters of the neighborhood could also spot a stranger the minute he crossed Linden Street. And strangers were looked upon with wariness. There was a kind of a "What are you doing around these parts, mister?" attitude toward unfamiliar faces.

North Camden had no specified commercial areas. Rather, most every corner and a rare middle-of-the-block location housed some kind of store. On the corner nearest my house at 8th and Birch was a grocery store/butcher shop owned by Joe Mazzarella; across the street was a jewelry and watch repair shop owned by Leon Flamini, Sr.; one block north on our side of the street at 8th and Elm was Litwin's grocery/butcher shop; on the opposite or northeast corner 50 feet away was Miller's grocery/butcher shop; 50 feet across from the whitebread Miller's was Lou and Syl's variety/soda counter/ice cream and sundries store; and on the other remaining corner at 7th and Elm was the Luncheonette which served sandwiches and the like to the neighborhood.

My own house was the location of Tony's Shoe Repair and Dry Cleaners, owned by my dad, who was a superb cobbler. At 8th and Pearl was the Armenian candy store and sundry shop, and across the street from that was Molotsky's dry goods store, where one could buy every manner of clothing. If I walked from 8th to 7th up Birch, I found "Jew Benny," who sold candy, soda and loose cigarettes, three for a nickel. Across the street was the ubiquitous local tavern. There was even a store dedicated exclusively to selling freshly ground horseradish. All of these stores were within 50 yards of my house, and this was only one block in each direction on 8th Street. The pattern was repeated on many blocks throughout North Camden.

On "our side" of town, there were two local movie houses within blocks of everyone's house. Here you could spend an entire Saturday for the nine-cent admission fee. And I do mean an entire

Saturday. For the price of the ticket, you got to see two feature films (a double feature), four or five cartoons and at least one serial. This was a time when the word "serial" was not associated with "killer." No, these serials were just that, short films which ended with the hero about to go over the edge of an escarpment while trying bravely to halt the runaway horses of a stage coach that had a beautiful woman on board. The film would abruptly halt in mid-fall with the words "to be continued" appearing on the screen. We were a gullible bunch back then, and we couldn't stop talking about it during the week. There was always doubt as to whether or not the hero would be killed, no matter how many times we had seen him escape in previous episodes. I guess it was like children's soap operas.

There were also several movie houses "downtown" on Broadway or Market. They seemed far away, even though the most distant could be reached with only a short nickel bus ride. The admission price there could get as high as 25 cents, but even at that it was the cheapest baby sitter around. The Roxy, the Lyric, the Savar, the Midway, the Broadway, the North Camden and the Elm were all safe places, and the transportation modes were reliable and safe as well. This was true notwithstanding my first encounter with a pervert in the front row of the Elm Theater. A man, whom I took to be "old," sat next to me and suddenly pulled my hand into his lap. Much to my utter shock, my hand came in contact with his exposed and erect penis. I bolted from the chair shaking from fright, and, although I had nightmares about it for months, I never shared the story with anyone until now. These sick people have always been in our midst.

One hardly needed a bicycle, let alone an automobile, to tend to one's needs or be entertained. Walking would do the trick. If that was not enough, there were two different buses that ran up

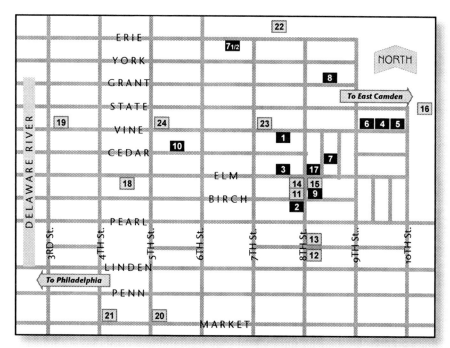

The Neighborhood

1. Mario and Teresa Monarca - 734 Vine
2. Tony and Dora DiSibio - 523 N. 8th
3. Anna and John Iannetta - 725 Elm
4. Louise and Joe Vitagliano - 933 Vine
5. Lola and Mil Iannetta - 935 Vine
6. Mike and Lucy Monarca - 921 Vine
7. Pat and Bob Jamison (1) - 642 Willard
7½. Pat and Bob Jamison (2) - 629 Erie
8. Lydia and Mel Mathews - 827 Grant
9. Mike and Lena DiSibio - 530 N. 8th
10. Dad and Eleanor DiSibio - 437 Cedar
11. Joe's Meat Market - 525 N. Eighth
12. Molotsky's Dry Goods - 490 N. 8th
13. Dad's Second Cobbler Shop - 500 N. 8th
14. Litwin's Grocery - 565 N. 8th
15. Miller's Grocery - 560 N. 8th
16. 10th Street Bridge - 10th & State
17. Lou and Syls - 600 N. 8th
18. Elm Street Movie House - 440 Elm
19. North Camden Movie House - 3rd & Vine
20. Savar Theater - 5th & Market
21. Stanley Theater - 4th & Market
22. Pyne Point Park - Erie
23. Sewell School - 7th & Vine
24. Holy Name School - 5th & Vine

8th Street and down 7th Street heading to East Camden and, in the other direction, to Philadelphia with all the stops in between. This bus line would cart workers to and from their jobs and later would be my transportation to Veteran's Memorial Junior High School and Woodrow Wilson Senior High School. In addition, of course, these buses would haul those who could afford it to the big shopping areas in the city like those on Broadway and Kaigns Avenues, as well as to a great adventure in Philadelphia. We almost always hoofed it to all of those locations. The truth is that you didn't have to go very far to be entertained for nothing. Every store had a different feel, every proprietor a different personality.

With a store on practically every corner, there was potential merriment all around. Within 50 feet of my house were three grocery stores, Joe's, Litwin's and Miller's. While the parents would never go into Litwin's or Miller's if they were customers of Joe's Meat Market, the children had no such loyalty and would pop in or out of the three groceries, mostly to join friends who frequented the other stores. There were, however, reasons for the loyalty of the elders. In addition to the fact that you were treated well in "your store," the fact that Joe or Ed or Bill would extend you credit drove you to be steadfast in your shopping habits. One would never be running a tab at more than one store, for if anyone found you out you would be cut off at both places. This particular system of credit required no computer or accountant to record the ongoing records.

All of the groceries had the same "system" of keeping tabs. It consisted of a military green metal box with a hinged top designed to hold index cards. Inside of the box were five by seven lined cards separated by thicker cards with raised letters for the entire alphabet. The "complex" transaction was completed when Joe rang up your purchase on a little Burroughs machine able to do the simplest number calculations. Joe would enter the amount on the shopper's card and replace it in the box, while handing the credit seeker the small perforated piece of roll tape for her records. Some of the ladies would dutifully keep it in a jar or other safe place. At the end of the month or other prearranged time, usually dictated by payday, the customer would ask for an accounting and pay all or part—"put something toward the tab"—of what was owed.

The credit system was somewhat universal in grocery stores, a carry over from the company store with the same notion in mind—maintain loyalty. Unlike the company store, however, the grocers had no control over the paycheck. I can recall Joe bitterly asking no one in particular, "How could Mrs. Smith go on vacation to Wildwood and still owe me $35 for groceries?" Or, worse yet, he would sometimes see the moving truck pulling away, without prior notice, with all of the worldly possessions of one of the debtors. The other nuance of the system was always knowing who had the right to put something on the tab in a particular family. Rarely were minors allowed the trust. But that was not the case at Litwin's, where Benny Jones had carte blanche access to the credit line, thus prompting our frequent visits. Many are the Tasty Cakes and sodas that we picked up on the Jones tab. Such was the world of high finance in North Camden.

The Litwin boys, Eddie and Phil, contributed to some of the negative Jewish stereotypes. They were brash, loud and often foul-mouthed, but always engaging. Like many store proprietors in North Camden, they lived elsewhere, in their case in East Camden in what was known as "the Jewish section." Underneath their rough exterior, they were warm and good-hearted people who prided themselves on being entertaining. They were overtly complimentary of the ladies and conspiratorial with the men. They always shared gossip and were highly knowledgeable about what gossip was most sought after and by whom. Even though Litwin's was the most unkempt of the three groceries, they always managed to maintain a substantial clientele due, in no small part, to the sale items they would boldly advertise via posters on the walls of the building.

The Millers were another story. Like most of the white-breads, they were devoid of personality. They were unfailingly polite and soft-spoken, and the store was always neat as the proverbial pin. But they serviced the smallest clientele, catering to those like themselves who didn't trust the Jews or the Italians. Bill was the owner, and he would get help on Saturdays from his friend Russ. Russ possessed a little more in the personality department, a fact that was highlighted one day when Russ pulled up for work in a brand-new pink Oldsmobile. It was the talk of the neighborhood. Some customers began to be concerned that perhaps they were paying higher prices so that Russ could afford such a fine car. Indeed, cars were the status symbol for nearly everyone in that era, and I was bitten by "the car thing" early in life for a variety of reasons, among them the admiration that Russ garnered just because of the pink Olds. The car bug that I caught way back then continues to infect me to this day.

Joe's Meat Market was "our store," and we knew it was the best. Joe Mazzarella, who had bought the business from his boss, and later partner, Dominic Salenzi, was the owner and butcher. Joe was the opposite of the picture many people had of Italians. He was quiet, neat to a fault, openly adoring of his wife and child and honest. Charming in his own way, he could cajole with the best of them. And he was very deliberate in everything he did.

While Joe had a gleaming new Buick in his garage in Pennsauken, he drove to and from work in an old grey Chevrolet. The paint was dulled from the exposure to the elements, and the upholstery was worn and ripped in places. He explained to me that he did not want his customers to think that he was getting rich on their hard-earned wages. It was the same car that he used to provide delivery service to the nearby towns of Runnemede and Woodbury and others. He provided this unique service to long-time loyal customers who had moved to better areas but still remained faithful to Joe. An indefatigable worker, Joe never took a day off for illness in the decade that I was around him. He worked six days a week from 7:00 a.m. until 6:00 p.m.—except Fridays when he was open until 9:00 p.m.

Joe's was the first real job I ever had. At first, I was "on call." When the weekly delivery truck came to unload the cases of goods that replenished what had been sold in the prior two weeks, Joe would wave me over from the corner across the street where I would be "hanging" with the gang. I would help Joe unlock the steel doors imbedded in the sidewalk and uncover access to the cellar of the store. This exterior door was the companion to the interior trapdoor leading to the storage space below. There were no staircases because it would take up too much room in an already crowded interior space. Case by case, I would haul the heavy boxes down and stack them, for which Joe would give me a small reward of 50 cents in addition to a Pepsi.

Joe would also call on me to deliver groceries to those with the phoned-in orders or to ladies who could not carry their own purchases home. For this, I might be rewarded with a dime tip, which was my pay. Of course, there were those who gave me nothing, but this was made up for by ladies like Mrs. Lloyd who always gave me a quarter, a munificent sum at the time. I was then all of 12 years old.

When I was 15 and still delivering groceries, I was once offered other favors, of the sexual kind, by one of our more attractive customers. This was a different type of education. On this and many other occasions, I became an observer of human behavior. I was always present when the guys would come in to "shoot the breeze" and tell bold and often risqué stories. I was treated like an adult. Joe's was a cornucopia of human interaction, and I became a voracious student of what motivates people. Joe set a great example and was a kind and patient teacher.

By the time I was 15, I was working for Joe full-time in the summer and as many hours as my schooling would permit during the school year. For the financial rewards, I was willing to eschew any hopes of making the high school baseball or football teams, although I had shown an aptitude for both sports, as a little leaguer and midget football linebacker. I liked the work, I liked the people, I liked the commute (30 feet from home), I liked the comfort of another father figure in my life, and I liked the money. Life was good. The experience of working at Joe's had a profound impact on my education and maturation.

The rest of my world was more problematic.

3
Tony and Dora

Mom and Dad were a dashing couple. He was a little dangerous, and she cut quite a figure.

The little shack at Lake Worth was our residence for the best two summers Elaine and I had as kids. We were "somebodies."

Tony and Dora

*"We would put the stopper in the drain and pour
in the hot water...We were now ready to clean up with a bar
of Lava soap, or whatever was on sale that month."*

DORA TERESA MONARCA WAS BY MOST ACCOUNTS rebellious. She was the middle female born to the Monarcas. Louise and Anna were born in the old country and would always have a countenance of the old world. Lola, being the first female born in America, would be the bridge between the competing cultures. Dora was the personification of the rebels, who founded and grew this country. She was strong-willed and stubborn, but without the facility to lead others to her causes. While her older sisters and brothers assumed their duties without question, she often bridled at the orders given liberally by her siblings. And, of course, as the youngest of the brood, she was often given those chores that others found beneath them.

By the time Dora was born in 1920, the family was in a routine of hard work. Teresa was spending more time birthing other families' children and tending to her husband. Louise and Anna were old enough to be relied upon to care for Dora and, like any children newly invested with the power over others, they were no doubt hard on Dora. So it is not surprising if Dora resented being low child on the totem pole and began to rely more on sympathy then on fight to get her way. She was the last child born in Jamesville, and by the time she had someone of smaller stature, Lydia, to lord it over, Camden offered a different environment which did not lend itself to such a stiff hierarchy. Lydia recalls the stories of

Dora disappearing for long afternoons, much to the chagrin of her mother and father. The parents would send the boys out to fetch her from whatever adventure she had sought.

While all of the Monarcas were ordinary in the looks department, Dora was described as plain. Unlike Anna with her likeness to Teresa, there was nothing distinctive about her. And bearing the brunt of the officious behavior of her siblings who were given charge over her, it is likely that she often felt unloved. Under these circumstances and at a very young age, she began to date and eventually ran off to Elkton, Maryland to marry the handsome—and charming—Anthony James DiSibio.

"Tony" was the eldest son of Raffaello and Domenica DiSibio, immigrants from Abruzzi, Italy, to whom there would be 10 children born in all. A later chapter will provide some detail, but suffice it to say that while the Monarcas were a gentle, caring and compassionate family headed by a matriarch, the DiSibios were a harsh, often violent and selfish, clan who were reared in a dictatorial patriarchy where there was no appeal from physical and mental abuse.

No more stark a difference could be drawn between the two families than in the views they held of Italy. To this day, the Monarcas visit the little town of their ancestors, keeping abreast of the births and deaths that are interspersed with visits going both ways. The DiSibios, on the other hand, could never even be heard speaking of their relatives left behind. One would be hard put, even with research, to uncover the name of the village from whence they came. In fact, even today's spelling of the name is suspect, with other supposed relatives spelling it differently. There never appeared to be any curiosity about the old country among the DiSibios, who had no love of nostalgia.

The "old man" ran his house with an iron fist. He would bring his fist or shoe down on all who would challenge him or disobey his dictates. It was not unusual to have him waiting with open hand on payday as the offspring would come home for meals. They would turn over the entire contents of the envelope, left to make do with what he doled out of their earnings, at his will, for their sundries and the like. Anyone returning after the curfew he set would find the doors locked, and, with no possibility of an entry, the latecomer would spend the night on the stoop or in the backyard.

Raffaello's whiskey-fueled tirades had no bounds, and he was as feared throughout the neighborhood as he was in his home. In no small part, this was due to the straight razor he carried at all times to confront any would-be affronter. His gentle and kind wife Domenica often took the blows meant for her children if she had the temerity to defend them. On more than one occasion, the wife-beater she had married would kick her down the cellar steps or give her a huge black eye with his shoe when he was not satisfied with her behavior or look or whatever. Late in life he calmed down. This was not because he mellowed, but rather because his son Mike, fresh from a marine's tour of the World War II Pacific, put a bayonet to his father's throat, promising to kill him if he ever touched his mother again.

The scars of brutality left by that world often resurfaced as Tony sought to make a life for himself and his new bride. Tony was not completely the tintype of his father. His mother Domenica was gentle, loving and generous, traits that Tony was fortunate to latch on to as he fought the negative lessons offered by his father. He would be torn between the Yin and the Yang, and be caught up in the good, the bad and the ugly of his youth. Through it all, there is no doubt that he was far and away the most charming of the DiSibios. He had a well deserved reputation as a raconteur, and he was much in demand as a friend and paramour. By all accounts, Tony was handsome, with wavy black hair that came together at a widow's peak on his forehead and green eyes that were often referred to as "bedroom eyes."

The courtship of Dora and Tony was as intense as any in the family, but it was met by admonishments from her older sisters that Tony did not come from a very good family and would break her heart. By this time, some of the siblings had settled down with men who were "safe," hardworking and willing for the most part to take direction from their wives. Tony, on the other hand, had some danger about him. He hung out on corners with "the boys" and gambled at sidewalk craps and late night card games. He had jobs, but not a job. No, Tony wasn't good enough for Dora. This, of course, drove her to him, and off they went to a marriage that would not be uneventful. The sparks flew from the beginning. The relationship of this pair, unlike the gentlemanly courtship of Joseph and Louise or of John and Anna, was passionate and as torrid as the staircase scene in "Gone With the Wind." Tony was Dora's Rhett Butler, and she would think of the dark side of Tony tomorrow.

While Tony's family had settled in South Camden along with the hordes of other Italians, he and Dora set up house in North Camden. Their first house, in the middle of the block on 10th Street between Vine and State Streets, happened to be just around the corner from sisters Louise and Lola and brother Mike. The house faced a gas station across the street and the 10th Street Bridge which was the demarcation for the beginning of East Camden. The better part of Camden, lying on the East side, did not really commence at the bridge. Instead, there was a stretch of open fields and garden patches on the right beyond the bridge and an open garbage dump on the left. It was almost as though this section of the city was saying to the residents of North Camden, "Leave your refuse and trash behind before you are welcomed to the pristine East Camden."

The little row home with its tiny rooms was similar to every other row home in the city that was described earlier. The lower level consisted of a living room, a dining room and a smaller room housing a kitchen. The upstairs had two bedrooms and a solitary shared bath. There was a small porch in the front that was three steps up from a sidewalk that was made of the same bricks as the houses. These are the same kind of sidewalks that are being re-installed today after tearing up the cement ones that the original brick sidewalks were torn up to install. I guess what goes around does, indeed, come around.

My first memories were of this house. My father, referred to as "Dad," "Pop" or "Daddy," depending on the decade, was a brakeman on the railroad, a job he got because of Uncle Phil, who began his four decades with the rail system at this time. The pay was good and certainly adequate for a growing family. Dora was 18 and Tony 24 when the couple was blessed with Elaine, born on April 27,1940. Born 18 months later, on September 8, 1941, I was named for my tyrant grandfather. Dora was honing her cooking skills and tending to her family. These were the times of shared meals, cooked as much out of love as for sustenance. Life started out with as much normalcy as any whitebread house might hope for.

I remember one particular morning at a breakfast of pan-cakes showing my Dad my loose tooth. He calmly said, "Oh, let me see." He reached for the loose canine and unceremoniously yanked it from my mouth. No warning, no string around the door-knob and not so much as a "How do ya do." This was his way of teaching me to suck it up. I cried briefly but finished my pancakes, with some blood in the syrup, to the encouragement of my mom and the amusement of my sister. Dad swatted me gently on the head and said, "Good job, Butch," using what would become his nickname for me. I remember little else of that house, with most of my memories from this time being from our next home. The tooth incident introduced me to the "Walk it off" approach to injury that we often practiced.

Elaine did not escape unscathed on 10th Street. It was in the dining room, while Mom was ironing and Elaine and I were cavorting about, that I reached up and grabbed a metal coat hanger with the notion of using it in some game of imagination. The hook of the hanger hit Elaine in the left eye, and the resulting injury left her "cross-eyed" for several years to come. This flawed her natural beauty until the damage was repaired, much to my relief.

We moved to 523 N. 8th Street, to a house on the corner of 8th and Birch, sometime during the first half of the 1940s. As a corner property, this was one of the houses constructed with a "store front," and the store changed the configuration of both the interior and exterior of the house. Instead of a porch on the front, there was one oversized step overlooked by a large picture window, approximately six feet by five feet, and a front door. Along the side of the property facing Birch Street was a side entrance consisting of a set of four marble steps providing an entry through a door that led to a kitchen and stairway.

The interior consisted of a very large room at the front (12 by 24 feet), at the left rear of which were three steps leading to the kitchen and shed. The kitchen was for cooking and eating, and the shed was for washing clothes. The kitchen was just large enough to contain a stove, a small sink, and a refrigerator (Kelvinator). There were stairways going up and down. Down led to a dirt-floored cellar with a coal bin and large furnace. The stairway up led to the three bedrooms and single bath. As you reached the top of the stairs and turned right, you were in Elaine's bedroom, which was over part of the kitchen and shed. Since the shed was unheated, this bedroom was brutally cold in winter.

Opposite Elaine's door was a hallway. If you took a couple of steps, my room appeared on the left. The room resembled an upside-down reverse L-shape. The long part of the "L" was just wide enough for a small twin bed, but not long enough to open the door all the way with the bed in the room. The short was large enough for a 30-inch set of drawers, but not wide enough to stand in front of and open the drawers all the way. Next to this room was the bathroom and then, at the head of the hall, was Mom and Dad's room. The "master bedroom" was generous enough to hold a full set of bedroom furniture.

The house had most "modern" amenities (for 1940), with some exceptions. There was central heat, provided by a coal-fired furnace that required constant attention to build, stoke and feed the fire. While there was indoor plumbing, there was no hot water. Any hot water was provided by way of what could be heated on the range and carried to the sink or, on a once-a-week basis, to the bathtub on the second floor. This situation led to many a minor burn and at least one major burn when Mom tripped going up the stairway, spilling scalding water over her torso and legs. Like the trooper she was, she "walked it off" and continued her chores for the day. She remained more mindful in the future of the dangers forced upon us by the lack of plumbing conveniences.

In addition to putting us near the bottom of the economic ladder, the lack of hot water had other impacts as well. In the morning, before school, we would have to go down to the kitchen and heat water for washing our extremities. The stopper used to hold water in the small bathroom sink was rubber and tethered to the faucet by something resembling a keychain that ensured that it would not be lost. Before bringing the heated water upstairs, we would put the stopper in the drain and pour in the hot water, adding enough cold to ensure we would not be scalded. We were now ready to clean up with a bar of Lava soap, or whatever was on sale that month. We would have to finish before the water turned tepid, and, of course, the water got dirtier and dirtier with every dipping of the washcloth to rinse. This morning washing ritual was always an adventure, because, in our haste, we would often accidentally grab the keychain device, causing the water to be lost down the drain. All that effort, and in an instant the water would be gone. We would either start over after heating more water or, more often, finish up using cold water.

But the most difficult—and humiliating—effect of the water situation was bathing. Because of the huge effort and dangers involved in carrying many pots of water up the stairs and to the tub, the bath was at most a once-a-week event. My sister, Elaine, would take her bath first, during which time we would be heating one more large pot of water. When Elaine was done, Mom would carry the one last pot to the bath and add it to the now tepid and unclean water used by Elaine, and I would get my bath in the newly heated but dirty water.

Other than the hot water issue, life at 523 was not unlike that of any other family in the area when it came to living conditions. We were essentially all in the same social strata, although there were small but noticeable differences which distinguished one stratum from another, causing envy among those who didn't enjoy the benefits. The ownership of an automobile, for example, often separated one class of families from another. A refrigerator, instead of an ice box, was also a differentiator. And having goods delivered to your house was a real status symbol. Uncle Mike DiSibio, who lived across the street at 530 N. 8th, would have half a dozen Italian rolls delivered every night, and milk was delivered in the early morning hours to many neighbors as well as the white bread that led to the name of the recipients. These amenities were coveted by me and many other neighborhood kids who were not the beneficiaries of such niceties. Beyond the indication of class, these kinds of services defined the living conditions of the city in the '40s and '50s. Nowhere in America has this atmosphere been replicated, despite the attempts of modern-day developers.

Another sign of the times was the way the neighborhood pulsated with street activities. While the commercial stores, described earlier, provided all that today's Kroger's or the local Giant can offer, there was an array of specialty good and services that were provided daily in a way that will never be duplicated in the suburbia we now have, or even in the faux retro neighborhoods that abound. Nearly every day, the usual hubbub of the thousands of people interacting in a small area was supplemented by the cacophony of street vendors shouting out their presence to gain the attention of would-be buyers.

There was, among others, the ice man, conveyed by an old truck with a canvas covered flatbed that protected the large blocks of ice meant for those homes with ice boxes in which perishable items could be kept. These boxes were just stand-up models of the ice chests that are now taken to the beach or ball game. The truck always had a step that extended down to make it convenient for the ice man to climb up and cut a quarter, half or full block for delivery to a waiting client. This step was also ideal for the neighborhood toughs to hitch a ride to the next street, much to the horror of the neighborhood wags.

The ice man was just one of many who shouted their arrival. The rag man as well would come by to collect rags, material scraps or other such throwaways for eventual delivery to the junk yard for a per pound price. He would be shouting, "Any old rags?" at regular intervals to seek attention. The green grocer meanwhile would be in competition with the corner store shouting out, "Fresh fruit, tomatoes, peppers picked today!" aboard his flatbed truck laden with baskets with an array of items taken from his garden that morning. The women could be seen surrounding his truck, squeezing and sniffing his goods to ensure ripeness before purchase. These were among the normal and constant daily deliveries.

Then there were the specialty services. The knife man carried his manually operated round wheel that, when pumped with his foot, would spin and allow for his expert hands to apply the blade of a knife for sharpening. This contraption was carried on leather straps much like very large knapsacks that are in vogue today. His only announcement would be his shouts of "Knife man, knife man!" a plaintive cry that would send housewives searching for knives and scissors long in need of a good edge.

Desserts and treats were also part of the daily landscape of sounds. The waffle man, perhaps the most unusual of these purveyors, would arrive in a horse-drawn open conveyance much like a stagecoach. The open area was large enough for him to stand in and also house a gas-fired burner attached to a waffle griddle, as well as the necessary ingredients for his preparations. The wooden structure had a large, 4 foot by 4 foot, opening on each side so customers could order and pay for freshly made hot waffles topped with powdered sugar. What a treat! Before you heard his announcement of "Waffle man, waffle man," the clip-clop of the horses' hooves would signal his arrival.

If that wasn't enough in the way of constant noise and activity, you would regularly hear the strains of "Yum-yum, yum-yum!" and see the young person pulling a wagon on top of which was a tapered barrel open at the top so as to hold a steel container surrounded by ice to keep the contents semi-frozen. Those contents were what we know today as Italian water ice. For three cents for a single scoop or a nickel for a double, you could quench your thirst and relieve the heat and with this cold confection delivered with a smile. Can the inhabitants of our today's antiseptic environments even begin to imagine this fascinating tapestry of the sights and sounds of my youth? This was the feel and smell and look of my small world on the streets outside my house as I was growing up.

In its own way, 523 was idyllic in the early days. Dad had settled on what he wanted to do for a living. The railroad had provided a good living, but also required the discipline of studying for a field test as a brakeman and being dictated to, as regards shift changes and destinations, on a daily basis. This was not for Tony. Although more suited to some occupations than others, Dad was never out of work; in fact, he often held two jobs. While a brakeman, he moonlighted as an apprentice cobbler. He quickly excelled at the art of shoe repair, and his easy way with people made him a natural to apply his newly-acquired skill to opening his own business. Indeed, the first-floor store entrance at 523 was likely the attraction that prompted the move from 10th Street.

I can clearly recall the configuration of the "shop," as it was called. The entrance door was on the right side of the building, while the entrance to the home was at the back and to the left of the long shop. The entire length of the left side of the shop, from the picture window to the steps leading to the living quarters, was a glass-fronted cabinet behind which was a leather repair sewing machine; and behind that was an iron stand with a cobbler's shoe form resembling an upside-down shoe on top. Shoes in need of work would be slipped over this form, and Dad would hammer away putting them into a state of good repair. Along the back wall, behind the counter, were the electric-powered machines that were used to trim, sand and stitch the heels and soles of shoes and boots. Dad would stand behind the counter made of a beautiful piece of white Italian marble and accept the shoes of customers, giving each a receipt torn from a perforated and sequentially numbered piece of cardboard. This would ensure that a customer would retrieve the right pair of shoes at the promised delivery time.

I never failed to marvel at Dad's ability to magically transform a dilapidated pair of dirty shoes, with holes in the soles and rundown heels, into a sparkling pair of Sunday-go–to-meeting kicks worthy of Dorothy in the Wizard of Oz. There were chairs along the right of the shop so customers could avail themselves of the "while you wait" service, a service that was, of course, necessary because many of his customers, like Elaine and myself, only had one pair of shoes.

Mom and Dad worked hard to prepare the store front. Mom was devoting herself to helping her man get the shop ready for opening. She would make the picture window shine to assure that all who passed could see the new neon sign that Dad had commissioned. It was made in the outline of a large shoe with the words "Tony's Shoe Repair" emblazoned across the bottom. The shop and the sign were the pride and joy of the whole family. Dora and Tony also took great pride in wallpapering not only the shop but the entire house. They were a great team when it can to that skill. She would paste and trim, and he would apply and smooth roll after roll, even on the ceilings, until the entire house was transformed. In one day they could repaper the entire house.

It was the neon sign and the ice truck that figured prominently in an unforgettable punishment I received about the time I was seven years old. Dad was toiling away in the shop making magic with a pair of soon-to-be refurbished shoes. Even though I had been warned many times about not hitching rides on the backs of moving vehicles, I could not resist the temptation. The ice truck was an easy target, but snow and ice storms could turn hitching rides on cars into the Olympics of hitching. As the cars slowed down because of the inclement weather, my more adventuresome comrades and I would use the opportunity to assume a deep crouching position and grab hold of the prominent rear bumper of a slowed vehicle; then, planting our feet squarely beneath us, we would let the auto pull us, sled like, for block after block to our new destinations. Neighbors who spotted us heaped curses upon us to let go and get out of the street. But we paid no heed until, as fate would have it, Charlie Crumuller had his leg severely injured when he slipped under a rear wheel. This, of course, put a crimp in our style and stopped the snow hitching, but not so the rides on the ice truck.

On one such ride, I lost track of how far the truck had gone, so self-satisfied was I with having jumped successfully aboard the rear buckboard step. I was blithely moving up 8th street, waving like Caesar to my friends, when I turned and saw my red-faced father using the handle of his trimming knife to bang on the picture window to get my attention and wave me off the ice truck. In his anger, he accidentally hit the corner of the neon sign and broke it. To say he was furious would be akin to saying that Jews were a little upset about the holocaust.

Recognizing danger when I saw it, I immediately leaped off the truck and headed in the opposite direction from the shop. My father leaped over the counter like a high jumper and got to the front door while I was still in sight. "Ralph, get over her *now*!" he bellowed. The one thing we knew as kids was that we came when we were called, never mind that this time I knew that all hell was about to break loose when I got there. With my head held low and many neighbors watching the drama unfold, my father grabbed me by the scruff of the neck and dragged me into the shop.

All eyes could still see through the plate-glass door as my father glanced about for a weapon. Along the wall were some six-foot sections of new wooden baseboard awaiting final installation in the fledgling shop. He grabbed a section, broke off a piece of 30 inches or so, and proceeded to haul me over his knee and administer blow after blow to my butt and upper legs. Alerted by his curses and shouted admonishments and my screams of pain, my mother came running from the second floor to my aid. Faced with a warning to her of a similar punishment if she interfered, she chose discretion over valor and retreated to the kitchen, where I ran for sympathy when I was finally released.

This vignette is by way of relating that few children of the era, least of all Elaine and me, were spoiled by the sparing of the rod—or the baseboard or whatever. I received a similar beating when my friends and I pulled the back seat out of my father's car and used it as a trampoline, leaping on it from our side step. And both Elaine and I were on the receiving end of many a backhand at the kitchen table, delivered in an effort to teach us manners or to emphasize that children should be seen and not heard. Incidentally, a "backhand" was a blow to the face or head delivered by the back of my father's hand after his fully winding it up across his chest. You would think I could have seen it coming, but I never did; Dad was quick with his hands. I note, however, that I never thought of my father or mother as abusive. Mostly, I thought I deserved the punishment I got, and I knew that, unlike Raffaello DiSibio, neither one of our parents enjoyed hitting us. Corporal punishment was a way of the times, and I don't think any of us were scarred by its administration.

Dad became fully engaged in making the shoemaking business a success, and his reputation as an expert grew throughout the area. He began to have shoes brought in for repair by his brother Mike, sent by the workers at Campbell Soup, and by Uncle Phil, who delivered work shoes from his co-workers on the Reading-Seashore line. Tony could do it all, from stitching a torn seam almost invisibly to applying full soles and heels to completely worn through bottoms. When he was finished, he would use the last section of machine fitted with soft brushes to apply polish and buff the shoes to a mirror-like sheen. If your shoes were too tight, he would insert a wooden foot-like mold, then turn a corkscrew that moved the sides of the molds out from the center, thereby stretching the shoe. He would then submerge the offending shoe in water for a day or two until the leather had taken on the new shape. He was a magician with footwear.

Mom, in the meantime, was tending to her family in all of the traditional ways. She served up her specialties at dinner time -meatloaf with hardboiled eggs hiding inside, red-sauced stew, roast pork peppered with garlic, liver and onions, and, of course, the Tuesday, Thursday and Sunday servings of spaghetti with meatballs and braciole. These were the times that Elaine and I can associate with normalcy. School and work occupied the week; and the kids went to the movies and played on Saturday, while the work in the shop, a six-day-a-week effort, continued. But for all of us, Sundays were special.

A typical Sunday was dedicated to family activities. More often than not, it would find us visiting family or hosting visits by other family members. We would put on our best, if modest, clothes and be inspected by Mom for cleanliness behind our ears and on both sides of our hands. Any stray mark would be cleaned by Mom wetting her handkerchief with spittle from her mouth and wiping it away, a far cry from today's oversensitivity to germs. Pop might go into the shop and use the machines to polish our shoes, and off we would go.

The visits would usually start at Grandpop Monarca's home, or, later, at Aunt Anna's where he took up residence. There we would "pay our respects" and sample homemade Italian cookies or ricotta pie. The adults would have coffee, and the kids would occupy themselves by playing with cousins or each other. We were always accorded a status a wee bit lower than others because of Mom's being the little sister, and there was always a residual resentment occasioned by my father's having run off with his Dora. Mom was forever getting unwanted advice from her older siblings and often felt disrespected. There was no intended malice, but the older sisters still felt a responsibility toward the younger ones. This attitude lasted a lifetime.

Aunt Anna's was always the greatest fun, first because of Grandpop, secondly because Aunt Anna was a great baker and mostly because Cousin John had the best toys of all kinds. A metal machine gun, wooden blocks of every shape that could be used to make great forts, lead soldiers with British uniforms and more. I was always awed and envious of his vast collection. I used to satisfy my envy by reminding myself that I had something he didn't have, a sister, who in the earliest years, was my 24-hour-a-day playmate. We had our visitors too. On occasion, we would receive visits from the younger siblings at our house. Aunt Pat might visit with her new beau, or Uncle Mike would come by with his girl, Lena Perno, after his return from the war in the Pacific.

If we were treated like the upstarts at the Monarca's, such was not the case at the DiSibio's. On the Sundays reserved for the South Camden visits, we would pile into an old 1932 Chevrolet and trundle off to 233 Berkley Street. If we were lucky, the "old man" would be drinking homemade wine with his cronies; if not, he would be ensconced in his oversized chair in a small room just beyond the entry. Each of us would have to plant a kiss on his often unshaven face while he grunted approval. Once we escaped his presence, we would pass through the dining room and into a spacious kitchen with a wood-burning cast iron stove atop which were several pots with the delicacies of the day cooking away.

Domenica's face would light up at the sight of her oldest son and his family, and we would be greeted with the grand respect owing to the first son of the first son. Kisses and warm hugs would rain down upon all of us. We could do no wrong and were waited on hand and foot. As other members of the large family arrived, they would pay homage to my father after the obligatory kiss given to his own father. Unlike the always reserved environment of the Monarca homes, where voices were never raised above a conversational level, Sunday at the DiSibio's was as loud as a rock concert.

Around the large kitchen table, there was constant bickering among the siblings and the kids would be running around unbridled. Occasionally the "old man" could be heard to scream something that sounded like "Ungooled, ungooled," an Italian admonishment to settle down. Domenica would be perspiring over the stove and murmuring, "pew, pew," which was her own catchphrase meaning, "More, more." This was her way of saying, "All we get around here is more and more, let's take it easy." Sunday at the DiSibio's was Bruce Springsteen to the Monarcas' Pavarotti.

Occasionally, we would be treated to a Sunday drive. This would consist of getting onto the velveteen seats of the old Chevy and heading out of town. Admiral Wilson Boulevard was entered just at the terminus of Federal or Linden Streets. This wide avenue would take us to the Airport Circle, so named for the little airport that serviced the surrounding area. Beyond the circle lay the hinterlands of southern New Jersey. Routes 70, 38, 130 and more offered adventure for the taking and went in all directions. We could go off to Clementon, to Merchantville or Delair, Evesham, or to the pig farms of Woodbury and Glassboro. Real adventure took us to Bridgeton, which was the hometown of Josephine Monarca, the young bride of Uncle Jim, and in the general direction of Atlantic City (playground to the world) another 25 miles farther south. In all cases, the chosen adventure was full of potholes and unpaved stretches of road that caused more than one flat tire requiring repair. All of these places would play a role in our lives as the years rolled by.

We settled into a routine during our early years at 523. The shop was doing well. Dad was working hard and building a name for himself in the business. He invested in a little white panel truck that resembled a station wagon without windows and with a door above the rear bumper that hinged like the rear door of a hearse. On the side of the truck was a hand-painted sign announcing pick up and delivery of dry cleaning and shoe repair. Dad was expanding his business by picking up clothing and shoes, taking the clothing to a central facility for cleaning, the addition of the much-needed service he provided aided us in our ability to improve our lives. Later, he would abandon the dry cleaning business as neighborhood competitors encroached into his territory. Still, no one could compete with his expertise as a cobbler. Eventually, he was convinced to close his shop in North Camden and open a new and expanded shop adjoining the huge new Baltimore Markets that was opening just off of Admiral Wilson Boulevard. This was the forerunner of the strip mall, and Dad was going to be ahead of the curve.

The war years meant that everyone had jobs and money to spend, and life improved in the North Camden neighborhood. Radios became commonplace, and there were rumors of moving pictures coming into your home via television. At about this time, some neighbors actually had home projectors to show short films, cartoons and serials. It was during that era that our home became the center of the block. Because it was easy to clear out one side of the shop, an area that was later pressed into service as our living room, we were the only venue available with the kind of space needed to show these movies. Once every couple of weeks, Dad would set up the projector supplied by a neighbor and show films supplied by another neighbor to a gaggle of noisy youngsters. It was grand being the center of attention for such an event. Of course, all of the kids in the area wanted to be invited to the DiSibio's for this treat. Naturally, Elaine and I, along with our parents, were the gatekeepers, and I am sure we used this power to reward or punish the kids we played with. But I do not recall any feelings except joy at these productions. They certainly gave us both an easy avenue to popularity.

During the summer months, much creativity was required to fill in the many idle hours that the lack of school provided. While there were reports from Uncle Phil that there was a swimming pool open to the residents of Pennsauken, there was no such benefit in North Camden. Surrounded by unyielding structures, Camden was steamy during the summer months. The brick and concrete sidewalks with granite curbing leading to cobblestone or black macadam streets were broken up only by telephone poles from which extended an occasional street light. The brick homes and their wooden fences in the rear led to the only possible soft material like soil or wild trees. North Camden was essentially bereft of any vegetation excepting at the Pyne Point Park, the 10th Street Park or the fields across from the dump on State Street. The heat, confined by the houses and exacerbated by the automobiles and ever-present buses belching diesel fumes in all directions, was stifling.

These were the days when parents in the "'hood" would release the kids in the morning with the admonishment not to return until lunch time. In some cases, our moms would send us off until dinner time with the full knowledge that we would fend for ourselves by dropping in on one of the numerous family members close by or raiding our own fridge while our mothers were visiting or otherwise occupied. If we were lucky, we would be welcomed to the Sewell School Yard. Here the city sponsored a summer camp of sorts where counselors taught kids how to make pot holders or lanyards for keys or some other time consuming skill. These camps, such as they were, were offered for a five-week period at a supplementary fee of $3, cheap child care at twice the price. It is ironic that the camp was held in the schoolyard. The Sewell School Yard was a concrete square approximately 60 by 100 feet, fronted by a 6-foot wrought iron fence on the 7th Street side, a concrete 10-foot wall on the opposite end, and the school and private residence on the perpendicular sides. A kind description would liken it to a prison yard. This was the summer camp of North Camden.

When not in the school yard, we were in and around the streets engaged in play activities that were almost exclusively gender based. The boys had a variety of activities to test our creativity and while away the hours that were yet to be filled by TV. Before there was a Howdy Doody, there was Kick the Can, Ringoleavio/Ringoleario, Rover Red Rover, Buck Buck, and Bull in the Ring. Any and all spare time was filled by playing halfball or touch football in the streets. Our most challenging efforts were building stilts and racing carts. Some explanations may be appropriate.

To play Kick the Can, we chose up sides (sometimes even the girls were invited for lack of bodies), and an empty tin can would be placed on "home base." The defenders would remain at the base, covering their eyes while the opposing team found hiding places all up and down the field (in our case defined as Birch Street from 7th to 8th), which usually meant under or in cars parked on the little street, on or under porches or in the alleyways or yards that empty onto Birch. If the defenders found you, they would man-handle you back to home base and sit you down around the can, until all of opposing team was found. The caught members could be released if an unfound member could run to home base and kick the can—thus, the name—and that meant all of the caught members could scatter and hide for as long as it took the defender to chase down the can and return it to home. The game could take hours

Bull in the Ring was a tough guy's invention. We would form a circle with a diameter of 10 feet or so and call out one of the group to be the bull. The designated member would be in the center of the ring and run full force into a section of the ring to try and breach its perimeter. There were no rules against pushing, pulling, slapping or punching the would-be escapee back into the ring, and the assaults would continue until "the bull" broke free or quit in exhaustion or pain. Later, we often used the game as an initiation into the gang to test the mettle of potential members.

Halfball was played by lopping off the head of a used broom and using it for a bat, which we then would use to hit a tennis ball that we had cut in half. The half ball would be thrown flying saucer-like to the waiting batter. The game was usually played on Birch with my house serving as the backdrop for the batter and the pitcher on the opposite curb of the 10-foot wide street using Joe's Meat Market for the wall against which we would swat the ball. Joe's wall was perfect because it was windowless. A ball hit into the street was a single, onto the opposite sidewalk was a double, against the wall but on the first floor was a triple, against the wall on the second floor was a home run, and a ball hit onto the roof (a "roofer") was an automatic grand slam.

Scooter construction, another activity, was an art. An empty wooden soda case or any empty wooden case of 20 inches or more would act as the body of the vehicle. A piece of 6-inch lumber of 36 inches or so would be the rail. The lumber was usually purloined from an old broken fence in a yard that faced an alley or from the inside of an abandoned house. We would nail the rail onto the bottom of the short side of the box or crate, and then came the hard part. We would have to procure an old abandoned metal skate and disassemble it from front to back. We would nail half of the skate to the bottom of first one end then the other of the rail then turn it over. We now had a scooter and by stepping on the rail, could propel ourselves along the streets and sidewalks with our other foot. Old bottle caps would adorn each transport, and handles could be attached to the top of the crate to create handle bars with which we could steer these beauties. What a racket they made when several were riding in tandem down the block.

Buck Buck is recalled in the beginning of the Bronx Tale, a film that will be mentioned again later. Learning how Buck Buck is played is just one of many reasons to see that movie. Another reason is its neighborhood similarity depicted on film.

These idyllic times were about to change, as our father began to succumb to the temptations of the flesh. He was not a consumer of alcohol like his father, nor did he have tendencies toward homosexuality like his younger brother Joe; but he did have an eye for the ladies and they for him. No one has documented exactly when he started to stray or with whom, but the timing likely coincided with the moving of the shop. For that matter, no one knows why he started to stray, although my mother's sisters were quick to put some of the blame on her for not keeping herself attractive or being meticulous in housekeeping or creative in the kitchen. Of course, the insecurity that had always characterized Dora was not helped by Tony's actions or by the disloyalty of her sisters; rather it was fed by these developments.

The next several years included verbal and physical fights between my parents, often witnessed by my sister and me and too numerous to detail. I have to say that Mom gave as good as she got, and she could stand toe to toe with Dad for the first few blows, perhaps not surprising in that she had a reputation of her own in the neighborhood. When Larry Mazzi, during one of our many fist fights, was sitting on top of me holding on to hands full of my hair and banging my head against the sidewalk, she intervened to allow me to my feet. Mr. Mazzi, Larry's father who was a recently discharged paratrooper, told her to "Let 'em fight," whereupon Mom hit him with a solid right cross screaming, "As long as they fight fair!" He didn't retaliate, probably because she was a woman, but that is not how she told it. Her dogged and unflinching defense of me was as forceful as a mother grizzly bear protecting her young and lasted for many years to come. Lest you think that Elaine did not pick up this trait, just do something to slight her grandkids.

Our parents' battles, meanwhile, occurred at all hours of the day and night and were always about the same thing, my Dad's cheating. In defending himself, he would attack her for "letting herself go" or express his chagrin over her cleaning or cooking or long visits gossiping with the neighbors. In the beginning, he remained at home and the confrontations were served up as a steady diet.

He finally walked out, but the first time would not be the last. Over the years, he abandoned us on 13 separate occasions for varying amounts of time. Every return was carried out with a flourish, and he would always bring two things—some token of his repentance (could be anything from fresh rolls to a wringer washing machine) and a renewed promise to mend his ways and turn over yet another in an endless chain of new leaves. Each individual absence is associated with another chapter in our lives, and the absences accumulated to become part of the fabric of our makeup.

During Dad's absences, Mom would recount in detail, to anyone and everyone who would listen, her tale of woe. For us kids, it was just another constantly repeated reminder of why people felt sorry for us. Elaine and I reacted differently to those events. To this day, I withhold my pain and sorrow to shield myself from the sympathies of others, while Elaine has more of a tendency to share her sorrows, though only with intimates.

The most indelibly planted memory was of Dad's effort to make up for being caught after his first major liaison. He offered Mom a rare and unique treat, which he knew would enthrall her. It was an offer she couldn't refuse, something she would not only enjoy for what it offered in and of itself but for the opportunity it presented to have something that none of her sisters had: a summer "home."

Just beyond the little town of Clementon, which was nine miles south of Camden, was the small village of Watsontown. Watsontown's claim to fame was a roller-skating rink and a public fee-based lake. Inside the barriers that you could pass through after paying the admission collectors were large picnic tables, some pits for building cooking fires, four small structures built to house renters or, in one case, a small home lived in year around. All of the structures faced the lake. There was a snack bar along one edge of the lake and a small play area with monkey bars and a chinning bar made of steel. Lake Worth Park was a destination of locals from around the area, and people would come from as far away as Camden to partake of the fresh air of the "woods" and the refreshing cedar waters for a small fee of 25 cents per person or $1 for a family of five or more.

Lake Worth was a commercial lake fed by a cedar creek that was no more than 60 feet across and 125 feet long. It was more or less of an irregular rectangle in shape. At the long end of the rectangle was a "beach," consisting of trucked in sand that was mixed with the naturally sandy soil of the region. At the opposite end, across the water, was a 10-foot-high dive platform, and on the short side of the rectangle, in front of the snack bar, was the low dive. Across from the low dive, the lake continued unobstructed to the feeding creek.

One of the tiny structures, generously termed a "house," was close to the snack bar and was perennially rented by Dominic Selenzi, the former owner of Joe's Meat Market. Five feet away, still farther from the snack bar, was a three-sided, one room structure with a screened-in area that could best be described as a shack. On the other side of the beach that the shack faced was a tiny well-kept white house with blue trim. The little sign over the door proclaimed it as "My Blue Heaven."

"My Blue Heaven" was owned by John Leo, of Yum Yum legend. He was the founder and sole distributor of Italian water ice in and around Camden. His work force consisted of scores of pre- and early teens who would trek to South Camden, give Mr. Leo $10 as a deposit for that red keg of yum yum that they would hawk all day, then take back the empty for a return of $5 of the deposit; the teenage entrepreneur would be left with the $10 that a full can judiciously doled out could produce, thus yielding a $5 profit.

John took no risk; he, in effect, pre-sold all his goods, and if the kid ran off with the barrel, John Leo would keep the deposit. The kids were happy, and John was happy. He never worried about benefits or labor strife. If a kid pilfered yum yum for himself or his friends, so be it, because John already had his money. Leo's Yum Yum still exists at this writing and is owned by John's grandchildren. John's wife could be found every summer, not at Lake Worth but at the Leo home in South Camden, while My Blue Heaven was occupied by Mae, John's mistress for the last 20 or so years of his life. This fact was well known, but never spoken about, by everyone at Lake Worth.

My father had known both Dominic and John for many years. I suspect that as a result of some arrangement or other they let my father know that for less than $100, give or take, he could rent the shack with the screened-in front. This, of course, was the perfect re-entry gift for Dora and the kids on one of Tony's many returns home. It also provided him ample opportunity to continue to carry on the extracurricular activities that he had never intended to relinquish.

Notwithstanding the nefarious purposes behind the rental of the summer place, the two summers spent there were the best of our young years. A lakefront villa on Lake Como could not have provided more allure. For one brief shining moment, we felt like we were the envy of the entire family. For once, other family members wanted to be like me and admired what I had. I am sure that some of the older ones saw through my father's subterfuge, but, if that was true, I did not sense it then. I only reveled in the bliss of those glorious summers.

At Lake Worth, every day was literally a day at the beach. Elaine and I would be dark as mulattoes by summer's end. Mom would be within eyesight, or we could hear the sound of her voice as she visited with Gloria Selenzi or Mae. Gloria's daughter, Mary Jane, became Elaine's constant and loyal companion, and Mae's sons, Chuck and John, took on the role of my platform diving coaches. I guess we were cute enough to be generally adopted by the lifeguards and the manager; we were there every day and were like mascots.

At Lake Worth, we were "somebodies." We swam good enough to win medals, Elaine Silver and me a Bronze, in swimming contests. And we looked forward to Sundays when Uncle Mike DiSibio and his family would come down for a big Italian feast served on a picnic table. Mom did a remarkable job with only rudimentary cooking tools. Some of the Monarcas also came by for a dip and a meal. Elaine and I slept in the screened-in area, and Mom and Dad shared a small bed in the kitchen/sitting area. We did not miss the hot water that we never had to begin with, and the toilet facilities were of the outdoor variety. But we loved the entire experience nonetheless.

Alas, the good times were not to last. Dad used the time when none of the family or extended family could observe him to expand his infidelities. He roamed as far as Baltimore, Maryland when his waitress paramour moved there from Camden where they had had a long-term illicit affair. Now even the shop at Baltimore Markets was in jeopardy. He was taking time off, hanging a closed sign up when he was scheduled to be open, and generally becoming unreliable. Customers went elsewhere in large numbers. And then we moved again.

Not for the first time, we found ourselves without the ability to pay the mortgage. In 1948, we were evicted when Dad walked out. We were then further humiliated by being taken in by the largesse of Aunt Lydia, who we lived with for several months. This time, we would move not just four blocks away but instead to another world. It is little wonder that my bedwetting was the least of my mother's worries. Everything went from bad to worse.

Aunt Louise

Aunt Louise and her men, Joe and Joe Jr.:
the pinball champ and the star athlete.

The inset is my idol on the day he became
my confirmation Godfather.

Aunt Louise

"When she was in her early twenties, Louise married her first love, Joseph Vitagliano, who came from a strong Italian family that included several siblings."

AUNT LOUISE WITNESSED MORE CHANGE in the extended family than anyone, because she experienced all of the changes up close and personal. She buried and grieved for parents, siblings, and offspring. Still the holder of the family record for longevity, she was deservedly held in the highest esteem throughout her life · by all who knew her. As the eldest of the clan, she assumed adult duties while still a pre-teen. She learned at the knee of Teresa for longer then the rest and became a teacher of her siblings.

Louise was a great baker and an excellent cook. I rarely heard her raise her voice, but when she raised it above a conversational tone, all in earshot would listen. She was well kempt and was seen without makeup only by her husband and, presumably, by some intensive care nurses. Her makeup was always appropriate to the occasion, and her hair followed the same discipline. She was rarely without hose and heels and never dressed in slacks or shorts. She had high expectations of those around her, which were only exceeded by her expectations of herself.

I have heard Louise described as many things: warm, funny, intelligent, witty, and tenacious—but never soft. She was a taskmaster with a gentle nudge but could be harsh if the circumstances called for it. She could build you up with praise or cut you down with a pointed remark, always deserved in either case. I include here the eulogy I delivered at her funeral services because it best describes my thoughts at the time, and they remain my thoughts today.

And then there were three - October 15, 1998

They all went before her. Joe, Sr., Joe, Jr., Jim, Mike, Phil, Anna, Lola and Pat. And then there where three. This is not a sad day for her because she is enjoying the company of those who went before. Philadelphia has the Liberty Bell, London has Big Ben and China has the Great Wall. All are symbols of national treasures. She was the Monarca family treasure.

Louise: born in Italy, raised in Jamesville and Camden. She was toughened by adversity but always gentle of touch. She was often a woman of contrasts.

A gentle word of praise was given when deserved, but a sharpened tongue of rebuke when called for. Few in this place cannot recall the sting from a dressing down from sister, aunt or Grandmom Louise. She could burn you on the one hand and sooth you with the breeze of love on the other. On reflection, we knew we deserved it. She did it out of love. She was a surrogate mother to many.

She seemed sophisticated beyond her education, always wise, but never smart in the shallow sense. That sophistication could come tumbling down when she told a ribald story that required that skirts be lifted and that cannot be repeated here today. Many remember a particular one which had her dancing around the room with skirt lifted that had uproarious results.

You remember when they used to say in school, "Neatness counts"? I think she made up that phrase. When she left the apartment to go see Dora at the nursing home or went across the complex to join the ladies for tea, she had every pin and seam in place. How many times as a kid did I hear her tell my mother in sharp tones, "Dora put on some makeup and straighten your hem!" She was always guiding, always teaching, by word and deed.

Few among us can count the number of friends she maintained for many years. Wherever she went, new and additional ones would be counted among this number. At 89, when friends typically predecease us, she was adding new ones. When family dwindles and grows apart by miles and interests, she was blessed to expand the circle and deepen the love. How she treasured the growing closeness of her beloved grandchildren as she entered the twilight of her years. She told me it was the thing that surprised her more and gave her the greatest joy. That they would still display the loyalty and love to her and to one another.

By her very life and her example she was always consistent. In many ways wonderfully predictable. She has left us a testament and a legacy.

To her siblings she leaves her love and only regrets being a burden lately. But, whether escorting her to the casino or sharing your dinner table, she knew the respect and love you always displayed to her. How charming it was to see two accomplished woman in their seventh decade still behaving like little sisters. She wants you to take the time to tell stories of the family so others can share the traditions.

To my generation she hopes we continue to show the respect we have for the elders and the family. And that we continue to try to help and guide each other, as well as our own. Each of us has heard her make a request, not for herself, but to help someone else in the family. "Why don't you give so and so a call, I think they may have a problem." She often acted as the Dame Corleone.

To the next generation she offers a challenge. Don't let our thing, our family, drift apart. This will take more of an effort then ever before. No one lives around the corner, like the old days. But you must take the responsibility. Attend the picnics, visit, call, care. This is surely your job as much as it is to raise your own family. Nurture this family.

I, Louise Monarca Vitagliano, expect nothing less.

When she was in her early twenties, Louise married her first love, Joseph Vitagliano, who came from a strong Italian family that included several siblings. Aunt Louise and Uncle Joe settled into a house at 933 Vine Street, by any standard a spacious home with some grand features. All of the houses on the north side of Vine Street between 9th and 10th Streets sat well above street level so that they took on an air of aristocracy. Even the front lawn was elevated from the street. There was an imposing 5-foot stone wall that held back the dirt in which the lawn was planted and three steps built into the dirt that you climbed up to ascend to the lawn level. At this point, you were looking at the front porch that lay beyond the 12- to 25-foot section of lawn. Still farther up were the three steps to the front door.

When you turned toward the street from this vantage point, you felt like a king surveying his lands. On either side was more lawn interrupted in places only by the walkways leading to the steps of each house. Once inside, you were in the living room with a fine staircase leading upstairs. Beyond the living room was a large dining room, and beyond that was a large kitchen. The kitchen had a door at either end, the rear one leading to a covered back porch and yet more lawn beyond. There was more lawn then I had seen outside any major park. The other door led from the kitchen to a real basement with a cement floor, a veritable playground of space. Yet another unique feature of the home was a skylight in the ceiling of the dining room, allowing for light to enter even the one room without a window. Was this neat or what?

Here was the home into which Louise and Joe brought Joseph, Jr. to be raised. He was the first son of the first born in the Monarca family, and, as such, he had praise heaped upon him from the outset. Little Joe could do no wrong. If he had been a baby that was challenged in the looks department, he still would have been praised; or if her were slow of mind or body, he would have received accolades. But no-o-o-o-o, this was a handsome boy who met and conquered every challenge presented to him all the way into adulthood. He was cursed with exceptional talent and charm, attributes that would later prove to be a liability.

Joe and Louise were justly proud parents. Louise worked at various jobs before giving birth, and Joe had a position with public service. He was a bus driver for the largest public transportation provider in the region. He, too, was someone to be proud of as he donned his attractive dark gray uniform every day to take on this awesome responsibility of carting people to and fro while fighting the narrow streets and avoiding daring pedestrians and shaky drivers. He often drove the #9 or #12 buses that plied their way through North Camden en route to downtown Philadelphia. On occasion, he would handle the #80, which traveled the far reaches of the area, from the end of East Camden to the end of Broadway at Kaigns Avenue. A huge treat in those days for the kids in the family was to wait for Uncle Joe's bus to pull up and get a free ride to your destination. It was like the Robert DeNiro movie, "A Bronx Tale" (in which, you might recall from an earlier chapter, Buck Buck was played by the kids in the street).

With the birth of Joe, Jr., Louise discontinued work, and Uncle Joe had to pick up the slack. He dusted off his old tools and took up barbering again. In the basement beyond the kitchen entrance was a real barber's chair that sat in the middle of the room a safe distance from the oil fired furnace. Directly in front of the chair was a large mirror that had been relegated to its place in the basement because of huge chips on two sides. While the mirror had lost its charm as a dining room piece, it was perfect to impart the ambiance of a real barber shop. Joe had a built-in clientele, with an entire family as customers at 25 cents a haircut. And for 25 cents, the customers got pretty much what they got at Nick's Barber Shop in the 700 block of Vine, nearly next door to the original home of Mario. Each customer got a professional haircut, completed with a flurry of talcum powder administered with a soft-bristled blonde brush. And a benefit, in addition to the 50 percent discount off Nick's prices, was the latest gossip about the rest of the family and the neighborhood. The extra money supplemented the money Louise had made, and Joe, Jr. wanted for nothing as a youth.

Uncle Joe liked to gamble a bit. He liked the horses and ball games and often wagered on both. Unfortunately, he passed this fondness on to his son, who took his father's fondness for gambling to a whole new level. Another natural attribute that Uncle Joe passed on to his son was his outstanding hand-eye coordination, an ability exemplified not only in his driving skill but, much to my liking, in his achievements as a great pinball player. He would take a nickel and play an entire night at Lou and Syls on the hot new machine in town. There wasn't a machine he couldn't beat, and I used to marvel at the rotund little man shifting his weight and cajoling the little steel ball to do his bidding with a little nudge from either hand at just the precise moment of need. He was a master and had a reputation to prove it. After I had observed him for hours, he would eventually look at his watch and nod for me to take over the machine that still had the many games that he had "racked up." Yes, Uncle Joe was king of the pinball. This is high praise from a guy who was pretty darn good himself, to say nothing of John and Joe and their considerable skill levels as well.

Joe inherited his father's love of sports, his penchant for gaming and his hand-eye coordination, while taking his intellect, his passion and his style from Aunt Louise. He got his charm and storytelling ability from both and his innate sports talent from God. Joe mastered everything he pursued as a boy. You name it, and he did it better than most, and often better than any. He could shoot the center cork out of any dart board, kick a football fifty yards, or throw a no-hitter or hit for average or power on the baseball field. But the basketball court was where he made history. As I proclaimed in his eulogy (included here), he was magic on the court before there was Magic Johnson. His talent was his blessing and his curse.

AUNT LOUISE

Joseph Vitagliano - 1935-1996 - May 1, 1996

I am blessed. I knew them all: JR., Joey, Joe, Tag, Vitag, Vittese. He was all of these and more.

He was a man of great appetites and, like us all, a man of many flaws—as well as many talents.

His pure athletic talent, forty years beyond its peak, is still spoken of with awe. Suffice it to say that on the basketball court, he was magic before there was a Magic.

His wit, charm, and storytelling ability made him a sought-after companion by man and beast. He was a Damon Runyon character in the flesh. A day with Taggy at the track was a scene from Guys and Dolls.

He spoke of regret when he reflected on his unfulfilled potential, but at a time when the family needed a symbol of its pride, all of the sports headlines helped us expand our collective Monarca chests and walk taller.

When, as a boy, I was in need of an idol he filled that role superbly!

Sometimes his regrets and flaws made him withdraw and retreat. But always he was drawn back by his love of family. The last several years saw him mellowing and growing close to loved ones.

In the fall of '94, he, John, Bob and I went to Italy to share a glorious time which we each knew could never be duplicated. Oh, how he treasured that trip and, barely two weeks ago, the four of us had a "reunion" at his request. We laughed together for the last time.

An event in the fall of '95 where Joe wasn't even present perhaps best illustrates the impact he has had on all of us.

In Maryland I was thrilled with a visit by three successful men of considerable respect: Cousin Sam, Cousin Bob and dear friend Peppe. It was a wondrous day of limo rides, feasts, and championship golf. It doesn't get better than that!

With all of the sophistication, worldwide travel and business experience, what did we speak of that brought on hysterical laughter and tears of joy to our eyes on that day? We shared Tag stories one after the other, as if it were a wake, and he wasn't even sick then. You know the kind: he was racing down the Atlantic Expressway going over 90 mph, attempting not to miss the daily double bet, when he was stopped by the police. As only Joe could do, he was aggravated with the cop. As Joe lowered the window, with that look that he had, the cop said "Do you know why I stopped you sir?" Joe replied, "If it wasn't for speeding you got the wrong !@#$%^ car!!!"

What high praise—to each of us, and to you, he brought memorable moments of joy. Like his athletic skills, these stories will last for decades to come, for that is his legacy. He was memorable. It's hard to think of him without smiling. And that's a true story.

When Joe and I talked about this moment I told him I didn't think I could get through it, he said "I'm laying 8 to 5 that you can." Well, pal, I did it... So when you get to heaven, go to the pay window.

You're a winner!

His exploits on the court have often been recounted, but for the youngsters who are reading this, allow me to regale you with some of them. He has been elected to the South Jersey Basketball Hall of Fame because of these accomplishments, which include leading his Woodrow Wilson team to a state championship in 1953. At just short of 5 feet 9 inches, he held more scoring records than anyone before his time and for a long time afterward. His foul shooting percentage is still among the top ten in the school's long history. He scored 53 points against Bridgeton and often joked that he would have scored 100 if they had two balls. He was recruited by schools from all over the country and was honored with a basketball scholarship to Annapolis if he would just first attend Bullis Prep, a preparatory school in Maryland. He chose Annapolis and went off with much fanfare in 1953. It was a shock to Joe to be surrounded not by adoring fans and awed opponents but by guys with similar talents trying to make the team without any privileges.

Our house at 523 became the refuge Joe sought when he surreptitiously left Bullis Prep and stayed a couple of nights with us to get a story together for his parents. Word spread through the family that Joey had quit school but was entertaining offers from Albright College and Muhlenberg University, both of which had offered him full scholarships to play basketball. He attended both for brief periods, each with the same result of returning to 523 for a night and then to Vine Street to break the news of quitting again. Still, Joe was the pride and joy of the family that continued to bask in the vestiges of his glory of the previous school year. He was still welcomed, although underage, to many bars and to all sporting events in the area. He was still a very big fish in a little pond.

Eventually, Joe found meaningful employment at RCA Victor and Campbell Soup, because they each had a basketball team in the Industrial League and Joe was a stellar addition to their squads. He worked in those factories as a timekeeper or doing other easy jobs that allowed him to be fresh for the evening games. He was treated as a celebrity by most all around him. While his sports talents would fade, he would always be treated as the respected elder of his generation even though his lapses in good behavior did not always set a good example. Only Uncle Emilio tried to instill humility in Joe, but to little avail. I was the biggest Joe Vitagliano, Jr. fan.

I followed Joe around like a little puppy dog. There was no task that I would not undertake on his behalf. From shining his shoes to fetching him a Coke, I was his guy. Joe was not unaware of my adulation, and he always responded by treating me as if I was older then my chronological age. He took the time to teach me lessons, not only showing me how to throw a curve ball but also instilling in me the value of a neat appearance. I was his "Pal," and Pal became my nickname for many years to come. His last call to me before his death at age 60 began with, "Hi ya, Pal, how's it going?"

He had an impact on my life from a positive as well as a negative perspective. My fear of failing at college stemmed from knowing that, with much more talent than me, he had failed. Succeeding chapters will attest to our lifetime of shared experiences. His life of the huge highs of success and the lows of failure needs to be studied by all in the family for the lessons it can teach: Humility is more valuable than the pride that comes from the adulation of others. Fame can be blinding. Work is as valuable as talent. Never give up.

Louise and Joe prepared for Joe's wedding with great anticipation. It would be the first wedding of the new Monarca generation, and everyone anticipated a gala affair. Joe, true to his celebrity stature and his natural charm, had attracted one of the beauties of the region. Charlotte Smith was beautiful by any standard. Her family was a prominent Anglo-Saxon type (a disappointment to some old-timers in the clan) that lived in upscale Erlton, just a few miles from Camden. Charlotte was as charming as Joe and was going to be a great addition to our family. The months leading up to the event were like every other major milestone, with the impending wedding the topic of every Sunday dinner conversation. Who would be invited? Would the Morronis make it up from Bridgeton? Who would be the best man and maid of honor? The whole family was immersed in facts and gossip. Nothing could spoil the events leading up to the celebration or the big event itself. But something did.

Two months before the big day, Louise was preparing for bed. Joey had yet to come in, and big Joe was prone on the sofa watching that newfangled TV. Louise, who enjoyed reading herself to sleep, often preceded Joe to bed, and on this night she followed that habit. Joey came in late as usual and quietly ascended the staircase so as not to wake big Joe, who had once again fallen asleep in front of a now snow-filled TV screen. Louise awoke chagrined at the empty space next to her. With a touch of anger she thought, "Damn him, he fell asleep on the sofa again and will have a stiff neck all day." She came to the top of the stairs and could easily see him unmoving in his pants and undershirt. "Joe," she hollered, "get up here and get cleaned up!" Uncle did not move. "Joe!" she yelled again to an unhearing Uncle Joe. He was dead. Aunt Louise did not know this until she ran down the steps and shook him over and over again. Next door, Aunt Lola could hear the screams of her sister, as did Joey from his bedroom upstairs. They too felt the shock and disbelief before grief. Joe, a man in his 40s, had died from a massive heart attack without warning just two months from becoming a father-in-law.

The wedding went on as planned, because, as people say at such times, "Joe would have wanted it that way." Louise was never really the same without a mate. She made up for it by doting on her son and the grandchildren that he and Charlotte produced. She was most notably involved with her youngest grandson, Jesse, who was also the apple of his Dad's eye. Like others in the Monarca family, Jesse counts Gram Louise as one of the most influential people in his life. He and his siblings, Judy, Joyce and young Joe, have grown up to fully understand their mom and dad, who often had a tumultuous relationship but never fell out of love, only marriage. The grand dame, Aunt Louise, went on to dole out advice and give direction to the entire clan, always out of love.

In Search of Courage

The DiSibios. At the occasion of Uncle Mike DiSibio's wedding, all of the clan was captured on film.

My dad was standing on the left, with Aunts Maida, Mary, Lena, and Uncle Joe and Aunt Minnie to his left. Seated was the bridegroom, Uncle Mike, Grandmom Minnigale, Grandpop, Raffaello and Aunt Lucy.

In Search of Courage

*"The neighborhood had more than its share of weird inhabitants,
people who would carry on conversations with no one in particular
and the ever-present drunk..."*

THE SHOE REPAIR BUSINESS WAS HISTORY. We had not paid on the mortgage in many months, and Mr. Vidigleone gave us notice to vacate our home. We were once again evicted. Dad had to scramble now and find us a home, while he was trying to break free of his latest girlfriend. He knew of a property at 4th and Berkley in the center of South Camden and quickly moved us there. One day I found him and his brother Mike piling our modest belongings into a borrowed truck, and off we went. The year was 1951. Dad had already made a revolving door of our front entrance, but this move was particularly traumatic for many reasons.

It is a lesson in economics as to how all of this selling and buying of properties could transpire without any formal paperwork. At the heart of these transactions was Mr. Vidigleone, like the company store a holdover from another time. Today, he would be called a slumlord, but in those days he was an investor who owned many houses in Camden. If you wanted one of his houses, you would abjectly approach him; and if he found you worthy and with a means of support, he would "sell" you a house. In his case, selling you the house meant that he would give you a small booklet the size of a passport. There were lined pages inside the booklet, and every time you came to him with your monthly cash payment he would mark the amount paid and date of the payment and initial the entries. I have never seen any other paperwork on our house. I saw the book, because on occasion my dad would give me the book along with the cash to deliver the payment to Mr. Vidigleone at his tiny office on Cooper Street.

Elaine once made a payment with one of her incessant questions aimed at the old man. "When will our bill be paid?" she inquired. He booted her out, with an Italian curse for her temerity. If you paid the entire loan, as evidenced by the booklet, he would then give you a deed in your name. If you missed enough payments, he would evict you and start the process over with another aspiring homeowner, because he never took his name off the deed. Such was the state of financial justice in Camden.

The trauma surrounding the move to 4th and Berkley ensued because we were about to be torn from our deep roots. Elaine and I had already started kindergarten and first grade at Sewell School, on the corner of 7th and Vine, and were admitted to Holy Name Catholic School for the upcoming year. Holy Name was a beautiful stone structure with attached church at 4th and Vine. We couldn't wait to go there with our Catholic friends; we did not want to go to school with the "publics." At Holy Name, we could wear uniforms and be taught by the nuns who were so very good, and smart too. We actually liked the rituals of "first Fridays" and morning prayers. We felt special—until the move to South Camden that meant we would leave our school and our friends. We had no idea where we would go to school, since we heard from the adults that Mt. Carmel School was full and no new students were to be admitted. Everyone knew that the publics in South Camden consisted mainly of colored kids and roughnecks. For some illogical reason, we thought of ourselves as above all those lower classes. This attitude, I am sure, was fueled by the adults who heard the story from my mother. We soon found out that we would be attending St. Peter and Paul on Spruce Street, just off Broadway. The school was almost eight blocks away, not quite a bus ride but a long way by our standards. Once again people felt sorry for us.

St. Pete's, as we called it, was not so bad. It had the same basic rituals as Holy Name with some new wrinkles. Each first Friday of the month we would have to take Holy Communion. This, of course, meant that we could not have any food for three hours beforehand, resulting in no breakfast. As a result of this rule, the school made provision for the kids to go down to the activity room to have hot chocolate and fresh cinnamon buns after mass. But there was one catch—the cost was 5 cents for each or a 10-cent total tab for both. This tasty snack did not come cheap.

To make matters worse, every Thursday the nuns would call the roll to see how many of each of the goodies the kids wanted. This came as a surprise on the first Thursday. The guys in front of me were showing off by ordering three cups of hot chocolate and three buns each, when Johnny Sturgis, just before me, proclaimed, "I want three cups of hot chocolate and five buns." All I could think of was, "Where in the hell does he plan to get 35 cents?" Now it was my turn, and I said I wouldn't know until the next day, but the nun demanded an answer so she would get a proper order. I finally said I would have one bun. Now I had to break the news to Mom. After a very stern lecture on never committing before asking, she agreed to give me 5 cents and an equal amount weekly for chores I would do so I could save the money and get hot chocolate next time. Elaine got the same lecture and to this day hesitates to make a verbal contract and is still wary of written ones.

Unlike the school, the house was never acceptable. It was a corner property with the store front facing Berkley and the residence entrance facing 4th Street. The store was unoccupied but was blocked off from the residence. Like the side entrance on Birch Street, there were four steps to reach the side door. Once inside you were in a tiny living room with a full staircase filling one side and a kitchen to the right through an archway. Up the stairs were two small bedrooms and a tiny bath with one tiny room at the back that had an exterior door leading to the lower rooftop. This little room was mine, and every night I slept there I imagined someone breaking through the door to get me. I spent many a terrified night there without my Dad around to protect me. Not fun.

The neighborhood was similar to North Camden but seemed a little more run down and the worse for wear. Directly across 4th Street was Gino's grocery store, a poor imitation of the great Joe's Meat Market. On the next street south on 4th was Nick's Candy Store. This is where the local Italian toughs hung out, day and night. Across Berkley from our rented house was a nondescript public elementary school. The same macadam street and brick and cement sidewalks, going on and on except for an occasional tree to break up the monotony, was a replica of North Camden. There were no buses on either 4th or Berkley, but they were plentiful on Broadway which was only four blocks away. Worst of all, there were no Monarcas.

Perhaps the one saving grace was the fact that the DiSibio house was at 233 Berkley just a block and a half away. This was fortunate for many reasons. Like the Monarcas, the DiSibio girls tended to stay close to the nest, thus several of my father's sisters lived only a few blocks away on Roberts Street or Evans Street. Grandmom DiSibio was the only grandmother I remember, since Teresa Monarca had died several months after my birth. Domenica, aka Minnie, was a gentle woman who personified the classic stereotype of an old-time Italian wife. She was completely subservient to her bully husband and doting and protective of her children.

I know of no redeeming qualities possessed by Raffaello, save for the fact that he worked hard all his life and retired with dignity from RCA at 65. We have a Courier Post photo to prove it. He ruled over a very unruly group of offspring that included three boys, Anthony, Michael and Joseph. The girls were a jealous bunch who, with few exceptions, thought little of others. Maida, Mary, Lena, Lucy and Minnie were all born at 233, and the lot of them were hard workers and taskmasters as spouses.

I have memories of all of them, but they are far dimmer and suffused with less affection than those of the Monarcas. The exception was my father's younger brother, Mike, who was a surrogate father to me in the absence of my own. Mike was the DiSibios' contribution to WWII. He was a Parris Island-trained Marine who was part of the "Greatest Generation" that Tom Brokaw memorialized in his book. He served in the Pacific in the battle for Okinawa and returned a hardened veteran. Mike married the demure Lena Perno who lived up the block on Berkley, and they had two great kids, Michael and Joseph, who would be like brothers to me. This family would go on to play a major role in my maturation.

The youngest of my father's brothers, Joseph, was unfortunately emotionally torn growing up and hiding his homosexuality. He suffered at the hands of his peers and endured the physical abuse of his older brothers, who, in ignorance, thought they could beat his feelings out of him. Joe was a gentle man who, in the last forty years of his life, found peace with his long-term companions, self-estranged from the family excepting for major events.

The girls were as different one from the other as any group of individuals seeking attention within a large brood. Aunt Maida married Mike Morroco and had one son, Dominic. They were as conservative and bland as any family carving out a life in South

Camden in that era. Aunt Lucy married the gentle Armand Pi-
toscio, who had a resemblance to Perry Como, a popular singer
of the time. They begat two children, Carman and Patricia. Aunt
Lucy was the loudest and most aggressive of the girls and widowed Uncle Armand when she died in her '30s from heart failure
during the Easter season in 1959. Armand, as quiet as his wife was
loud, did a fantastic job of raising the kids without fanfare, always
maintaining contact with the family.

Mary was the sweetest and most timid of the sisters and
married Donald Pearson; together they had Margaret and Barbara
and settled on Roberts Street. Uncle Donald sustained a back injury at work that left him disabled enough to receive a large cash
settlement. He invested the money "on the street," as they say—he
became a shylock. He lent money at usurious interest rates and
made a good, if dangerous, living.

Minnie was the youngest sister and suffered some malady,
perhaps epilepsy, which affected her throughout life. She married
several times without bearing children and became estranged from
the family in her late '20s, eventually turning up in Florida before
her death in her '50s. Lena was the DiSibio's answer to the Monarca's Milena (Pat). She was dramatic, with a slight resemblance to
Lana Turner, and domineering as the wife of Mike Recchia. Together they parented Sammy, who enjoyed a somewhat more
enlightened environment, but a society still marked by prejudice,
when it came to his homosexuality. The Recchias settled on Evans
Street between 4th and 5th, joining Maida and Lucy and eventually
Grandmom following the death of the "old man."

Uncle Mike Recchia was a diminutive man of modest
wants. He was capable but unwilling to challenge his wife on most
domestic matters. Instead, he carved out his own life outside the

home. He was renowned as a consummate card dealer for all the big card games the mob types would put together. He had a reputation for honesty and integrity beyond reproach and could be trusted with large amounts of money or secrets. He worked at many legitimate jobs, including at the Courier Post and the Garden State Race Track, but supplemented his income with the pay and tips he received at all-night card games.

His reputation was never more soundly tested than when the Garden State Track was set ablaze by an electrical fire in the middle of a busy racing day. The fire resulted in many injuries to workers and spectators alike, to say nothing of cash that went up in flames. Uncle Mike was serving as a teller at the $10 window when the fire caused a panicked rush toward the exits. Mike calmly piled all of his cash into a large sack and left for the exits amidst outgoing patrons and incoming firefighters. Mike made his way home and called the main offices of the management of the track, informed them that he had saved about $11,000 in cash and inquired as to where he should deliver it. Of course, he was berated by his wife and ridiculed by my father and others for his "stupidity." For once, he defied his wife and simply shook his head at his detractors knowing he had done the right thing and that they just didn't get it. These were the opposing moral forces I was surrounded by as I continued to be exposed to the two families.

The similarities of North and South Camden ended with the closeness of family members. In North Camden, I had a father, a familiar school and friends cultivated over years with whom I had established a reputation of daring and courage. In South Camden, my father was mostly absent, and playmates that were more mature tested me every day. The biggest difference was the impact on my sense of safety and security. For much of the year we spent in South Camden, I was scared. Fear was part of my day and night.

During the day I was fearful of not living up the expectations of the local tough guys with whom I began to hang. They had begun to comment on the physical assets of the passing girls and women and of their desire to have carnal knowledge of them and I, at 12, was struggling as I tried to understand what the attraction was and why anyone would want a "piece of ass." From that, I learned a valuable lesson. I would listen to the banter and smile and nod when I felt it was appropriate and, thus, would appear to be knowledgeable. This tactic worked more often than not but did not relieve the constant fear that I would be found out for the naïve kid that I was. If I listened long enough, I could often ferret out enough information to actually understand, for example, that the reference to a piece of ass wasn't meant literally but instead meant intercourse. The story of the birds and the bees was related to me not by a patient father but by foulmouthed guys hanging on the corner of 4th and Berkley.

My fear related to physical security was even more deep-seated. North Camden was an enclave of likeminded people who shared much the same goals of social and financial advancement. I was surrounded by caring and loving family members who had a genuine feeling of responsibility for my safety and wellbeing. The need to lock one's homes was never felt, and I never was fearful for any reason other than the rare nightmare occasioned by a Bud Abbott and Lou Costello Mummy movie. On the other hand, South Camden was lacking in loyal friends, and relatives looked at us as a liability whom they might have to help feed or clothe. Add to this a population that was interspersed with people of color who we feared out of ignorance, and you can well imagine that this was not fun.

The ignorance about people of color was not diminished on one particular night when my mother sent me down to 233 to return a large empty bowl and platter used to cover the now eaten hot spaghetti that Grandma had sent up for us to have for dinner. My grandmother and the aunts would often send us leftovers, knowing that my father was not providing for us in his absence.

On this night, the bowl was very large and, in addition, my mother topped it with a large pressing iron that she had borrowed earlier to iron some of our meager clothing. The three items combined to make an unwieldy bundle, and I carried them by encircling them with my arms and heading off to cover the block and a half to 233. As I walked the darkened street, I noticed, in the dim light of the street lamp, a tall young colored man coming in the other direction. I was a little nervous because my hands were occupied, and I could do little to avoid him if he confronted me in some way. There was no confrontation; he just calmly passed close by me and reached over, grabbed the iron which was on top of the bundle and ran off. I was dumbfounded. I ran back home, still encumbered by the bowl, and cried while telling my Mom the tale upon my arrival. While she gave me sympathy, she implied that I should have done something to prevent the theft, like crossing the street when I first noticed the man. The iron theft incident, coupled with the dreaded exterior door in my bedroom, certainly did not aid and abet my sense of security.

To further exacerbate my insecurity, there was an additional string of events that deserve mention. The neighborhood had more than its share of weird inhabitants, people who would carry on conversations with no one in particular and the ever-present drunk who would while away the day hanging on corners with paper bags that covered half pints of vodka or rum. One particular large colored man took up the habit of making crude remarks to my mother when she walked by on her way home. These remarks got increasingly lascivious and loud as the days passed. My mother ignored him for a time but soon found his behavior turning more aggressive. I can remember more than one night being awakened by this drunk banging on our entry door and hollering for my mother to let him in; eventually, he would go away when my mother would not respond to his shouts. For some reason, his behavior ceased as mysteriously as it had begun. Perhaps he stopped because my dad had reappeared for a brief period around Christmas time. The entire incident added to the terror I felt in the tiny bedroom as I awaited for dawn to bring some modicum of security.

My father returned shortly before the happening of an un-related event that was the most memorable occasion during our South Camden tenure. In July of 1951, Arnold Vincent Cream de-feated Ezzard Charles for the heavyweight championship of the world. You may have heard of him as Jersey Joe Walcott. This was at a time when boxing championships were as cherished as World Series rings. Walcott was a hometown boy, and the spontaneous celebration that erupted in the homes and in the streets after his victory was an unforgettable sports memory for me and Elaine. People were banging pots and pans and whooping and hollering, all of this on a summer's night with windows raised to fight off the heat. Charles' defeat in Pittsburgh instilled pride and gave the whole town a reason to celebrate. Walcott would forever be intro-duced as Jersey Joe from Camden, New Jersey.

Some years later, I remember my dad introducing me to "the champ" in Frieda's Luncheonette at 2ne and Berkley where Joe had stopped to have a sandwich. Still later when I was in Junior High, I ran into "the champ"" when he was lecturing me and my gang in North Camden, where we were engaged in a race war of sorts over the integration of Pyne Point School. By this time, Joe was the Sheriff of Camden County and engaged in gang control and race relations efforts. That did not ever take away from the pride that

Joe gave us all in 1951. It was proof positive that success knew no color bounds; the white folk took pride from every source, even if the lessons that could have been learned were ignored.

Dad's return was almost as dramatic as the knockout of Charles. My father appeared after a frantic phone call to my mother, asking her to let him return because he was injured and was finally finished with his fling with Eleanor of Baltimore. Mom, who caved as usual, was unprepared for what appeared a short time later. Dad came through the door with a couple of bundles, one containing his belongings and the other with his dirty clothes. Hidden at first by the two bundles, but revealed when he dropped the packages onto the sofa, was a bloodstained shirt, still freshly wet. As Mom ministered to the gaping wound in his chest, he told her how Eleanor had stabbed him with a pair of scissors during a fight. Elaine and I were in awe and listened and watched as Mom expertly mended and bandaged the wound. No matter the injury; we were delighted that we were together again and naively thought that it would last.

Mom has often told the story of how no sooner would she finish washing and ironing his dirty clothing than he would abscond again. When my wife Carol heard the story for the first time she advised my mother that she "should have ironed slower"—a funny line for a sad story. He stayed long enough this time to give us some real hope. He vowed to move us back to North Camden, and this was one of the few promises he kept.

Our year in South Camden left us with few memories of note. Elaine made no friends she can remember, this from a girl who has always been a magnet to whom loyal lifetime friends are drawn. As for me, most of the memories were dark ones. To further accentuate the clouds that hung over us at 4th and Berkley, this was the place that rheumatic fever began to take hold in my body. Elaine can recall better than I the screams of pain I expressed as I doubled over with abdominal pain. All of my joints were wracked with pain, and there was considerable consternation as to the cause. I had dark circles under my eyes, even on my best days, and people began to notice that my complexion was just not right.

Eventually, my condition was diagnosed correctly, and treatment included daily multiple doses of iron medicine preceded by many hours spent in the waiting room of Dr. Bonier and others. In those days, a doctor's appointment was much like the cable guy today—be there for your appointment at one o'clock but you may not see anyone until 5. Of course, if you arrived at 1:15, you might find that you had missed your appointment and had to reschedule for another day.

Rheumatic fever or not, we were happy at the prospect of returning to North Camden. Once again, it was a mystery to me as to how my father was able to somehow resecure the old 523 N. 8th house, but he did. While we were making plans to return to our roots, however, we heard of distressing news: the Holy Name School had no room for Elaine and me. Mom told us that we would, after all, have to go to school with the publics. Woe unto us. Later we would come to realize that the story concerning the availability of space was bogus.

The sad truth was that Elaine and I would be going to Sewell School, because Dad could not afford both the arrears payments to Mr. Vidigleone and the small amount of tuition that Holy Name required. Now we would have to return, not to a school with Cousin Johnny and our other friends and the beloved Sister Veronica, but to a school surrounded by the unfamiliar. On balance, we were happy to get back to all the other comforts and the security of our old haunts, but the school issue once again made us the subjects of sympathy.

6
Aunt Anna

Aunt Anna holds Cousin Johnny as Grandmom Monarca looks on. The photo was taken in front of Monarca headquarters at 734 Vine. Take note of the brick sidewalks.

Uncle John cut a dashing figure in his fedora.

Aunt Anna

"Uncle John was a kind and gentle man who was perfectly suited to the strong-willed and traditionalist Anna."

AUNT ANNA COULD EASILY BE DESCRIBED AS HANDSOME. She was not a beauty like Marie, nor was she tiny like Lydia; but she possessed the most regal countenance of all of the Monarca girls. Together with Louise, she came to the "promised land" of America guided by Mario and Teresa. She and Louise would take on adult responsibilities long before puberty set in. She was a student of her parents but was nearly the equal of her sister, and, together, they would forever be the closest of any of the siblings, regularly parceling out their counsel and advice. They would often be spoken of almost as the alter egos of one another when the family referred to their thoughts. "Louise and Anna think . . ." this or that. But Anna was not the mirror image of her older sister or her mother, Teresa, or of anyone else for that matter. She was one of a kind.

Aunt Anna was deliberate and meticulous in all things. No one could compare to her as she prepared a meal or a snack. She always approached the activity with the precision of a paratrooper on a night jump, starting with the donning of the proper apron. The image of her in the kitchen that I recall was of a woman in a full apron, one with short sleeves and full front. She unfailingly would protect the food from falling hair by encasing her head in a neat hair net. She would then put out all the proper instruments to be used in preparation and be sure that the proper bowls and plates were at the ready. The correct place settings would include all of the instruments required to consume the meal. In all of this, "proper" was the operative word: Aunt Anna was proper.

Many words could describe her, in addition to some of those I've mentioned—meticulous and deliberate, dignified, regal, conservative, staid, reproving and uncompromising come to mind. Like Louise, she could not be described as soft. Yet, although the word "warm" was not apt, her love of her husband and son were as fearsome as that shown by some of the more gregarious and demonstrative family member. She was too candid to be called charming. Once she quit smoking, she had no discernable vices, and many spoke of her as self-righteous. If the family had a moral compass, it was Anna.

The Iannettas settled at 725 Elm Street. The tiny backyard practically abutted her parents' home at 734 Vine Street. It was just half a block from my house on Birch, closer if I used the alley behind Joe's Meat Market and exited the other end of the alley at the back of Litwin's Grocery Store. Aunt Pat's house was just three-quarters of a block away on Willard Street.

The Elm Street home of the Iannettas was impressive. There were four steps leading up the entrance, and upon entry you found yourself in a tiny vestibule beyond which was a staircase inviting you to the upstairs. Just right of the vestibule was a very large living room, nearly the size of our shoemaker shop, replete with well-kept furniture, including a large overstuffed chair under the front windows. Next to the chair was a beautiful console radio with an "RCA Victor His Master's Voice" symbol emblazoned on its rich woodwork, which could not help but catch your eye. There was a full-sized sofa on the long wall to the right and a large delicately carved table under yet another set of windows beyond the sofa. The left side of the living room, which held a couple of chairs, also had a very unique feature: there, in the middle of the wall, was a door beyond which was a closet. I was very impressed with this, because we had no closets in my house, either upstairs or down. What a luxury!

Beyond the living room was a beautiful and fully furnished dining room. As you moved through the dining room on the left side of the table in a path that put you between the table and the serving piece on its left, you entered a small kitchen, nearly running into the refrigerator. On your right, with the dining room wall on the other side, was a small enameled table and chairs, and on the opposite windowed wall was a sink and modest counter space. Wooden cupboards finished the windowed wall. On the left side of that wall was a door leading to a tiny porch and down a couple of steps to the small yard. This path would take you to yet another unique feature of 725 Elm. At the far side of the yard was a wrought iron gate that brought you to a cement walk all along the side of the house and back to Elm Street. Instead of attached neighbors on the east side of the house at 734, Aunt Anna's Elm Street house had this 8-foot separation between it and the next house, allowing for a number of windows on its east side. Every one of the three bedrooms had windows facing the "courtyard" or the front or back. In effect, it was a corner house in the middle of the block. You could hardly be unimpressed by such a structure.

This extraordinary house was made a home by the efficient touch of Aunt Anna. She had taken a spouse after she and her sister Lola fell in love with a couple of brothers, both of whom would soon join the Monarca family. Uncle John was a kind and gentle man who was perfectly suited to the strong-willed and traditionalist Anna. Her domain, like her mother's before her, would be a matriarchy. Uncle John, who came from a strong Italian family, in South Camden of course, was steady as a rock.

Uncle John was as unflappable as any man I knew as a child. I never heard him raise his voice, express anger beyond the frustration of a father/uncle at the antics of roughhousing boys or be anything but pleasant. He worked for as long as I can remember as an electrician in the New York Shipbuilding Corporation. The "yard," as it was known, was a massive shipbuilding enterprise at the very tip of South Camden, necessarily fronting the Delaware River. It was here that the mighty war ships would be built to confront the Nazis and the Japanese war machines.

In my mind's eye, I can still see Uncle John sitting in front of that beautiful radio in his grey sweater, reading the Courier Post and smoking his unfiltered Camel cigarettes. With his great dignity, he was a perfect mate for Anna. He was generous with his labor and in his acceptance, without comment or complaint, of Grandpop's move into his home and his stay of many years. His little snicker at an amusing comment can still be heard today, echoed to perfection by his son. He was not a man of extremes or of consuming passions. He would gamble at a friendly card game, but not to excess; he would have a highball or glass of wine, but no one ever saw him tipsy; he enjoyed sporting events, but they were not his major topics of conversation. His only known passion, which he engaged in quietly, was his family. He demonstrated his love in many ways, but never so tellingly as when he referred to his wife as "my dolly." When she would declare it was time to leave a family event, you could hear Uncle John gently reply, "Alright, Dolly, let's go."

Together the dignified Anna and the taciturn John produced their only child, John, nine months after my birth. To this day, we are as close as any cousin in the family is to another. John, a cute youngster who grew into a handsome adult, enjoyed a life as an only child born to conservative parents who were never prone to drama. His family was never forced to deny him anything but doled out gifts and toys carefully, with admonitions to care for them. Like all of us, he has assumed many of the attributes and frailties of his parents. He is dignified, sometimes to the point of seeming cool or even imperious, though he can be uproariously witty and wry; he is conservative but has owned motorcycles and Corvettes; he is modest but can wax on with passion about his grandchildren; he is introspective but willing to share considered thoughts about himself and others; he has rock-like fidelity to family and friends; he has cultivated a reputation of frugality but can exhibit great generosity; and his integrity is unchallenged. He is a truly a product of his parents and is a child of North Camden as well.

My life is intertwined with Cousin John's because of our closeness in age and the relationship that grew as we shared of the neighborhood. Many are the hours I spent at 725, and we both spent many hours at 523. At 725, we were closely supervised, excepting the times when we were in the basement playing war. At 523, we were mostly without adult eyes that could observe us when we moved the sofa or overstuffed chairs around, pretending that they were the opposing linemen on the football team, running at them at full speed and throwing ourselves into them with all of our force, knocking them over without regard to the possibility of breakage. I loved going to Johnnie's house, because he would open that magical closet door and pull out cardboard boxes with neatly packed sections of his well-preserved toys.

We could play for hours with those wooden blocks or the tiny cowboys and Indians; I was always the Indians and, rightly so, since they were Johnnie's toys. Occasionally, Aunt Anna would make us some Kool-Aid and put out a ginger snap for us to snack on. These, of course, were served only in the kitchen at the table after we had properly washed our hands. At 523, we would rummage, with soiled hands, through the cabinets to grab a soda and bring it to wherever we were playing, often spilling the contents in the process. I loved the order of his house, and I suspect he loved the freedom of mine.

Johnny and I had different circles of friends but were constantly drawn together by our contrast. As we grew into our teen years, he would often be with Michael Gartland or Freddie Rumbach, usually in their houses across the street from 725. I would be hanging on the corner with Skippy Flamini or Dukey Kirk, playing in the street or acting like young toughs. Johnny and I shared a teenage attraction to Carolyn Massi, daughter of the fabulous seamstress who made the Easter outfits of which we were so proud; in neither case, though, was the "relationship" ever consummated, not even by a stolen kiss. Cousin John was always conservative, while I was flashy. In every way, I was the sizzle and he was the steak. In our choice of clothing, for example, I had the latest fad when we could afford it, and he fancied timeless fashion. I was daring and adventuresome, and he was steady and productive. Our differences abounded, but we would always be drawn together by our mutual affection and respect, as well as the interests in common we discovered over the years. Our love of family, our eye for beauty, our boundless search for knowledge, our keen insight into people, and our desire and commitment to try to "do the right thing"—and do things right—are the glues that bind us together. Over the years, I have learned many things from John Baptista Iannetta.

My affinity to John was often derived of envy. Of course, I envied his "Leave It To Beaver" family (even before there was a "Leave It To Beaver"), and I envied his "stuff"—his toys, his bedroom, his house. I envied them in a good way, not a jealous way; I aspired to have these things myself and was inspired to emulate the lifestyle at John's and so was motivated by what I saw there.

Johnny became proficient at playing the accordion after Aunt Anna and Uncle John purchased the instrument and weekly lessons for him. Unable to afford either, I nonetheless found a way to mimic his musical accomplishment.

In Sewell School, there was a band, and when Mrs. Johnson, our fifth grade teacher, asked for volunteers to take up the French horn, the only instrument that no student was looking to play, I quickly raised my hand. Bursting with pride, I lugged the huge black case from school, along with a sheaf of the first lessons. My first stop was at Aunt Anna's. I knocked on the door, and Aunt Anna invited me in with a distinct look of curiosity. Johnny was still not home from Holy Name, so Aunt Anna and I sat across from each other in the grand living room while I unpacked my newly-adopted hobby. At moments like these, and there were many, Aunt Anna was patient and caring, making inquiries as to why I had chosen this instrument and wishing me success. She was gentle and kind as she advised me to practice hard and learn well. She was warm and encouraging. It was a special moment between an aunt and a nephew.

My arrival at 523 that day was decidedly less encouraging. Mom was flabbergasted by this turn of events and expressed concern that I would break this fine item and we would be responsible for it. She also peppered me with questions about when and how I intended to learn to play and made faces when I put it to my lips and produced horrible squealing sounds that did not portend the likelihood of long-term improvement. Further, she surmised that I had no real interest in music and only wanted not to play it but to play with it. My relationship with the French horn mercifully ended the next day when Mrs. Johnson informed me that lessons would each be $1; this settled any doubt as to whether I might have a lasting relationship with music. This was no loss to me or to the musical world, for, alas, I have proven that, except for the nine chords I can play on the folk guitar, I have zero musical talent. Failure with the French horn was a foregone conclusion.

In addition to his talent with music, Johnny was a terrific athlete. He received none of the adulation of Joey but was nonetheless superb in his own right. We were young boys together when the neighborhood began to be formalized enough to have organized and uniformed sports teams. The little league teams had the names of their sponsors, Flexetalic Gasket and Hunt Penn among them, emblazoned across the top. John and I both made the same team, he as a catcher and me as a short stop. One year when I was made captain and John was the MVP of our championship team, we had a gala team party at which we received our first trophies and went home thinking we were now like Uncle Phil or our big cousin Joey. Uncle John was at many of those games, if his work permitted, and Mom, and occasionally Uncle Mike DiSibio, would cheer for me.

Football was our most exciting endeavor. We could not wait to don pads and helmets and become gladiators. But there was one catch. There were weight limits, and both John and I were each two or three pounds over the limit just two days before opening day and weigh-in. This was not a problem for the geniuses like Pat Pagent that were coaches. We were told to bring our heaviest winter coats to practice the morning before the game. When we arrived at Pyne Point Park, we put on full equipment, topped by our winter coats, and were ushered into the coach's waiting car which was running with the heater on full blast. Once in the back seat the coach put a blanket on us and slammed the door shut until we sweated off the offending pounds. This may have been creative leadership, but in looking back it's easy to see that no one was concerned with the dishonesty—or the danger we were put in.

John went on to become a standout as a defensive end for a talented Camden Catholic team as well as a light heavyweight boxer
for the school. I forewent sports after junior high school so I could
work after school and on Saturdays at Joe's.

While Johnny seemed to have it all as a young man, from
his rearing by an intact and providing mother and father to being blessed by having our grandfather as a housemate for several
years before his passing, no piece of good fortune could compare
with his choice of the woman he would take as a wife. The delightful and ever-optimistic Margaret McMonical agreed to become his
bride during the summer of 1964.

There are few unions that could be described as nearing
perfection, but I would suggest this is one of them, the conservative John joined with this woman of Irish decent who would exhibit
behaviors that he might disdain in others but always cherished in
her. When others would become raucous at parties, John might
shake his head with a suggestion that the revelers should display
more decorum. But when Peggy was the life of the party or the
instigator of boisterous antics, John would smile in approval with
Uncle John's little "heh, heh" giggle and intone proudly, "Isn't she
something?" Another Yin and Yang, Peg and John are like clapper
and bell—they go together. Indeed, who else but Peggy would find
it cute when John disappears during shopping mall visits only to
return in two hours or so, responding, without remorse, to queries
regarding his absence by saying, "I went to the movies, is there
a problem?" With all that's been good in his life, fortune failed to
shine upon him for a time when he prematurely lost his beloved
mother in 1972.

As adults, both of my wives and I have delighted in the
company of John and Peg. In early adulthood, we would settle for
coffee and cake or pizza at each other's homes, and would always

gravitate toward one another at family events. In later years, we would rendezvous at more exotic venues. We got together in Seattle, embarking from there on a fog-filled hydrofoil trip to Canada; we also shared a condo in Lake Tahoe for a long weekend during which John and I revived our competitive early years with fierce paddle ball games until we were exhausted. Incidentally, I won, but who was keeping score? We met in San Francisco, where we went to bars suggested by Danny Iannetta, John and Peg's son, and saw all of the sights of the city; the day after Carol and I left, John and Peggy experienced the great San Francisco earthquake of 1989—and lived to tell about it. We all shared a fondness of a good drink and saw the inside of many bars. John and I would rarely fail to propose the toast first created by Peggy's late father, "How could anything this good be so cheap?" In 65 years of my life, I cannot remember a year without spending some time with John, and I have no memory of any of it ever being without reward.

In Search of a Father

Elaine and I with Dad. We are sitting on the steps of what used to be the side entrance to Joe's Meat Market.

Dad was in his cobbler's clothes, and we were in our Easter finery, handmade by Mrs. Massi.

In Search of a Father

"...Elaine and I got in the habit of coming home from school and... checking Dad's sock drawer. If there were socks, we knew he would be home for dinner; otherwise, we would have to wait some number of weeks for his next return."

WE RETURNED TO THE SECURITY OF NORTH CAMDEN in time for school in 1951, settling into Sewell School with far less trauma then we anticipated. Elaine and I learned to respect Mrs. Johnson and Mrs. Quinlin, who were among the dedicated teachers we came to appreciate. We embraced the schoolyard, and it became an extra play area for us to supplement the confines of 8th and Birch.

Our house had changed fairly dramatically. While we had been gone for a year or so, the storefront was rented to a fishmonger. The odors of the fish that permeated the walls lingered for a couple of years, despite the wallpapering magic performed by Mom and Dad. And that wasn't the worst part. North Camden, like any inner city neighborhood, had a rodent population, mostly rats, that moved through the sewers with occasional forays into a few of the backyards where garbage cans were left uncovered. But the morsels of crabs and flounder and the beckoning smell of the fish attracted these scavengers to 523. Somehow the rats found nests in the dirt cellar and eventually made their way into the spaces between the uninsulated walls and ceilings. It was not only a constant source of embarrassment, but yet another reason to fear the night.

Elaine and I can separately recall specific times that we had friends over when the rats could clearly be heard scampering up the walls and across the ceiling. On one visit by an early suitor of Elaine's, they could hear the racket caused by the rats. The sound startled the young man, and he inquired, "What was that noise?" Elaine, feigning calm replied, "What noise?" Needless to say, she was mortified. As well as being a source of mortification, the rats were also the source of fear. We had heard the story of an infant that was killed when rats crept into her bassinette and chewed on her neck, right through her jugular vein. Whether or not this story was apocryphal or not did not change the impact it had on me. For the next several years, my habit was to sleep on my stomach with my right hand over my throat. While the fear has gone, the habit lingers.

Eventually, my mother called on her big brother Phil to be our Pied Piper and rid our house of these beasts. He arrived one weekend morning bearing poison he had gotten on the railroad to spread in our cellar. His efforts were largely unsuccessful and had an unintended, and unpleasant, consequence. The poison did a partial job, and when one or more of the rats died, the smell of the decaying of their flesh overwhelmed the fish smell until the other rats consumed them. The rats did not abandon 523, but Dad still was problematic.

Dad's behavior continued with long absences punctu-ated by brief returns, when he would bring fresh rolls and short interludes of normalcy. Our times at 523 became more crowded on at least two occasions when, first, Uncle Mike DiSibio and his bride and, then, Aunt Pat and her husband lived with us until they "got on their feet." This was not extraordinary in ethnic families; it was in fact somewhat commonplace. What may not have been so usual was that Dad would use these opportunities to expand his involvement with Eleanor. His promises of fidelity were hollow, his abandonment of us more or less regular. He was no longer in the cobbler business, excepting for his weekend part-time work at Sun Shoe Repair on Broadway. His full-time job at the Shipyard or Campbell Soup or RCA meant that he was not at home when we returned from school. Not knowing if he was gone on account of his job or for some more enduring cause, Elaine and I got in the habit of coming home from school and going into our parents' room and checking Dad's sock drawer. If there were socks, we knew he would be home for dinner; otherwise, we would have to wait some number of weeks for his next return. Eventually, there came a time when he did not return, and we were informed that our parents were divorced.

Strangely enough, this had a stabilizing effect on Mom, me and Elaine. We knew, once and for all, that Dad had found another life, and we could live without the constant anticipation of a return—that would be followed by the anxiety of waiting to see what would happen next. When would he leave? When would he return? We now had the definitive answer to both questions: he had left and never would return. Divorce in general was rare, more so among Catholics and unprecedented among the Monarcas or DiSibios. Mom didn't help by broadcasting the sordid details of the years of abuse and abandonment to anyone who would lend an ear. Of course, this turn of events resulted in yet a new and increased wave of sympathy from family and friends.

We now had a smaller nuclear family by one, and each of us reacted differently to this turn of events. Mom sought refuge in more time spent with the neighborhood wags, senior among whom were Florence Buss and Jean Carlucci. In the company of her friends, Mom would be looked upon as an equal, get sympathy and not be reminded that she had contributed to the dissolution of the union by her less-than-stellar performance as a wife. Elaine, meanwhile, began her search for a father replacement in an older boy for whom her hormones were raging. Buddy Mills became the target of Elaine's ardor. I attached myself as often as possible to Cousin Joey and to Uncle Mike DiSibio, both of whom filled some of the emotional voids left by Dad.

In addition, I was spending more time in the streets, seeking opportunities to exhibit my physical skills by fist fighting my way to respect. These were not major brawls, just one- or two-punch events in which I thought I was defending my honor. By the time I was in junior high, I had a reputation as an accomplished local tough. In many ways, the reputation was overblown since I had had only a couple of fights, but such was the power of gossip. John Ryan was among those who tired of the "razzing" that our guys often gave him on the bus ride from East Camden to his house at 7th and Vine. When he shouted to me that he was not going to take it any more, I calmly told him that he knew where he could find me when he wanted to do something about it.

At about six o'clock that evening, he knocked on the door at Uncle Mike's, where Elaine had told him I was, and said, "I'm ready." I came out, closed the door and calmly proceeded up Birch to a vacant lot between 6th and 7th Streets. John Ryan followed me, along with my Cousin Johnny, and we were joined by another friend, Art Oppman, who had seen us passing his house. There had been some bad blood between Ryan and me, so this looked like the culmination. As we were walking, I was wrapping my hand with a handkerchief for some protection and Ryan was unzipping his jacket. When we turned into the lot, I made sure that Ryan's back was to the cement wall, and I turned toward him. As he began to remove his jacket, I hit him as hard as I could with a right hand; his eye was swelling before he hit the wall and then the ground with me on top of him, flailing away and raining punches from every direction. For a minute or two, I was merciless until he shouted, "I give, I give up!" I was relieved, since my flurry was as much from my fear that he would hit me back if I stopped as from my anger at him calling me out in front of my Uncle and leaving me no opportunity to talk my way out of the fisticuffs.

Needless to say, this event secured my reputation as a tough guy for several years and elevated me to the position of leader of my modest little "gang," the bunch of us that hung around and talked tough about "protecting our turf," a phrase we heard in "The Blackboard Jungle" movie. We were an odd lot of kids, as diversified as Ryan and Kirk and Oppman. James Loving was one of those kids who hung out because he had no discernable home of his own. We were not sure what race he was, we only knew he was cool and could play left field.

Sewell School gave way to Veteran's Memorial Junior High, and Mrs. Johnson and Mrs. Quinlin gave way to Mr. Krimpetts and Mr. Udy. Mr. John, the math teacher, became Elaine's latest fantasy, while I was looking to maintain my reputation by generally being a wise guy when the opportunity presented itself. Mr. Carlton Holmes was a brilliant English teacher who used the term "by the by" instead of "by the way," which always impressed me, and who provided me with an early lesson in conduct.

Robert Russo occasionally would flick his ink pen at the back of Mr. Holmes's gray and black suit, a prank that resulted in a spatter or two of ink soaking into the fabric. The first time it was hilarious, and Robert was thrilled at his new popularity. For four straight days, the teacher wore the same jacket, which struck me as odd. Each day, when the teacher's back was turned to Robert, the new center of attention would plant another small spot or two with another flick of his pen. On the fifth day, after passing by Robert, thus allowing for another ink attack, Mr. Holmes turned back and removed his coat, looked at the fresh stain and announced that Robert would report to the principal and not be permitted to return to school until his parents had made restitution for the cost of the suit.

Later, Mr. Holmes described for us how each day he would go home and observe the pattern of the stains; he removed his jacket after each period until he had discovered which period held the offending class—and, finally, which nitwit was the culprit. I learned many lessons from this incident. Teachers were smarter then I thought. Patience was a virtue. Planning was as important as execution. And a spotlight can be a good thing, but if you gloried in it for too long the spotlight could end up highlighting your failure.

Junior High also taught me to have confidence in myself. I was on the baseball team, since I was only working on Friday nights and Saturdays. I was the starting shortstop, having beaten Ray Kaiser out for the position. During the second game of a short season, I made an error on a ground ball. When I came in at the conclusion of the inning, I sat next to the coach and declared, "I stink, you should put Ray in." Of course, I was doing what my Mom often did, looking for sympathy and a "keep your chin up, you'll do better next time" kind of response. But, instead of the pep talk, the coach followed my suggestion and put Ray in at shortstop for the next three games. That lesson was not lost on me either, particularly since it wasn't the first time I had been in this situation. I was in the chorus, and then, unlike now, I had a strong voice. The director selected me for the honor of singing a solo section of the Lord's Prayer at our opening production. At my first practice alone with the director, I did not hit the note perfectly, and I turned to her with a grimace and said, "I'm not good at this, maybe you should get someone else." Whereupon she acted on my suggestion. Those were the last times I would make the mistake of denigrating myself by denying skills that others had given me credit for. My demeanor and approach changed from those experiences.

The neighborhood activities continued unabated. Mom was working at Futernick's department store just off Broadway and often had to work nights. Elaine began to take up more of the motherly chores, including the washing and the cooking, around 523. Her skills in the kitchen were somewhat limited, with scrambled eggs, hot dogs or pancakes being the standard fare, but my meals were supplemented by visits to Uncle Mike's at strategic times—like when dinner was served; and I would sometimes provide dish-drying services by way of a modest repayment. On occasion, Mom would give Elaine enough money to get the two of us a blue-plate special at the Garden State Restaurant, where I would steal some of the food from Elaine's plate when she wasn't looking.

At the rarest of times Mom would meet us at H&H. Horn and Hardart was a popular cafeteria where you took a tray and headed down a long aisle balancing the tray on three continuous stainless rails. The familiar order of the food layout was comforting. First, you would have the choice of cold drinks which were already arrayed in a dozen or so glasses in order—ice tea, lemonade, or water—and, finally, hot coffee or tea. Next were offered two different kinds of bread, white squares or small rolls with accompanying pats of butter, each on its own little square cardboard platter. Desserts, even if out of order, came next, with chocolate and vanilla pudding, the signature rice pudding, tapioca pudding and, of course, Jell-O. Now came the steam table with assorted meats—Salisbury steak, hamburgers, liver and onions, hot dogs with sauerkraut, one or two kinds of fish. Finally was a variety of vegetables—corn, peas, string beans, creamed spinach, home fried potatoes and, the most beautiful of all and my favorite, the baked beans and bacon served in still warm individual little brown crocks.

The scary part, the cash registers where ladies would scan your tray and add up the damage, came last. Drinks were 5 and 10 cents, bread was 5 cents, desserts were 10 cents apiece, meats were 20 or 30 cents, depending on the selection, and each vegetable was 10 cents. Mom, Elaine and I acted out the exact same routine every time we went through the line. We would each pick up a free glass of water. Mom would get coffee, no roll, no butter, and then rice pudding for me, tapioca for Elaine, no dessert for Mom since she got the coffee. There was no meat for any of the three of us, but, finally, three vegetables of choice. I would invariably get home fries, creamed spinach and always baked beans. This wonderful repast would set Mom back $1.20, no tip needed. We loved it!

The job at Futernicks required Mom to "dress up," and we would often sneak a visit to her department and have a brief chat if our adventures along Broadway brought us close by. Broadway was a beehive of activity, with a profusion of wonderful stores, what today would be called boutiques, in addition to H&H. It is easy to remember some of them because of their uniqueness. Above Horn and Hardart's was the Paramount Pool Hall, which allowed me to while away many hours as I honed my abilities with the cue stick. If you headed north, you would be in the shadow of a beautiful City Hall and County Court House, and after you passed The Sacred Heart Church and School, you could spy the Savar and Stanley Movie Houses.

A look farther north brought a look at the Walt Whitman Hotel, then the Garden State Restaurant and, across the street, the White Tower Hamburger Shop, home of the 25-cent freshly cooked-to-order burger, would come into view. Beyond The White

Tower was the entrance to the great Delaware River Bridge, later renamed the Ben Franklin to differentiate it from the other bridge crossing the Delaware River at Gloucester City. The original Delaware River Bridge was taken for granted, even though it was a magnificent modern engineering achievement, among the largest in the world. Beyond the bridge entrance laid the streets of North Camden.

From H&H, if you walked South on Broadway, at the very next door was the Midway Theater, so named because it was at about the center of Camden. Across Broadway was the rail station that whisked you off to Philadelphia across the bridge or up to New York or to Baltimore or Washington, D.C. Farther to the north was the Sun Shoe Repair, where Dad often moonlighted on Saturday, and still farther along the way was Adams Men's Store. Adams would become important to me in later years when my needs outgrew Molotsky's Dry Goods at 7th and Pearl. Mel, the manager, would always have suggestions for how certain colors should be worn together, and Cousin John helped me pick out a timeless sport jacket that lasted me 15 years. There were doctor's offices, with lawyers and other professionals represented as well. Continuing along, three more movie theaters would soon crop up, the Lyric, Roxy and Towers mentioned earlier. Close by was the original Spars variety store that has become an international hobby supply chain. Eventually, you would pass Berkley and then get to Kaigns Avenue, another grand shopping and fresh produce haven. What better way to spend a non-school day than being a participant in the everyday entertainment of Broadway.

The neighborhood could still envelop us in comfort and reliability. It was a rare day that was not much the same as the day before. I was running errands for Joe's and generally hustling to make some spending change to quench my newly developed thirst for pinball. Unlike Uncle Joe Vitagliano, I often spent a quarter before I was able to rack up enough games to pass whatever time was available. I would often go in partnership with Cousin John or Skippy so we could pool our money. While they may have relied on me to get some games, I always trusted myself to do better than my partners. Like Joey V., I had developed a "give me the ball, coach, I'll take the last shot" attitude. Many hours were spent inside Lou & Syls or at the Elm Street Luncheonette where the gang, such as it was, would gravitate to watch the players of the now lost art of pinball.

At about this time, Johnny and I devised a way to make some cash. Having seen the ragman collect old stuff on his way to the Ballentino's Junk Yard, we thought we could practice this trade with the touch of personalized service. We would go the six blocks or so down Elm Street near the river to borrow a wheelbarrow cart. This contraption was a large, triple-wide wheelbarrow, with the extra convenience of two oversized wheels, that we promised to return at the end of the day full of salvage that we would be paid for in return for our efforts.

After we made the deal for the wheelbarrow, we set out to all of our relatives and friends with another proposition: we would clean out their basements, in return being allowed to keep any scrap metal, rags, cardboard and newspapers. Everybody was happy—Ballentino, our customers and us. It was this concept that allows us to claim that we invented the "win, win" approach, only we didn't call it that; we just called it another way to make a quick buck. The problem was that we soon ran out of family and friends who had no more need of our services, at least not for a year or more, once we had cleaned out their basements. Since no strangers were going to permit the likes of us into their basements or otherwise inside their homes, we could easily see that we had the labor supply but there was no demand; thus, another lesson was learned in economics.

To break the monotony, we would quickly choose up sides for street football, played with the street as our field, notwithstanding the regular interruptions of the buses running up 8th Street. Using certain porches or parked cars or parking signs or the like, the quarterback could tell his trusted offense to "Go down to the telephone pole, cut hard right towards Mr. Long's car, and I'll hit you with a pass." Or, "Dukey is getting to me too fast; knock him on his butt before you go long towards Miller's picture window." How it was that no one got seriously injured or killed upon crashing head first into some granite curbing or while barely avoiding a moving bus, often used as a decoy, is still a mystery to me.

I still have a slight scar on my forehead caused by running full speed into the steel pole of a parking sign as I was reaching for a well-thrown ball that touched my outstretched hands just as I turned into the pole. I crumpled like a rag doll. Of course, like any street kid, I "walked it off" and was ready for the next play. The small scar was next to the large one that I sustained at the age of six when I jumped over a stair railing, directly into and through a glass-topped coffee table. This was another offense worthy of what I suspect was a well-deserved beating after the bleeding stopped.

It was sometime around my late Junior High School days that I became friendly with David Molotsky. David was the youngest son of Nathan and Sylvia Molotsky and the younger brother of Stanley. David was rarely permitted to play outside and never in the street. At most, he would be seen playing catch alone by throwing a new pink ball against his row home/store combination. The store was larger than Joe's and was completely full of large tables which were stacked with men's and women's clothing of every description. The walls on both sides of the long room had shelves that went up to the ceiling, neatly stacked with items of male and female apparel. Toward the rear was a counter that stretched almost the full 12-foot width of the store, with a small opening that allowed only the owners to get to a register that was on a separate table. Next to this table was the entry to the living quarters. The lower level had only a large kitchen just beyond the store exit and one other room that was barely able to contain a small chair and telephone table. The rest of the room was taken up with a sizeable staircase leading to a large second floor. It would be many weeks before I would be invited up.

David and I became acquainted on the bus to South Camden. An unfamiliar tough began to pick on David because he was wearing a yarmulke. It did not take a leap of insight to see that David, who refused to make eye contact with the punk, was frightened. I got up and went to where David was sitting and sat next to him. Starting to believe in my own reputation, I stared down the punk without a word. I asked David how business was at the store. We chatted a bit until he got off at his stop, the Jewish synagogue just off Broadway, where he attended shul in preparation for his Bar Mitzvah.

On that bus ride, I was on my way to my grandmother DiSibio's, who now lived on Evans Street, on the same block as three of my father's sisters. I engaged in this ritual every week for a year, because Mom worked late on Thursday night, and at my grandmother's I would be assured of a great spaghetti meal with the additional benefit of being treated like a Crown Prince by Grandma and the gentle Uncle Joe DiSibio.

On my next bus trip, I found myself with David again, and this time we talked sports. He had a phenomenal knowledge of everything having to do with the Phillies or the A's. He was dignified but, at the same time, passionate about sports, although he never engaged in games around the neighborhood. He invited me to come by for a visit the next time I was in the store. Fact is, I was in the store on a regular basis, sometimes running up there to get my Mom nylon stockings (size six, ten denier, whatever that meant) or to fetch my Dad socks, to replace the ones that he had just torn beyond the help even of my mother's considerable sewing repair skills, or to pick up other items they carried, like needles and thread.

With no announcement to my gang about visiting the "fruity Jew kid," as he was referred to in the 'hood, I did stop by and ask Mrs. Molotsky if David was home. She knew me from around the area and apparently David had told her of my protective gestures, because she smiled and put her head in the kitchen, yelling up the stairs, "David, I'm sending Ralph DiSibio up!" With that, she directed me through to a small but lovely kitchen. I ascended the grand staircase and found David at the top beckoning me up. The stairway emptied onto a long hallway that ended at the entry to a living room about the size of Aunt Anna's. The hallway ran down the windowless side of the house, and there were three doors along the way and an additional door in the back over the garage that faced Pearl Street. The doors led to three bedrooms and a bath. I was stunned by the living room for, although it was no larger than Aunt Anna's, it was elegant in every way, from the thick carpeting to the glass and marble-topped tables to richly adorned lamps. Most of all, I was struck by a large console television with a screen that must have measured at least 16 inches. Looking at "Zenith" in gold letters with a little lightning bolt across the front, I thought, "No wonder David never comes out to play."

It turned out that David and I spent a lot of time together in that house. I did not abandon my other friends, but with David I discovered, for the first time, something of culture. David introduced me to chess. I saw magazines, expected at Dr. Bonier's office but surprising in a private home. On the occasions when I was invited to dinner, I marveled at the China and the fact that the maid put out sections of paper towels as placemats. We had ice cream and pretzels for dessert. Mr. Molotsky would smoke his pipe and inquire as to how my summer was going and actually carry on a conversation with David and me. Like Cousin Johnny, David was someone I envied, although in a good way. Around him, I wanted to be more intelligent; I wanted better things; and I wanted to understand the classical music that played in the background when the TV was not blaring. I wanted culture and class.

David and I carried on a friendship throughout high school. In the beginning, I would go up to his house and we would play block ball for hours. Or we would trade baseball cards and discuss the statistics on the backs. We sometimes played two-man stick ball, each of us pretending to be a team, either the Yankees or Phils, announcing each batter—who, as it happened, was also the announcer. Invited to sit at David's right side at his Bar Mitzvah, I donned my very own yarmulke at the official service and rode with his parents and his brother Stanley. I was the only goy at the event and honored to be so. We were never part of one another's crowds—he was college prep and I was distributive education; I acted as his campaign manager, when he ran for president of the sophomore class and lost. We finally drifted apart in my junior year, but I will forever be indebted to him and his family for their hospitality and for the lessons they taught me. They opened my eyes to the possibility of a different life. I also remember the kindness they showed me by never asking why I didn't bring David to my home.

By September of 1956, I was turning 15. I had quit school sports to begin full-time work at Joe's during that summer. I had been working a few hours a week for a couple of years, and Joe was teaching me the rudiments of butchering. I began by cutting up whole chickens into six pieces and graduated to stripping beef neck bones of every available shred of meat to be used to make hamburger. Eventually, I would be trusted to cut slices of round steak and to section quarters of beef into many saleable pieces. Joe was a patient mentor who would teach me well. He was a workaholic and a fine role model in every regard.

To add to the color of Joe's, on weekends, Joe's brother, Pete, would help with the increased business from shoppers who had a day or two away from work. Pete was younger than Joe and was as frenetic as Joe was steady. He was quick of wit and always ready with some wild tale that he would share with great gusto. When he was at the store, he provided additional wit and charm. Pete and Joe made a great team, as they worked together to aptly handle the many personalities that frequented this microcosm of society. I tried to absorb the lessons that were offered as I observed their talents unfold.

Joe's and 523 had the same footprint, but where we had a kitchen beyond the three steps, he had a steep staircase up to a second floor that was used as storage for every conceivable item that could not be stored in the basement. Past the staircase was a walk-in cold storage room called a cold box. The cold box had two rows of meat hooks near the ceiling and a wooden slatted shelf across the back. The box was no more than 6 feet by 6 feet and was repository for all of the fresh meat Joe sold. Hanging quarters of beef, veal and lamb were placed on the large hooks, using the space between the hoofless ankle bone and the large tendon that attached the ankle to the shin bone as a natural opening strong enough to hold the weight of the carcass as it hung upside down. The shelf held boxes of Italian sausage and hot dogs and other packaged meats. I marveled at how Joe could heft hindquarter pieces of beef, weighing almost as much as he did, up those three steps to be hung in the waiting cold box.

The main room housed all of the rest of the products available for sale. Chickens were stored in the cold case which ran down the middle of the store separating the customers from the butcher. The case had a large window that satisfied the curious as to the available lunch meats and cheeses. Large butcher blocks flanked each end of the cold box, and beyond the block at the rear was the slicing machine for the cold cuts and then, back, toward the front, was a large counter that could hold the orders of the customers as we pulled items from the rows of shelving that surrounded the store both in the front and back of the counter. Behind the scale near the rear butcher block was a magnificent huge cash register that had many push buttons with various denominations of money. Joe would punch in the correct buttons and turn a large handle, prompting the corresponding total to appear in a large window across the top of what is now a relic cherished by collectors of grand antiques.

Not a square inch of the store was wasted with empty space. There was only one bar-type stool, upon which weary customers awaited attention or rested while their orders were being butchered of their order. The wooden floors had fresh sawdust spread in the morning to ensure easy cleanup at closing. This environment was the scene of more hours than I spent anywhere else for the next four years.

Elaine was every bit as magnetic as I when it came to attracting friends, and she seemed always to be surrounded by a gaggle of pubescent girls. She had taken to putting her hair up in pin curls and covering her head with a bandana, and jeans with rolled-up legs and bobby sox became her preferred dress. Elaine was the first to decry the state of our home; she couldn't rest until she changed it, showing early on the tenacity that has never left her. She finally shamed Mom into surrendering the books of the tiny, gum-backed S&H green stamps that were usually, but not always, given by local stores with the number you got depending on how much money you spent.

The stamps were pasted into the books that the merchants supplied (for free) until the entire book was full of stamps. To fill one book was a real challenge that took many months. When your books were finally filled, you could take them to Philadelphia, where you might redeem them for everything from a shirt (four books) to a washing machine (200 books), with many possibilities in between. By hook, crook, begging, borrowing and everything short of stealing, Mom had amassed enough books to enable Elaine to pick out our new living room furniture and rugs. We were about to redecorate!

The well-worn hand-me-down sofa and overstuffed chair, further dilapidated from the use as football dummies by Johnny and me, were given to even poorer neighbors. They were replaced by a little love seat and two chairs and matching tables that can best be described as something that would serve as lawn furniture today. The seats and backs were covered, not with cloth but with plastic, and the legs and arms were made of thin wrought iron. But the real gems were the two 9-foot by 12-foot "carpets," each two shades of green and made of woven paper. Yes, that's right—paper. The new items, combined with another overstuffed sofa that had survived the assaults of Johnny and me, made for what can kindly be called an eclectic look. I thought it was sharp ("cool," in today's vernacular), and Elaine thought it was downright elegant.

She was growing up fast and beginning to assume a mothering countenance when it came to our relationship. Because Elaine was 18 months my senior, Mom put her in charge of me when she was absent, and Elaine took to her new power with vigor. She bossed me around, as if to test her new-found responsibility, and I bridled at any direction regardless of its purpose. These conflicting attitudes, fueled by estrogen and testosterone, escalated to the level of dislike for one another. Gone were the days of playful teasing and the nights of slumber parties at which Elaine's friends might come into my room and practice kissing. No, this was all supplanted by Elaine's demand that I be banished to Aunt Pat's to sleep when her friends stayed over. Still worse was Elaine's punishment of me. She would stand directly in front of, and two inches away from, the television during my favorite show, making it impossible to view. She gave new meaning to the word "spite." But I was forbidden to touch her in retaliation, because she was a girl, a dictate stemming from earlier times when I would hit her with a broom, then swear to Mom that, "I never laid a hand on her, I swear!"

In the interest of candor, I must admit that I abandoned all vestiges of anger management when I threw a paring knife at Elaine that struck her in the arm and then dangled there to our mutual shock. I was now subject to a prohibition against touching because of my growing strength, and Elaine took full advantage of her protected status. She always did have "a bit of a mouth on her" and even took on Mom once too often when she announced, "I hate it here, and I'm leaving and going to live with Jean Carlucci!" Mom, used to threats of people leaving her, grabbed Elaine by the arm as she was getting underwear together for her trip; she opened the window in Elaine's bedroom and pushed her out, holding only her ankles. Mom was shouting, "You want to go to Jean, then you can take the short cut!" Elaine was screaming, "I'm sorry, I'm sorry, *please* don't drop me!"

As was demonstrated by this incident, Mom could occasionally do a pretty good imitation of Sonny Corleone in the temper department. Mom finally pulled in her distraught daughter, who learned a lesson—I think. Elaine and I eventually grew out of the conflicts that are inevitably suffered by siblings and implicitly reached a mutual non-aggression pact in high school. Ultimately, we developed an ever-deepening love for one another that continues to grow.

The time to put away childish things was quickly approaching as the summer of 1956 was drawing to a close. Elvis Presley was changing the way music was appreciated; Ed Sullivan replaced Howdy Doody; and James Dean was rumored to be the new Marlon Brando. Elaine had been staying on the morning bus past Veteran's Memorial Junior High School, where I got off, and continuing on to Woodrow Wilson High School at 27th and Federal Streets, and I was preparing to join her for what I thought would be the closing chapters of my formal education.

8
Uncle Phil

Uncle Jim with Grandpop Monarca and Uncle Phil. On the steps at the Monarca headquarters is Aunt Louise and Uncle Phil's dear daughter, Phyllis. Note the ubiquitous stogie in Mario's hand.

Uncle Phil

"A visit to Uncle Phil's was a delight. All of us had the same first impression—this was a paradise worthy of the king of the Monarcas. The second thought was, 'Wow, he has a driveway!'"

U NCLE PHIL WAS A GIANT. At 5 feet 5 inches and 185 pounds, he may not have been perceived as a big man by many, but he was nevertheless a giant in the hearts and minds of all of the Monarcas.

Fillipo Monarca, aka Phil, was the third child born to Mario and Teresa. The order of his birth was far less important than the fact that he was the first born in the USA. Even more importantly, he was the first male child, and Phil was all boy. It was a part of his birthright that he was superior to the seven children who came after him. As to his older sisters, he gave them their due because of age, but he was spared any normal duties of the youngest in the family because of his gender. Deference was paid to him at meal time and when decisions were made. He would, however, sometimes be called upon to lift heavy objects or perform other masculine tasks usually seen to by his capable sisters. He took to his role with humility, but with a certain sense of entitlement.

By the time Mike, Lola, Jim, Dora and Pat were born in Jamesville, Phil had assumed many duties around the home and in the small town. His feats of strength, even at a young age, were often the subject of proud bragging, and one wonders whether the tales told were, at least in part, the exaggerations of adoring sisters, much like their references to Uncle Jim as a rakishly handsome and tall fellow. Even so, there is no question that Phil was possessed of great strength, and the proof was his exploits on the athletic fields of South Jersey. He excelled at football as an offensive and defensive standout on the Zuni Indian semi-pro teams. On the baseball diamond, he had a Babe Ruth body and Ruthian power. In his adult years, he achieved a regional reputation of legendary proportions as a bowler.

Phil was the first to escape the confines of Camden when he and his wife moved to Delair, some three miles to the north of East Camden. It might just as well have been 300 miles, because such a move made walking to his house impossible, and there was no regular bus service out to the countryside where they had settled. This physical move added to the mystique of this gentle giant, and his frequent visits to town would be marked by the excitement of a returning traveler. When any of the family members was lucky enough to visit him, it was a day-long event worthy of several days of retelling.

River Road became nationally known in 1951 when Howard Unruh became the first mass murderer in modern-day America. One clear day, on the 6th of September, Unruh, a WWII veteran and bachelor living with his mother, "snapped" and went on a shooting rampage, killing 13 people and injuring 13 more, all within a matter of minutes. He was captured after a brief standoff and, now an octogenarian, is still incarcerated in a prison psychiatric ward. We never went to Uncle Phil's using River Road without someone pointing out Howard's second floor room and recounting exactly where they were when the radio broadcast the events as they were happening.

The ride down River Road led to the home of Uncle Phil and Aunt Mary Monarca, nee Sambucci, whom he had married in large part without the blessings of her family. She was very young, and her folks would have preferred a formal event to the elopement that took place. The Sambuccis were a warm and gregarious family with a proud Italian heritage, and Phil would have to prove himself worthy of their only girl. Actually, the Sambuccis were a family much like the Monarcas. They were hard working, honest, and compassionate and with a closeness that much resembled that of the Monarca clan. Phil and Mary's move to Delair was not the result of a new job or the love of fresh air or even to escape the mass of Camden humanity that could become suffocating. Rather, the move was to allow the young couple to be next door to the heads of the Sambucci family. Going to a place where the Sambucci boys were only a short distance away, Uncle Phil paid homage to the time-honored tradition of the male leaving the nest and becoming close to the family of his spouse.

Aunt Mary was as regal as Aunt Anna, as hard working as my mother and as wise as Aunt Louise. She was, by anyone's estimation, a gem. Uncle Phil had found his soul mate. Aunt Mary, who was large for a woman of that time, nearly as tall as Uncle Phil was tiny by the standards of the era, tended toward the Sambuccis in stature. I particularly recall her in a formal picture as a bridesmaid—she made the lilies she held look ugly by comparison.

A visit to Uncle Phil's was a delight. The trip took us past the city limits to Derouse Avenue, where we turned left and drove for several hundred yards until just after the railroad tracks. Beyond the tracks, we made a right turn into the dirt driveway. All of us had the same first impression—this was a paradise worthy of the king of the Monarcas. The second thought was, "Wow, he has a driveway!" We had never seen a driveway before. The house was huge by our standards, with a front hall containing a big staircase. The first of three archways leading from the large entry hall led to a huge living room, the second to a generous dining room, and the third invited us into an ample country kitchen. Every room was decorated with care and taste, neither in the overdone, nouveau riche style or the plastic seat-covered way.

They had all the modern conveniences, including a TV and a washing machine and a sewing machine as well. The kitchen had a side entrance that led to a set of stairs and down to the best part of all. At the bottom of the stairs spread a hammock which extended between two large trees. You could lounge in the hammock, or, like all the kids with the good fortune to find themselves there, you could romp around in it. Either way, you were within arms-length of the purple grapes, the fruit of a large grape arbor that was reminiscent of the old country. It was all quite grand and engendered universal envy.

Christmas was always a great time to visit all the family members. Everyone was excited to show you what they had gotten from Santa or Mom and Dad. We DiSibios, regardless of some hard times, never went wanting at Christmas; Mom would do whatever it took to make sure we didn't feel left out. Mom earned holiday money by taking in things to iron, a skill at which she excelled; and she cleaned Aunt Anna's house once a week to earn a little extra, enabling her to afford a "lavish" Christmas. But few among us could compare with the assortment of gifts we could view at the Delair house. Box after box of blouses and sweaters, with shoes to match, were arrayed. The boxes were open and the tissue paper carefully tucked in to allow for easy viewing. It was a sight to behold. Uncle Phil and Aunt Mary spared little for their daughter, and the Sambuccis added even more to the riches on display. Aunt Mary's home was modest, but she was proud of her girl and her family and showed it with her generosity.

Even though she was challenged with a heart condition that occasionally left her bedridden, she worked for many years of her illness-shortened life. She had various jobs, but there is one in particular that I recall. She was a "floor lady" in the sweatshops along Arch Street in the Philadelphia garment district, and a great one at that. Her job description was keeping the product (usually sport coats, winter jackets or trench coats) moving, out the shipping doors to the waiting department stores throughout the city. That responsibility required making sure that the bolts of material were cut, tagged, and doled out properly to the forty or so seamstresses who were bent over their hot machines, working on a single, repetitive sewing application for eight straight hours. From one seamstress to the next, the product would move along, taking on more and more shape as it continued its journey. There might be a collar here, a lapel there, then pockets and button holes and linings. The penultimate stop was at the pressers where the wrinkles were removed before the goods were finally wrapped in plastic and shipped.

On the floor, Aunt Mary was the boss. She settled disputes among seamstresses, one of whom might be angered when she failed to get more of the partially finished goods she worked on because someone ahead of her or the Bundle Boy did not deliver a new stack before the last one was finished. This was a concern, because the women got paid by the "piece," which is to say that for every job completed they got so many pennies. Mary knew every operation and was firm but fair. She never had to raise her voice, and she was always heeded when she gave directions. She was at work as she was at home—respected, loved and revered.

At the sweatshops, there were many familiar faces, and several in the family knew of Mary's expertise because we were eyewitnesses. Aunt Lydia's second husband, Joe Cini, owned the shops where Aunt Mary worked. Before her marriage to Joe, Aunt Lydia worked as a bookkeeper in those same shops. My mother Dora was a buttonhole maker, and, alas, I was a Bundle Boy. In fact, I knew more about Aunt Mary's career than even Uncle Phil or their daughter Phyllis did. I would often be the driver of the car pool that crossed back and forth to Philadelphia. Aunt Lydia, Aunt Mary, my mom and I spent many hours together in this way during my sophomore year of college.

Uncle Phil and Aunt Mary begat Phyllis, the first girl born to the Monarcas and, indeed, the first with the family name. They were devoted to her from the day she was born. The fact that she was possessed of an extraordinary beauty that she has maintained to this day, more than 65 years later, is just part of the reason she is cherished. Even more compelling than her external beauty is the inner beauty that she has always exhibited. With her calming effect on all who are around her, she is literally the apple that fell very close to the tree that grew from the union of Phil and Mary. She is kind, caring, compassionate and exudes enormous warmth, and the miles of separation from the central unit of the Monarcas have only served to make her even more alluring. No one ever witnessed any flaw in her, and to this day, no one has recounted any evidence of inappropriate behavior.

When they heard that Phyllis was engaged to be married, few in the family were familiar with her beau. Her visits to Camden had always been with her parents, and never had anyone met this lucky guy. One thing we all knew was that he was not worthy. We imagined a handsome, square-jawed, male version of Charlotte Smith. Likely he would be the tall star quarterback at some private school. The gala wedding was the first look many of us had of her soon-to-be husband. We were taken aback. He was a little guy with dark hair who had a talent for social dancing. This Frank DeAmbrosio kid had stolen our Phyllis. Oh, sure, he had a twinkle in his eye and was quick to light up the room with a smile or witticism; but did he deserve Phyllis?

It turned out that he did and still does. He is a great husband and father, a terrific cousin, and, the best of all, he was a great son-in-law. Uncle Phil, with his gentle but insistent and constant advice, wasn't the easiest guy to get along with. And it could not have easy to be around a guy of so many accomplishments, built up into mythic proportions by a near-worshiping daughter, adoring sisters, and even bowling fans. It wasn't easy, but Frankie did it with great finesse and aplomb.

Uncle Phil, always deliberate in speech and in decisions, was a railroad man. After leaving high school, he surveyed the landscape searching for ways to earn money for his family and selected the railroad as his vocation. It was another marriage made in heaven. The job lasted a lifetime and provided him and his family with a comfortable living, one without the threat of strikes or the fear of economic downturns.

Uncle Phil was frugal, never giving into the temptation of tobacco or strong drink, but he tolerated those that succumbed to such vices without reproof. He was, however, prone to scold his female siblings on the inappropriateness of women engaging in the growing fad of smoking. He was quick to anger if he thought they were not heeding his advice in these matters, and the sisters were anxious to avoid doing anything that might bespeak disrespect of their big brother.

Aunt Lydia is fond of repeating a story that illustrates all of this so well. She was living at home at 734 and enjoying the ministrations of a fine cigarette while reading a book. It was summertime, and she was dressed casually in shorts and a short-sleeved top. Uncle Phil was returning from the Camden rail yards to his country home when he decided to drop by the family home to pay respects. Lydia saw his head through the window just before he pushed open the unlocked door. She panicked—what if Phil caught her smoking? Undoubtedly, she would get a tongue lashing and perhaps even a smack or two. Most of all she would risk the loss of her brother's respect for her. Without a second thought, she put the lighted cigarette between her thighs and put her legs tightly together, just before Phil came in and began to chat with her. Phil was a very slow and soft-spoken speaker on all occasions, but Aunt Lydia swears to this day that he knew what was going on and spoke even more slowly to exacerbate her discomfort and pain. The story shows a great deal about the relationships in the Monarca family.

Uncle Phil did his best, given his distance from the family, to be a big brother and to be an uncle to the kids in the family. I was often given a little extra of his time because of my father's absences, and I am grateful for the experiences he shared with me. On one occasion, he promised Johnny and me that he would take us on a railroad ride with him when he rode the line to Atlantic City. This was no wimpy trip on cushioned seats in a passenger train, but a ride on a freight hauler where we would share the caboose. That car, a replica of a small house on wheels, had bunk beds and a pot belly stove and was the center of many a great railroad tale. Uncle Phil made good on the trip. He picked Johnny and me up, and the three of us made our way to the central yard. We witnessed the respect with which other railroaders greeted Uncle Phil and quickly recognized that a conductor was quite an important guy. It was a great adventure, and one that John and I have always included when recalling our childhoods.

Uncle Phil, as noted, was a consummate bowler into his late years. He had amassed scores of trophies, newspaper clippings and, along with those, a great reputation. On at least two occasions, he picked me up on a Saturday morning and took me with him to one of his matches in the South Jersey area. It was great to see him in his element and a source of price when he received trophies on both occasions.

When I was in high school, I became somewhat proficient in woodworking class, and Uncle Phil asked if I could make him a trophy case if he paid for the materials. Of course, I agreed. I am sure he made the request because he wanted to show me he had confidence in my ability and to give me a mission. At times, I was a bit much for my Mom to handle, and I am confident she had shared that with her big brother.

I took the job seriously, even paying a pre-planning visit to Delair to check out the sizes and number of trophies that my work would have to display. I made some calculations, and off I went to create this "hummer." It was five feet wide, four feet high and 12 inches in depth. It had a one piece glass front framed by a plain 1-inch molding. Behind the glass were three shelves of different heights that would handle his treasures. The single piece in the rear was of quarter-inch plywood and was removable by turning two latches on each of the four sides. Made of white pine with a walnut stain and finished with two coats of shellac and two of varnish, this was not a work of great furniture. It wasn't Ethan Allen, but it was functional.

Uncle Phil helped me transport the case in a borrowed truck, and together we hauled it into the long vestibule next to the staircase. He was effusive in his compliments and allowed as to how I should continue to hone my skill and perhaps become a carpenter. I was beaming with pride as he carefully filled the shelves with his hard-earned hardware. As big as the case was—and the vestibule would not have allowed it to be larger—he could not fit in all of the booty. For several years, he told every visitor to his home that his nephew Ralphie had made the case for him. It was, and is, an honor to be part of his heritage.

In Search of Manhood

*The North Camden Cardinals at our championship banquet.
I am dead center, and Cousin John is on my left.*

*We had special trophies emblematic of my Captaincy and
John's MVP award. Jimmy Loving is the tall guy in the center,
and Skippy Flamini with the big body and
long crew cut is in the forefront.*

In Search of Manhood

'The best dances were in private homes... About an hour into the night, we would begin to play 'flashlight,' the best part of these events to be sure."

WOODROW WILSON HIGH SCHOOL SAT at the intersection of 27th and Federal Streets, an imposing structure of massive proportions. It was one of two public high schools in the city, and it had a built-in fierce rivalry with its older sister school, Camden High. Woodrow Wilson was in the "upscale" part of Camden, but it could not match the beauty of Camden High School, with its look of a Camelot castle. What Wilson lacked in beauty, though, it amply made up for in academic reputation. The victor in the sports rivalry varied, with first one school then the other being ascendant, depending on the year and the sport. WWHS's student population reflected the eclecticism of the part of the city—North and East Camden—it relied upon for students. South Camden, with its increasingly colored population and naturalized citizens, provided Camden High with its students.

My sister and her coterie of friends, including Patti Whittick, already had their sophomore year behind them and were able to give me warnings and tips that would prove useful. Buoyed by that intelligence, I had little trepidation about the first-day initiation ritual, a tradition that had the more raucous of the upperclassmen awaiting the buses that would drop off the new sophomores at the corner stop. As the wide-eyed kids exited, some of them stared, close-up for perhaps the first time, at the edifice of their new educational home. It was at that point that they would be met by groups of "superior" upperclassmen hurling eggs and grabbing the new arrivals to cover their faces with shoe polish and watercolors. The rookies that did not escape were generally made to look like clowns with egg-stained shirts. Those who were forewarned escaped by having parents or friends drop them off a block or so away and sneaking in the side door, and some got away just by outrunning the clique.

I was not among the wide-eyed as I got off the bus, but, rather, armed with advance knowledge, I proceeded warily, looking for the nearest escape route I could find. This was just like the Bull in the Ring game we played on Birch Street. All I needed to do was crash through the first cordon and I was free. As the bus emptied, I hooked arms with a kid that I had just met on the ride to school after he got on at High Street. He sat next to me and, unsolicited, informed me that nobody was going to egg him. I boldly replied, "Me neither!" Arm in arm, we knocked the first upperclassman down with our initial charge and, running over his prone body, escaped. "I'm Natale, the 'e' is silent," he intoned. That was my welcome to high school. I was infused with confidence and had made a new friend, Natale Girgenti; our paths would run parallel and from time to time cross for a lifetime.

The school's interior was a square, each length of which had classrooms or offices. The first and second floors had identical footprints but differed in minor ways. The third floor was unbroken by an auditorium or guidance and administrative offices like those that were the highlights of the first. The basement was the most interesting because it housed the cafeteria, shop rooms and the art classrooms. The shops fascinated me from the start; there were wood, electric, automotive, plastic and printing shops. In addition, there were well-equipped sewing classrooms and a modern cooking classroom as well. The center section of the square was a central courtyard that I do not recall ever entering.

At the impressive front entrance, consisting of a massive 25-foot portico held in place by four huge Ionic columns, you were invited to enter one of three sets of oversized doors. One got to the portico after ascending numerous granite steps which ran across its 50-foot width. Although the main entrance was rarely used by students, it was absolutely overpowering when seen from Federal Street. On the other side of Federal Street laid Farnum Park and a small branch of the Camden Public Library. Students usually entered WWHS from the side door on the west side, because entry there did not require the climbing of any steps. But, the main entry was most important to me for other reasons.

In the main hall at the front entrance, you could see a series of huge trophy cases, each of which made the one I constructed for Uncle Phil seem like it was built for a doll house. These were at least 8 feet long by 6 feet high and 1-1/2 feet wide. They were full of sports trophies from the decades past along with memorial tributes to past coaches, athletic directors and legendary players. My idol, Cousin Joe Vitagliano, was the sole subject of nearly one-half of an entire case. Every record was highlighted, 8 by 10 photos of him, uniformed as both a baseball standout and a basketball star, were on every shelf. Just as Uncle Phil told people of his nephew Ralphie building his trophy case, I never failed to announce to any one who didn't already know that this was my Cousin Joe. Every day I passed that case, my boyhood adulation for Joe was validated.

I must say that my high school days were not academically memorable. From a curriculum perspective, they were quite forgettable. While Cousin John was going to Camden Catholic on his way to becoming a very successful lawyer of real estate and property law renown, I was taking "General" classes. Just like it sounds, it was a little of this and a little of that, including "Junior Chef," where I learned the rudiments of cooking that still come in handy today. I took that class not because of any interest in owning a restaurant or even cooking, but rather because I could use the opportunity to eat free food. I might have been only a General student, but I was no dummy. I was always thinking.

Sometimes I thought too much. I remember insensitively extorting a doughnut a day from a "momma's boy" with the promise to protect him from other toughs. I warned him that if I didn't get the doughnut, I would let him fend for himself. After two days of freshly baked goods, I let him off the hook. I felt guilty seeing the fear in his eyes; and I continued to be his protector until he found his own little niche with a gang that went on to intimidate others. I was not above finding bigger fish to conspire with. I made a deal with a new study hall teacher that if she counted me present, I would get cigarettes or gum or fill other orders for her from the luncheonette across the street, where I would spend the period playing pinball. The deal lasted the entire year to our mutual benefit, another win-win.

But lest you get the wrong idea, I wasn't all that tough. I was not even close to the top fifty toughest kids in school, far from it, in fact. But I picked my confrontations carefully and avoided situations that were problematic, as I blossomed into someone of importance in my own little crowd. From my first day, when Patti Whittick spotted me in the stairwell after I had escaped orientation and remarked, "You're walking around like you own this place," I was never uncomfortable. I wasn't cocky, just not intimidated.

My bearing and approach led to a situation that cost one hapless teacher his job. I did not dislike school; in fact, I actually liked social studies and history, but I was not interested in doing more then was required to get B's and C's. I was the classic student that people refer to when they say, "Well, Mrs. So-and-so, your son has great potential, if he would only apply himself." I wanted to do only what I needed to do to get my "ticket punched" and use my considerable energies to make some money. In time, even that modest ambition began to waver.

Frank Labrizzi was our junior history teacher in the class before lunch. He was young, he was new, and he had recently graduated from St. Joseph College without yet having gotten a full certification to teach. He did not have the requisite tools to face our third-period class, full of young toughs with little interest in learning, or much of anything else for that matter, except for the girls who tended to be more serious sorts. We set out to intimidate Mr. Labrizzi from the first day. It was all very childish and included pranks that had the combined effect of enabling us to wrest control from the teacher. We would put our chairs together when he would announce a test and would call out answers to each other without fear; and we would take the wooden pass (the ticket to the lavatory) without permission and announce that we would be back after we had a cigarette. He feared us, but feared more the result of sending us to the principal and admitting his lack of control. The situation got worse by the day.

One Saturday afternoon, following a few racks of pool at the Paramount Pool Hall above H&H, we passed by the Sun Shoe Repair. Lo and behold, we spotted Mr. Labrizzi, adorned in an apron, finishing shoes. He spotted us and waved us into the store. We were taken aback at seeing him outside a classroom, sans suit coat and tie, but even more surprised at his invitation to lunch. He introduced us to his father, the owner of the store, who inquired about my father, whom he recalled as having been a part-time cobbler for him.

Mr. Labrizzi took us up to the Calico Kitchen where we each lunched a Texas Tommy (a hot dog blanketed with a piece of cheese and wrapped in a slice of bacon). He made his plea to us as we ate. "Guys, I need your help; your class is out of control, and I need you to help me." I hesitated because I didn't know how to tell him the truth. He went on, "Look, Ralph, you're the leader of some of them, and I know you can help. What do you say?" Natale had not stopped eating. I looked across the table and informed the young teacher that I couldn't help. It was too late. "Look, Mr. Labrizzi, even if it wasn't too late, I could only control my own guys. The class has guys from East Camden that I don't even know." I told him that I would like to help, and if I had known who he was, it might never have started. I apologized, and we finished lunch. He thanked us for joining him. Natale, Dukey Kirk and I never acted up in his class again, but Mr. Labrizzi was soon replaced by Mr. Jim Eulo.

Mr. Eulo took no prisoners. He whipped us into shape, figuratively, in short order. His first action was to announce that he would like to see me after class. We felt him out on that first day, but soon realized from his demeanor that he was not to be trifled with. After class, he coldly told me that he knew what happened to his predecessor and that he would not follow suit. He told me that he had looked at my records and had seen that I had some baseball ability; he was coaching baseball at Vets Junior High and wondered if I would like to give him a hand. I told him I could only help out on Mondays, since I had to be at Joe's for a couple of hours every other day after school. He took me up on my offer, and I on his. At the conclusion of practice, Mr. Eulo dropped me off at Joe's, asking about my ambitions along the way. I told him I intended to join the Marine Corps and most likely be an MP. He worked on me every Monday during the season, saying things like, "You have a lot of ability, and you should think about going to college." He always said, "You are a natural leader, and I see how others are drawn to you; that is a special gift, and you shouldn't waste it."

Mr. Eulo gave me much to think about, even though I knew I couldn't afford to go on to school, nor did I have the course work to get into college. But, the experience brought on by the mis- behavior with Mr. Labrizzi taught me many things. Actions had consequences. Life wasn't all fun and games. I had some worth, and I could perhaps aspire to more than I had contemplated.

I am delighted to report two things. Mr. Labrizzi went back to college, attained his certifications and went on to become a principal in the Camden city schools. He told me years later, at a wedding reception, that the episode at WWHS spurred him on to become a professional educator. Unfortunately, Mr. Eulo died prematurely of brain cancer, unable to enjoy his new marriage to a lovely lady. Coincidentally, there came a time when his widow worked for me when I was an assistant superintendent of schools in Gloucester City. She didn't know at first that I had known—and remembered—her husband. We cried together as I recounted the story of how her mate had played such an important role in my life by being the first to inspire me to go to college.

Things at 523 had not changed much during my high schools days. Mom was still working hard at regular and odd jobs. Elaine was spending more time with her girlfriends, when not providing me with occasional dinners and helping to keep the house in order. When Dad brought his new family to Uncle Mike's at 530, I could clearly hear them laughing and enjoying the visit. They were just 50 feet away, and the summer nights carried their voices through open windows. I was hurt and sad that I could not share those mo- ments, but at least there were no battles raging at 523.

The summer before I went off to WWHS, Dad tried to reprise his cobbler days. He rented an empty store, a tiny shop less than half the size of his former space at 523, at 8th and Pearl across from Molotsky's. It was just large enough to hold the minimum essential pieces of equipment for a professional. I loved the whole notion. He was frequently there at the shop, fixing up and preparing for the opening, and I often helped him. We covered the windows with paper, pending the grand opening. The paper had printing that I made in art class, announcing the forthcoming business. It was all very exciting. I thought he would be there every day for years to come and, although he lived three blocks away on Cedar Street with his new family, I would only need to go half a block to see him alone at the shop.

Elaine was now enamored of another handsome boy, since Buddy Mills had gone off to the Navy and was now looking, successfully, for a girl in every port. Then, as now, Elaine's choice in men is suspect to say the least. Call it bad luck or some version of "Looking for Mr. Goodbar" (fortunately without the same bad outcome), she has not been blessed with tender sorts as mates. Pooky Binder, her next project after Buddy's departure, was a handsome devil. His ready smile, which exposed deep dimples and flashing blue eyes, belied his darker side. It would be kind to say that William, aka "Pooky," Binder came from rough stock.

His was a hard childhood without any of the softening effects of a Monarca clan. His well-deserved reputation as a street punk was heightened by his equally rough-hewn brother, John aka "Chicky." These were two tough hombres. Your first clue to the nature of these two was in their nicknames; while John and Ralph became Johnny and Ralphie, William and John became Pooky and Chicky. And that was only the beginning of the differences. I fought because I had to and only then when I couldn't talk my way out of it. The Binder brothers, by contrast, enjoyed fighting, and by all accounts they were very good at it. The crowds they hung with were of like mind. They had no extended family or role models to round the rough edges.

With all of his hardness around the neighborhood, Elaine still fell in love with his charm, and I am sure she was somehow attracted by the danger. In some ways, he must have reminded her of Tony. As many hurtful things as my Dad did to his first family—the one with me and Elaine in it—there are few in the Monarcas that would not to this day describe him, with true affection, as charming and great to be around. Pooky was like that also. He was impish and cute, just as he was hard and nasty. In sum, I suppose he was hard not to like. And Elaine loved him.

He came from Abblet Village, which was "the projects" of the day. Even though the confines of "the Village" lay beyond the 10th Street bridge in the area where State Street met River Road, to say it was part of East Camden would impart too much class. There were many great families and their offspring that came out of those projects, but there were an inordinate number that were thugs, what today we would derogatorily call "white trash." Pooky was raised there by his grandmother and spent as little time as possible anywhere but in the streets. Considering how much time he spent outside of the house, he was ironically destined to spend many years in reform school and prison. For Pooky, my nuclear family, as dysfunctional as it was, was a step up the social ladder.

Dad opened the shop at 7th and Pearl, but his presence there did not last very many months. The failure of the business this time was caused not by his own wandering, but by prosperity. People were riding an economic wave; they had disposable income and used some of it to buy extra pairs of shoes. Shoes in general were cheaper and lasted longer. And if you had more than one pair, it would take even longer to wear them out. Even when one pair wore out, people would often throw them away because they could afford the latest shoe fashion. In a cruel twist of fate, the shop failed because people had more money to spend. While Dad was there, however, he wanted more details from me about this Pooky guy. He did not like what he heard about him. More importantly, he did not like the time Elaine spent with him and was dismayed at how often he could observe him coming and going from 523. Eventually, he confronted Pooky and lectured him about spending so much time at 523 when Dora wasn't home. But, of course, this had only a temporary cooling effect on the torrid relationship.

I began working full-time at Joe's during the summer of 1957 and began to focus on earning money. I was giving Mom $10 a week and started to use some of my money to acquire clothes as I began to be more concerned with my appearance. Girls were beginning to enter my mind as something other than a nuisance. The amusement of the slumber party kissing practices was yielding to desire, and desire was giving me a mission. Bandstand was a local Philadelphia phenomenon, as dances began to crop up at every club, school and community. I was smart enough to recognize that I could find a variety of potential "partners" of the opposite sex at those dances. I was always thinking.

Once again, I owe Elaine for the familiarity I had with dance. Not only would she practice dance steps with me, but her many girlfriends would do the same when they were not practicing with each other. To this day, I am challenged in the rhythm department; while I can dance without embarrassment to slow numbers, more upbeat tunes present me with difficulties. Thank God for the twist, without which I would have been lost in college. Elaine did teach me enough simple steps to fake it well enough that girls often agreed to step on the dance floor with me, and I began to attend the dances in the area. Abblet Village, St. Mary's and other places where dances were held began to be my destinations whenever I could leave work in time to continue my search for girls. An early visit to Bandstand was the highlight of my dance career before Cousin Bob became a regular on the expanded program.

The best dances were in private homes where a dozen teens or so would go with their favorite 45's (vinyl records) and dance to Bill Haley and the Comets or to Jo Stafford with the indulgence of some generous neighbors. About an hour into the night, we would begin to play "flashlight," the best part of these events to be sure. At a strategic moment in the evening, when the hostess believed that the dancing partners were compatible, she would turn out the lights and call for a 10-minute flashlight break. With that announcement, each couple would rush to the nearest comfortable chair or sofa and begin "making out"—and this was when all that kissing practice came in handy. You had to be careful how far you would let your hands stray, however, because the hostess would suddenly shine a flashlight on you and the partner you embraced— thus, the name of the game. In ten minutes, the lights would be turned on and blouses would be buttoned and normal color would begin to return to flushed faces and the dancing would continue. The dancing intervals got shorter, and the flashlight breaks longer, as the night progressed. When I think of the "good old days," I think about flashlight, not 25-cent gas.

As my wealth began to build by a few dollars a week, I began a lifelong love affair with cars, a love that was fueled by my two surrogate fathers. Cousin Joey had a 1952 Cadillac that he loaned to me for my junior prom. With Art Opmann behind the wheel of Joe's Caddy, we made our first foray into New York City. Uncle Mike DiSibio always displayed his stature with a new Buick every couple of years that I helped him polish in return for driving lessons. This was long before I got a driver's license or a permit.

I was never much for patience, and that flaw in my character has had the vices of its virtues over the years. This has been manifested time and again as I have impatiently searched for the perfect car. My frenetic nature is well illustrated by my initial passion for a particular car, the acquisition of that car, the waning of the initial infatuation and the trading of the car. That has always been my relationship with cars: hot, fiery, intense and short-lived. This is not a good thing, but at least my fickle nature has not exhibited itself in my human relationships.

Not long after I turned 16, I spied a 1948 Ford Coupe in the 600 block of Birch Street with a "for sale" sign in the windshield. I went to the house listed on the advertisement and negotiated

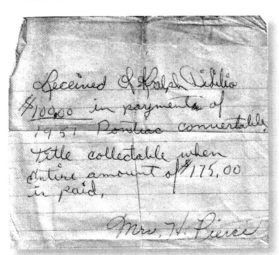

a deal with the female owner. I returned a half hour later, with a contract I had written up and $10. She signed the contract, took my money and handed me the keys to my "new" car. The contract was the first of many that I created for various transactions. A Pontiac would replace the Ford, and, again, I created a contract. I ran across the original (shown here), and my naiveté is clearly in evidence. You can note the lack of a date as well as other errors too numerous to detail. I am confident that law schools can use this contract to definitively prove the truism: "The person who represents himself has a fool for a client."

Any flaws in my draftsmanship notwithstanding, I did receive the title of what would be the first of the scores of automobiles that I would own over my lifetime. From the exotic DeLorean, Corvette and Mercedes SL, to the conservative Plymouth, Corvair and Pinto, I haven't missed much. One thing is for sure—if I had put 50,000 miles on each of the first 10 cars I owned, I could have retired 10 years earlier on the money saved by not buying the rest. Two thoughts come to mind, however: I would not have experienced the joy of owning those cars, and I would have likely spent the money on boats or other unnecessary but satisfying toys.

That '48 Ford Coupe was my first auto love and my first project. Cousin John and I spent many hours refurbishing the interior. He was a willing participant, as we sanded down the dashboard and the metal around the windows in preparation for new paint and pin striping. Since I had no license to drive, I had the car permanently parked on Birch Street at the first available space closest to 8th. It was the first thing I saw when I left the house by either exit or when I came and went from Joe's. I spent many spare hours preparing for my maiden drive, which I almost didn't get a chance to enjoy because of stupidity. In preparation for painting the interior, I had carefully taped paper as protection against any overspray, covering every inch that was not to be painted. The steering wheel, the seats, the door panels and the windows all received careful attention.

Finally, when all the preparation was complete, I armed myself with two cans of flat black spray paint, sealed myself inside and closed the door. I proceeded to spray away. At the start, I was pleased to witness the metamorphosis as the paint began to adhere to the dashboard. The cloud of paint got larger, and, as it did, I was inhaling copious amounts of the black mist. Needless to say, I had worn no mask or other protective device. Although I began to choke, I wanted to finish, (that impatience thing again), even as my lungs began to object. When I became faint and dizzy, I finally opened the door and, enveloped by a huge cloud of black, fell to my knees beside the now-transformed Ford. In true North Camden fashion, of course, I "walked it off."

Nine weeks later, I got the title to the Ford, as contracted for, and by this time I had turned it into a sharp car. I thought I was really something to behold behind the wheel, as close to James Dean in his '50 Mercury in "Rebel without a Cause" as I could get. But my love affair did not last beyond the classified ad that caught my attention in the Courier Post: "Will trade '52 Pontiac Convertible for any Ford Coupe '47-'49." I made the call, drew up a second contract, and for my Ford and $250 ($25 per week), I was the owner of a blue 1952 Pontiac Convertible. It was 1958, and I drove it all during my senior year at WWHS.

Toward the end of my junior year, I had to make some decisions about my upcoming senior year course work. I had heard about a Distributive Education program offered seniors that allowed for a shortened schedule and early release from school. Here was a formal program built around a practice I had invented and had been perfecting for two years. Is this a great country or what? I looked into what was required to sign up and was told that I had to be interviewed by the instructor of the program. A guardian angel, Mr. Raymond Granfield, became part of my life.

Granfield admitted me into his empty classroom at the appointed time and proceeded to explain his requirements for admission into his exclusive program that would accommodate 15 students: Suit and tie for boys, hose and heels for girls, a legitimate job in the retail business and regular attendance at both school and work. He went on to say that his program would be represented by those who were accepted, and he had very high standards. I had observed him carefully during his monologue. He was tall and lean and sporting a blond crew cut, with a well-creased suit and a narrow tie. He had a rather military bearing that I later found out was a result of his Marine training. I felt like I could respect this guy for the double classes I would be spending with him over the school year. I applied for the program and was accepted.

The class work was benign enough; public speaking, customer service, promotion and product display were among the highlights of our learning. I was less interested in excelling at the class activities than I was in having the extra time to put in more hours at Joe's. Early in the year, I was elected president of the class although I did not seek the position. This was the beginning of the skill of resume-building that I learned to rely on when I sought educational or career advancement. Granfield paid an initial and subsequent visit to all of the work sites. He found my original guardian angel, Joe, to be an interested participant in the program, although Joe's was not what Granfield had in mind for a typical site. He was more used to JC Penney and Sears as the workplaces for his students, but he recognized the benefits that experience in a local store setting could bring.

For the second time in as many years, a teacher took an inordinate interest in my future. In January, unbeknownst to me, Mr. Granfield called my mother and set up an appointment to visit our house and have a chat. Mom worked 3:00 to 9:00 p.m. on Wednesdays, so a 1:00 o'clock meeting was arranged. I arrived, as usual, at my own work at 12:30 and set about my beef-boning chores. At about 1:30, Joe signaled me to the phone and told me my Mom wanted to talk to me. She informed me that Mr. Granfield was sitting with her, and could I come home for a few minutes? I was in a panic. Mr. Granfield was sitting in my rat-infested, roach-populated house with the green paper rugs and the lawn furniture "bought" with green stamps. I didn't want to face him, but I had no option.

I crossed the narrow Birch Street, still wearing my blood-stained apron. I opened the door and stood in the threshold without closing the door. Mr. Granfield was in his well-pressed suit, sitting across from Mom. They were both smoking and appeared to be at ease. I was wondering at the purpose of my summons, but I soon found out. "Mr. Granfield thinks you should go to college," Mom offered. Mr. Granfield just nodded.

My heart was pounding, as I was hoping the rats would not take this moment to noisily change locations in the house using the ceiling as a causeway. Belying my agitation, I calmly said, "Look Mom, that's fine and good, but I can't afford to go to school, and, even if I could, I didn't take the courses I need to get into college." In hopes of escape, I lied by saying, "I only have a few minutes break, 'cause we're busy over there". Undaunted, my Mom retorted, "You can stop paying me board and save the money it takes." Seeing me begin to shake my head, Mr. Granfield added, "Let me worry about where you can be admitted." He went on, "Why don't you come by my apartment tonight, and we can look over some catalogs from Colorado State where I went to school, and we can chat about it?" Seeing this as an escape opportunity, I agreed to see him at his apartment and excused myself.

When I left work at 6 p.m., I did not bother explaining to Mom why I was aggravated about Granfield's visit; I just took the address he had left with her. I changed into a clean shirt and headed to East Camden, where Granfield lived with his wife on 26th Street, just off Federal. I had to make one stop along the way. Natale lived on High Street, off of 27th. The Pontiac practically found its own way, since I had picked him up there every day since I had gotten my license. We had become like brothers, not that he needed another; he already had five brothers and a sister to boot, all of whom shared a single home with their parents who had come over from Italy. I was like one of the family, I spent as much time there as in my own home, and an invitation or a knock was unnecessary. I burst into the side door, calling for Natale, who was also known as "Needles," as I went. He came bounding down the steps with a smile. Without formalities, I said, "Come on, get into the car." "What's up?" he replied. "Never mind, let's go, andiamo!" I said, using one of the few words I knew in Italian. Off we went. "What's up," he repeated. In a disconcerted state, I blurted out, "Granfield came over to my house and told my mother I could go to college. If I can go to college, so can you." "Are you !@#$%^ nuts!" was his considered response. Natale was no dummy either.

As we continued to Granfield's apartment, I shared what little details I had, and when I got to the part about Colorado, Natale stopped me and said, "Where the hell is Colorado?" I quickly answered, "How the hell do I know, all I know is it's cold!" This last bit of conversation was the result of neither one of us ever having been more than 100 miles from Camden and never having been on a train (save for a caboose) or plane. When we arrived, Granfield answered the doorbell in his sport shirt and desert boots, my first glimpse of him without a tie. I will be forever grateful to him for many reasons, but among them the fact that he saw the two of us and never even blinked an eye when I introduced Natale by saying, "This is my pal, Natale, he would like to go to college too." This was one of those life-defining moments for me and, needless to say, for Natale. We were soon to find out about Colorado State College and all of the hoops we needed to jump through for application and acceptance. It was already the end of January, and Colorado State started freshman classes in September.

In the meantime, we had to start thinking about earning enough for tuition, fees, room, board and clothes and meeting a million other challenges. From that night forward, I was someone who was going to college. I was just like Max, the Jewish man, who went to confession and, at age 75, told the priest that he was enjoying the sexual pleasures of his 30-year-old new bride. When the priest asked why, since Max was Jewish, he was telling him, Max shouted out, "Telling you? I'm telling everybody!" I had a mission, and I was going to be a somebody. I felt like I was running fast. But—what if I failed? After all, the only expectation anyone had for me to this point was to finish high school. Certainly, there was never any notion that I would go on to college. Cousin Joey had failed, and he was way smarter then me. I was staring failure in the face.

I certainly didn't look scared. I was confident that I could save the money needed to at least begin college. I knew I could hustle jobs and earn enough during the holidays and during the summer. Money would be a challenge, but not an insurmountable one. Meanwhile, I set about to do all the things necessary to make a proper application. With the patient help of Mr. Granfield—and with me learning enough to help Natale—we both got accepted, me without restriction and Natale on academic probation.

Things around the neighborhood took on a different hue now that I was a short-timer. Some things got better, some worse, and some remained the same. Elaine had graduated WWHS the year before, and by the time my graduation approached she was marrying Pooky, with Aunt Lydia and me as maid and man of honor. It was a small ceremony and subdued reception, more than a few remarking that there was little to celebrate. Mom capped off the evening by leaving in disgust when Dad came to offer best wishes.

My own love life was filled by the fair Marie Ciri of Berkley Street. Marie and I had met at a dance, and we were a hot ticket for some period of months. She was a sweet and charming Italian girl who had lost her mother at a young age and was now sister/mother to her older brother, Frankie, as well as a wonderful daughter to a hard-working and old-school father. They were a wonderful family, and I enjoyed being around them. Marie and I were "going steady," and I couldn't wait to tell her of my college plans. She was proud of me, and we talked of the future together.

To that point, the only argument we had ever had occurred as a result of my temper. I picked her up to take her for a 16th birthday dinner. Keeping a secret of the dinner I had planned, I told her simply that I would pick her up and we would grab a bite to eat. She was beautiful, as usual, that night in an attractive dress. I had saved big bucks to take her to the Hawaiian Cottage, a large and garish—and very expensive—formal restaurant that enjoyed popularity. Marie had never been there, and I was determined to give her a special treat. I avoided her insistent queries about our destination until I pulled my convertible under the portico at the front door. "Ta-da!" I said with great delight, "here we are."

Marie looked at me and said, "I can't go in there dressed like this." I was dumbstruck. I told her that she looked just great and that this was going to be a special night. "I said," she spit out sharply, "I will not go in there like this, let's go." I was livid. "Let's go?" I said, "Oh, we'll go alright, we'll go right back to Berkley Street!" With that, I slammed the car into reverse and smashed the accelerator to the floor, peeling rubber as I went backwards. I don't know exactly how many yards I traveled before I slammed the trunk of the Pontiac into an immovable telephone pole, but I had picked up enough speed so that I hit the pole with sufficient force to leave a huge impression of the pole in the steel bumper and halfway into the trunk. I had ruined my new convertible.

Without a good night or any other words, I dropped her off and returned to North Camden to explain to Uncle Mike, much to his amusement, the circumstances of my "accident." Mom and Elaine, of course, raved on and on about how that ungrateful Marie was the cause of the damage to my beautiful Pontiac. Such was, and still is, the perspective of my loyal mother and sister.

In the final analysis, it wasn't the notorious Hawaiian Cottage incident that broke Marie and me up, it was college. When we discussed our future together, we both knew that I would be gone for long stretches over the next four years. I told her that I expected that she would wait for me and would not go out with others. I also told her I would not want her to attend the dances we went to together, since I wouldn't be there. Reverting to Hawaiian Cottage Marie, she calmly informed me that she thought it was unfair of me to make such a request. She wasn't a nun, she said, and she would like to go to dances, but she would certainly remain true to me and not have any dates. Not to put too fine a point on it, I was, once again, livid. I guess I got livid frequently in those days. In the end, this led to the demise of the relationship. Marie was right, of course, notwithstanding my mother and sister, loyal as always, fully backing my position on this as well. A month later, in front of the trophy cases at WWHS, Janis Zeccola boldly introduced herself to me, and a new relationship evolved that would last a lifetime, nearly 25 years of which were in marriage.

My father and I began to develop a bit of a relationship when I would occasionally run into him at Grandmom DiSibio's. I knew and liked his stepson, Larry Carroll, from neighborhood sports, and Larry was also headed to college. Dad was firm in his belief that Larry would do well at Temple University in Philadelphia, while he thought that the Colorado idea was a bad one for me— and, besides, I was becoming a pretty good butcher. Dad wasn't big on psychology. He was doing house repairs and painting as a way to make a living at the time, and he was doing well. I told him I could use the extra money if he could use me on Sundays, and he thought it was a great idea.

I began to earn extra money with him and learned a great deal about painting and general home repair. He would also bring Pooky on as an extra hand on occasion, and I got to know my brother-in-law better and grew to like him. The circumstances lent themselves to humor once in a while. Pooky and I were painting baseboards on the third floor when Pop, suspecting we were taking a smoke break, shouted up, "What's goin' on up there, I don't hear any noise up there!" Rarely stuck for an answer, I shouted back, "How much noise do you expect from a paint brush?" We all got a kick out of it. Dad never realized how funny he was when he was just being his Archie Bunker self. When I was a little kid, I asked him why it was that there was a fathers' day and a mothers' day but no kids' day. He shouted back, "Shut up before the Jews hear ya and start selling cards!" He was Archie before there was an Archie.

Before I knew it, the summer was almost gone, and Natale and I were getting ready for college and the vagaries of Colorado. My bank account had swelled to nearly $1000, and Mom was using her ironing money to stop at Adams Men's to get me underwear, sweaters and a couple of pairs of trousers. (I had taken to calling my pants "trousers," because Mr. Granfield said only sailors and girls wear "pants.") Mom went to the Army-Navy Store and bought me a foot locker and a clock radio as a final gift. I filled the brown foot locker and locked it with a purloined Master combination lock from WWHS. I didn't know what to do with the locker, since it would never fit under my train seat. I searched the catalog I had gotten from the college and found out that there was a Director of Student Housing. I taped a large address label to the locker and took it to the post office, where I mailed it for a cheap three-week delivery rate. The address on the label read, "Office of Student Housing: Care of the Director: Hold for Ralph DiSibio." Again, I was thinking.

When the time came to depart, the scene at the North Philadelphia train station was crowded. It was made more so by Natale's family and mine seeing us off. Uncle Mike DiSibio, Mom and Elaine were misty-eyed as we tucked our set of matched Italian luggage—two cardboard boxes full of pepper and egg sandwiches and homemade cookies—under our arms, along with two cartons of Marlboro cigarettes. We pulled out to the whoops and waves of loved ones. Mario and Teresa would have been proud of the "unafraid of the unknown" attitude we exuded. Deep down inside, though, I was still running scared.

10

Uncle Mike

Uncle Mike and Aunt Lucy holding little Michele.

*This picture is taken looking at Joe's Meat Market across
from the side entrance of 523 N. 8th Street. Take note
of the resemblance of Cousin Jim Iannetta to Uncle Mike.*

Uncle Mike

"Cousin Johnny identified his college summer job there as the ugliest, hardest and nastiest that anyone can possibly imagine. Uncle Mike stayed on for more than thirty years."

MIKE WAS OUR HERO. In many ways, he was a human dichotomy, hard as nails but soft as pudding. He was macho, but he doted on his wife and daughter. He was harsh at times, tender at others. He could intimidate you with a look, but bring you to tears with some of his own. We did not need the bronze star awarded to him for his daring on D-Day as evidence of his worth; we only needed to be part of his life. Mike was our hero.

Mario, or Mike, was born in Jamesville, the forth child and second son of Mario and Teresa Monarca. He respected his older sisters and looked up to his older brother. Phil was modest and not given to bragging because, as long as Mike was around, there was someone who would do the bragging for him. Mike, who would regale everyone within earshot with the exploits of Phil, would wax on about his brother's strength, his athletic prowess and his wisdom. Jealousy was foreign to Mike in his relationship with Phil, indeed in his relationship with anyone. As the youngest, Mike was required to fulfill responsibilities that others put off on him, yet he took his duties to heart and performed them without hesitation, because he knew his role in the family hierarchy. Mike was to take duty seriously his entire life.

He and the rest of the family matured in Jamesville, where the first four offspring would be joined by four more—Lola, Giacomo, Dora and Milena—before the family moved to Camden.

Camden gave an urban setting to the family, and Mike flourished in it, as did the rest of the Monarcas. Mike continued to tag along with his big brother and carry out brotherly duties that related to the younger girls or to assist in other family matters. Occasionally, he would be sent off to fetch Dora who had strayed too far from 734 or to help tend to the little patch of land that Mario cultivated near the 10th Street Bridge. For the most part, life took on a routine of school, playing the sports he had been taught by Phil and getting into his share of scraps that toughened him up.

While Uncle Phil carved out a future on the railroad, Mike was looking for a working place of his own. Camden was a thriving industrial community, with Campbell Soup, Esterbrook Pen, the huge fabric mill on State Street and RCA Victor offering only a few of the opportunities for employment. School was never a priority for the family, and it wasn't until Lydia that anyone in the family came close to finishing high school. Like his siblings before him, Mike left school as soon as he was able to earn a living to help with the increasing expenses of a growing family. He chose to work at the John R. Evans leather factory.

JR Evans was located around 5th and Vine Streets, just a couple of blocks from 734. The factory produced finished leather products for shipment to shoe manufacturers, handbag producers and a myriad of other makers of leather goods that required leather. Here, in the Camden plant, truckloads of cowhide skins would arrive daily, freshly taken from slaughtered cattle. The pelts still had bits of meat and all of the hair attached, and the stench from opening the containers was worsened when the pelts were processed through vats of an acid-like liquid used to dissolve the hair from the hides. Most all of the operations, from dehairing the pelts to the multi-step tanning process, required manual labor and great physical strength.

The entire process reeked, and it was overwhelming. The malodorous aroma permeated the entire building and escaped to envelop the neighborhood for a block in each direction 24 hours a day. The work environment was suited to very few. Louise and Anna worked at the plant for some months, but they left as soon as more attractive factory work was available. Cousin Johnny identified his college summer job there as the ugliest, hardest and nastiest that anyone can possibly imagine. Uncle Mike stayed on for more than thirty years.

Mike was a charming, playful and popular guy around North Camden. He was less serious than Phil and always carried an impish grin that he passed on to Lola's son, Cousin Jimmy. He played the romantic field until, in his early '20s, he became enamored of Lucy Riggio. Lucy was a dark-skinned girl with parents born in Italy; her understated beauty and shy demeanor made her well-suited to Mike. She was always well kempt and neatly, but modestly, attired. She had a delicate constitution and was prone to illness, but when she was healthy she worked at the Strawbridge and Clothier department store on Broadway. The job not only brought in extra money but also got many family members a discount in "her" shoe department.

Lucy was a demure and typical hostess at home, in the Italian tradition. A visit to their house was always an occasion for coffee, cake or assorted foods. Together they produced, like Phil and Mary before them, a single female child. Michele was born in prosperous times, and the three of them could afford to purchase a lovely home in the 900 block of Vine Street. It was identical to the home of his sister Louise and her husband, Joe Vitagliano, only six doors to the west. By remaining in close proximity to the Monarcas, Mike broke with the male tradition of moving close to the family of the wife and strengthened ties to the Monarca family by choosing my own mother and father to be the godparents to Michele.

Family was always important to Mike, as was his work. But no event or activity or experience was more life-defining to Mike than World War II. Mike was in his early '20s when the attack on Pearl Harbor brought America into the war. Until then, the country had been committed only to sending material to our allies, who were engaged in the monumental struggle with the Nazis. Our declaration of war was the crucible that produced the greatest generation, one that demanded a human commitment; and Uncle Mike made a decision to enlist in the army to fulfill some part of that commitment. He and Lucy had just married and came to the mutual agreement that he had the duty to serve. Michele would not be born until after the war, and Lucy had his family and her own to look out for her wellbeing. He went off to war without trepidation.

Like many of his generation, Mike had life-altering experiences in the military. It did not change who he was, but it did change what he was. He was more confident, less frivolous, more focused and hardened at the end of his tour of duty. He was older than most that enlisted and was given more responsibilities from the outset. He quickly became a drill sergeant, who trained men for combat. Thus did he seem destined to continue preparing other men for battle and seeing them off to war while he remained in the USA and awaited his next cadre of green recruits ready for his tutelage. But that was not to be. He was granted his request to be shipped out with his men. He had an earned reputation for being a tough guy, and when one of the recruits threatened to punch him in the mouth, Mike quietly told the young man, "You might be able to do that, son, but I'll break you of the habit." All within earshot believed that he could and would fulfill the promise.

Sergeant Mike Monarca led his men when the landing craft dropped them knee deep in the English Channel at Omaha Beach on D-Day. On that June 6th in 1944, when all around him were cowering in the beach sand, it was Mike that stood up, surrounded by exploding shells and machine gun fire, and commanded his men forward. They followed their courageous leader, and those that did not die went on to complete the mission. For a lifetime thereafter, the men he led returned to reunions to praise his courage. At his funeral, many of these now old men traveled many miles to, one last time, pay homage and last respects to their fallen chief.

When Mike returned to North Camden after the war, he returned to work at the leather factory. Aunt Lucy continued to have health problems, and Michele presented problems of her own. Although she seemed to all to be a healthy and well-adjusted child, she would grow up to be strong-willed and socially challenged. She finished high school, and like all of the Monarcas, earned her way in various jobs. Still, as time passed, family members wondered about her overall ability and coping skills, and she was sheltered by her parents. Between Aunt Lucy's health problem and Michele's social issues, Mike took on more and more of the cooking and cleaning chores in addition to the hard labor at JR Evans. The family noticed all of this, but it was not because Mike ever complained or even mentioned these challenges that faced him.

Mike had other things to be concerned about: Michele began to date. Mike was more protective than most fathers, and on one of her early dates the young man came to pick up Cousin Michele, only to be met by Mike with important instructions: He was to have her home by midnight. Midnight came and went and finally, at 1:15, Michele and her date came through the front door where they encountered the waiting Uncle Mike. The startled boy listened as Mike shared an experience from his past. "When I was in the war, son, I killed 23 Germans. I didn't know them, they didn't know me." He paused for effect and to quell his anger. "The men

I killed didn't harm my family or hurt my daughter. Do you understand what I'm saying?" The boy flushed and left, never to be seen again. Such was Uncle Mike's love for his daughter.

Their rancher in Edgewater Park, just off of Route 130, was as modest as Mike and Lucy. You entered through a front entrance directly at street level, eliminating the hassle for Aunt Lucy caused by the many stairs that were required for entry to the impressive Vine Street home. On the other side of the door, the house emptied directly into the living room. Beyond the spacious living room was a formal dining room, and off to the right was a small but efficient kitchen. The furniture had all been taken from Vine Street and was crowded in this more petite residence.

These furnishings had some special memories for the couple. The coffee and end tables were covered with thick glass sized to precision, and Uncle Mike was proud to relate the fact that his army buddy had cut and beveled them specifically for these tables as a gift for his old sarge. On the large wall, facing you upon entry, was a strangely exotic work of art, a painting on which the image was applied on the reverse side of glass framed with mahogany. The representation of the moon was highlighted by sparkles, giving it a shine and exaggerating it in the sky over the quiescent village. They had proudly displayed the piece since marriage. The dining room buffet also held four brass pieces representing Venice, a foot-long gondola and its gondolier, complete with his delicate oar, and two of the lions that are the symbols of the city. These items adorned the buffet in both of their houses and were treasured by the family.

Through the kitchen, you made an exit into an expansive backyard that was fenced to contain Uncle Mike's dog. When his beagle mix had died, he had gotten a Border Collie mix and spent hours teaching her to fetch a Frisbee while leaping four feet into the air. The dog always followed us as we strode to the extensive garden that was separately fenced in the rear. There, Mike cultivated all manner of vegetables that he never failed to harvest for his visitors to take home.

Before he quit late in life, he would smoke or chew on a cigar constantly. I can picture him now, cigar in mouth, reaching into his pocket and opening a large jackknife. He never bent down at the knee, but always spread his feet wide and leaned over from the waist as he cut out a head of lettuce or a banana squash. He would rise, holding up the fresh food while still shaking the dirt from its foliage, wearing a look of pride and wonder, although the cigar clenched in his teeth partially obscured the grin of satisfaction. In his senior years he had become Grandpop Mario on his little patch on 10th Street.

I personally felt the depth of his love for family many times. He and I spent numerous hours at his home in Edgewater Park, 10 miles north of Camden where he moved to give Michele more opportunities, and we talked about his life and the family. After Aunt Lucy left him a widower, he got a new job that he had found after his factory closed. He was proud of the fact that he had a "clean" job at an electrical supply house and that Michele was building up a record number of days worked without a sick day, almost nine years. With a failed marriage to an abusive husband behind her, she had no prospects for another and was content to stay at home with her father. I had left Camden many years before, but on my regular returns I rarely neglected to pay a visit to my hero.

When my family and I made a home in Maryland, Dean was fulfilling his Army Reserve commitment at Fort Dix, some 10 miles from Edgewater Park. Dean was having a very tough time adjusting to the "in your face" ravings of his superiors. The ravings, of course, were meant to break a recruit's ego; I explained this to Dean in one of his phone calls to me, but he was still considering quitting. I contacted some of my friends who had the same experience, and they all wrote to Dean in an effort to bolster his resolve. But none of these letters impacted Dean more than the actions of Uncle Mike, who had heard of the dilemma.

Uncle Mike put his discharge papers, his silver star and his purple heart into his pocket and headed for Fort Dix. Dix is a huge military complex with the requisite security measures to keep out intruders and the uninvited. Uncle Mike went to the main gate and requested a meeting with the camp commander or anyone with decision-making authority. The MP escorted the civilian to the administration building, and Uncle Mike was able to meet not with a General but with a Captain who was the Officer of the Day. Uncle Mike took out his medals and his discharge papers, which registered all of the battles he had engaged in, and showed them to the young officer. He explained that he used to be a drill sergeant and knew that it was not customary, but he would like to see his great-nephew, Dean DiSibio. The wise officer made a command decision and drove Mike to the field headquarters.

Sergeant Mario Monarca awaited buck Private DiSibio in a large tent, while a corporal went out about a hundred yards to inform Private DiSibio that he was wanted in the command tent. When Dean double-timed it to the tent, he was shocked to see his Uncle Mike standing there alone. "Hi Dean, how's it goin'?" Still perplexed, Dean managed to reply, "Okay, I guess." Uncle Mike drew himself up to his full 5 feet 5 inches and embraced Dean. He whispered, "Dean, I want you to know how proud we all are of you and what you're doing for our country. If you ever need anything, you know I'm only a little ways away." He released Dean and said,

"You had better get back to your unit son." With tears welling up in his eyes, but with renewed resolve, Dean said thanks and left. Uncle Mike never spoke of the incident, but Dean related it to me some weeks later. Mike was our hero.

In Search of a Niche

Here I am moving into the AKL fraternity house at 1845 11th Street in Greeley, Colorado. I had just been elected as Social Chairman.

I had my ever faithful brown trunk that Mom had bought me and my switchblade knife, which solidified my reputation as a tough kid from New Jersey.

In Search of a Niche

"We slept late on Saturday, mainly because we were tired, but also, we thought, because it was a precursor to death by starvation."

JUST DAYS BEFORE THE MISTY-EYED DEPARTURE from the train station, I had gone to jail. On the day after my 18th birthday, I had gone to Camden Trust to withdraw the $1000 I had managed to save, which included the $150 I had gotten for the still unrepaired Pontiac. With a cashier's check for $800 and $200 in cash, I drove the '58 Ford that I had borrowed from Aunt Lydia to WWHS for some final farewells. I had not remembered that it was initiation day for incoming sophomores, but, of course, I got involved in the fun and the ensuing fisticuffs with unwilling participants. The police were called, and I soon found myself in the back of a paddy wagon. The bad news was that I was taken to the city jail at the court house; the good news was that I had enough cash, $100, to bail myself out, along with my friend James Loving who was also involved.

I sheepishly caught a bus back to get the car. By the time I returned to North Camden, Aunt Anna had already called my mother with the news that Ralphie was arrested. Such was the communication network of the Monarca's in 1959. In those days, you could, as the saying goes, use telephone, telegram—or tell-a-Monarca. We invented our own brand of Nextel: it was tell Louise, next tell Anna, and next tell Dora. I got my bail money back two days later when the miscreants appeared in court and were told by the judge to use our energies to polish our shoes and not other kids.

Those were kinder and gentler times. Still, the incident justified the "telemonarca" networkers in predicting that I would never make it out of sight of family, let alone in college. Nothing, however, could deter my own excitement and the anticipation of heading west.

West, to Natale and I, had always been West Virginia, but by this time I had gone to the school library and learned about Greeley, Colorado. It was on the eastern slope of the great Rocky Mountains and named for Horace Greeley, who had advised everyone who sought adventure to, "Go west, young man, go west." Much after the fact, we heeded his call and headed off in the suggested direction. The 34 hours required for the trip didn't sound like much, but on a bumpy train sitting upright in flimsy seats, it wasn't a day at the beach. We augmented our homemade sandwiches and cookies with snacks we bought when we had a short stop in St. Louis, where we marveled at the mighty Mississippi; and we would later be astounded by the barrenness of Nebraska. It was all new, all noteworthy, all exciting. We actually saw a herd of buffalo as we crossed into Colorado, at the same time as the conductor was calling out, "Greeley, next stop, Greeley, next stop."

Natale and I gathered up our belongings and quickly positioned ourselves near an exit stairwell. As the train slowed to a halt, he and I leaped from the train and down onto a patch of dirt. We stared ahead at a series of six small buildings, one of which had a Coor's beer sign, and we both had the same thought, "What the hell have we done. This is Greeley?" Our hearts sank, and the thrill of the adventure drained from us. Our funk was interrupted by the conductor's voice again calling, "Greeley, next stop, Greeley, next stop." In unison, we cried out to him, "Isn't this Greeley?" He laughed and told us that this was LaSalle, where the train was switching tracks, and he ordered us back onto the train. LaSalle, we later learned, was five miles east of Greeley, and the Coor's sign served to beckon customers to a bar where we would drink copious amounts of the 3.2 beer that was legal for 18-year-older in Colorado.

The train station in Greeley was attractive and spacious. We gawked at the sights as we made our way into the oversized men's room to freshen up. We unpacked some clean clothes and prepared to hit the streets. It was close to noon as we exited the station onto the sun-drenched main street of Greeley. Having gotten directions from a smiling, friendly clerk, we headed toward the campus some 10 blocks away. Neither one of us had any idea of what we were going to do next. Natale finally broke the silence with, "What now, chief?" I told him that all we had to do was find the housing office in Frazier Hall. It was an uphill climb, and by the time we got to the edge of the campus, we were perspiring in our new sweaters that we had donned as a result of my erroneous prediction that it would be cold. We were awed by the environment. There were hundreds of mature trees in every direction. In between the curved walkways were beautiful brick buildings sporting various Greek and Italianate architectures. We had died and gone to heaven in Colorado.

We inquired of a passerby as to the location of Frazier Hall, and, for the second time, we got a smile, this one accompanied by patient and careful directions. Natale waited on the generous steps of the entrance to protect our possessions, as I headed in search of the Director of Student Housing. I was confident that he would aid me in retrieving my footlocker that I had sent three weeks earlier to his care. I entered a room with a flag sign indicating that I was in the right place. An attractive young lady greeted me with a smile, the third in a row, and asked if she could help. "I'm Ralph DiSibio. I would like to see the director, please." At the sound of my name, her eyebrows lifted, and the smile got bigger. She went into a small nearby office and returned with the invitation, "Mr. Turner will see you now."

I entered the modest workplace that was barely large enough to contain the desk, chair for a visitor and a two-shelf bookcase. Behind the desk, I spied a smiling—making it four in a row—man. Just over his left shoulder, in the corner, nearly touching his small chair, I spotted my footlocker. Maintaining the smile, he said slowly, "Mr. DiSibio, whatever possessed you to send me your footlocker?" Recovering from hearing my name preceded by "mister" for the first time, I said, "Well, sir, I thought you would know what to do with it." He chuckled and told me that he did know what to do with it, but would I please retrieve it at the end of the day, when, he predicted, I would have a proper place store it.

Before escaping my first college embarrassment, I received a four-page list of "approved college housing"; the dorms were full, I was told, and I would have to use the list to find housing, since only those places on the list were acceptable. I returned to the entrance to find Natale on his third Marlboro and anxious to hear what the plan was. We headed out across the campus, now armed with the list and a map of the environs. The first stop was a revelation. An elderly lady answered our knock with a smile, making five in a row, and invited us into her well-kept little bungalow. According to the list, she had a basement apartment for rent. She bade us to sit and watch the TV in the living room, while she went into the kitchen, returning with two glasses of milk and some cookies. We thanked her, and, as we greedily ate and drank, she asked about our home town and our reasons for choosing Colorado State College as our school. We chatted briefly, then I got to the point—that patience thing again—with, "How much are you getting for the apartment?" She gave us a smile, our sixth, and said, "Oh, I'm sorry, boys, but that was taken this morning and isn't available." She wished us luck and thanked us for chatting with her. We left, puzzled.

This place was going to take some getting used to. Everyone was smiling, everyone was patient, and now a little old lady had, as we saw things, risked a mugging when she didn't even have a chance of getting anything from us. We might have been reminded of Stepford, except that "The Stepford Wives" had not yet been written. This Colorado was a little strange, but we liked it. Our next stop was just across the street from the newly constructed girl's dorm, and, of course, I liked the location. The potential housing was in a corner house that, according to the list, had three rooms on the second floor available for three students, who would have to share a bath in a common hall. We carefully inspected the rooms, and I made the landlady an offer she couldn't refuse. She was getting $100 per student, per room, per quarter, and I explained that Natale and I were willing to give her $150 for one room that we would share. Each quarter, she would get $50 extra, and we would save $25 apiece per quarter: another win-win. Thus it was that we shared a double bed in that 12-foot by 12-foot room, without even the thought of a complaint, for the next two quarters. The only adornment was that pink clock radio retrieved from my footlocker that now served as an extra set of drawers.

Money was tight from the outset. We each opened accounts at the Weld County Bank and allotted ourselves $10 per week for food and expenses. In this way, we could be sure that, with part-time work, we could survive the year, although the niggardly allowance required some creativity from the get-go. As we worked to manage the meager amounts of money we could spend, the Colorado mystique wore off when, on September 30th, a freak snowstorm blanketed us with 18 inches of the white stuff. We did not yet have the proper attire to fend off the cold, but we made do.

Natale secured a job in the kitchen of the girl's dorm, where he washed pots and pans. This required him, sadly, to dump serving tray after serving tray of perfectly good, but unserved, food down a giant disposal. He would eat as much as his lean body could contain and sometimes covertly ferret some morsels back to our room. For some extra cash, I worked two hours a night in a convenience store that was fashioned out of the basement of a private home.

Thanksgiving was approaching and, while we had much to be thankful for, we were not looking forward to our first holiday away from home. Neither one of us had tasted good spaghetti and "gravy" for a couple of months. The campus, which was about to shut down for four days, would become a ghost town when most of the students returned to their families. My own family was represented only by the letters we received from the faithful: Mom, Aunt Lydia and Janis, who, unlike Marie, agreed to remain nun-like until I returned for the Christmas break. Once in awhile, a dollar bill would appear in Aunt Lee's card or Mom's.

Thanksgiving Day dawned beautiful and crisp, and Natale and I agreed that we should treat ourselves to a "picture show" at the only movie in town. We luxuriated, able to sleep in since our respective places of employment were closed for the extended holiday. "On the Waterfront" was showing at the theater just across the street from the Canfield Hotel. What better way to mark the first holiday out West than watching Brando as a tough New Yorker fighting the mob? The Canfield hotel was a beautiful green-stuccoed, five-storied building that was the centerpiece of downtown Greeley. We stopped to gaze into the fancy dining room and saw the advertisement for a bountiful Thanksgiving meal for the munificent sum of $5.95. The bill of fare listed, in detail, all of the wonderful items to be served. Natale and I looked at each other and had the exact same thought—we deserved it.

We carefully counted our money and figured we could go to the movie, enjoy the sumptuous repast and still have about a quarter left over. We both knew there were three full days left in our $10 allotment, but we planned to make an early withdrawal of next week's allowance, rationalizing that we would replace the funds. We walked home completely satiated, indeed stuffed. We slept the sleep of the content, aided by the ample amounts of turkey we had consumed.

On Friday morning, we made our way to the Weld County Bank only to be shocked to find it closed for the extended holiday. Woe unto us. We were now broke, having spent the last quarter on Marlboros, and with three days remaining until either the dorm kitchen or the bank opened. Two active, healthy young men without food for three days is not a pleasant thought to contemplate. We made it through Friday by drinking copious amounts of water and talking a lot about the food we would get on Monday. We slept late on Saturday, mainly because we were tired, but also, we thought, because it was a precursor to death by starvation.

Our "sleep of the starving" was interrupted by our landlady with her incessant tapping on our bedroom door. "Boys" she whispered, "there's a package for you, just delivered by the mailman." We dressed and went to the door, almost falling over the large brown-papered box that had been left just outside with my name in bold letters. We tore it open, as if the paper itself were edible, and to our growing delight, we started to empty the contents one item at a time. There were three cans of Campbell's pork and beans, a whole cooked chicken in a can, a box of Oreos, two lemon TastyPies, two TastyKake butterscotch Krimpets and three cans of Campbell's tomato soup. We felt like the rescued prisoners of a concentration camp. There was a God, and it was my Mom.

Now that the body was handled, it was time for the mind. Upon our arrival in Colorado, I had appeared at the cattle call they referred to as freshman registration and tried to figure out how this process worked. I kept observing others meander through the maze of class abbreviations and boxes full of punch cards. Recalling my lesson from South Camden, I listened, without initiating or even responding to conversation, in hopes that, like the "piece of ass" puzzle, this one, too, would be revealed to me. My new guardian angel appeared in the form of Dr. John Welling.

Dr. Welling, who, as it turned out, was a world-class history professor, saw me perusing and observing and said, "What, pray tell, son, is your major?" His accent exposed him as hailing from the east coast, with a high class twinge that suggested Boston. "I'm thinking about history, sir; but I wish I were sure." He smiled at my accent and intoned, "The fact that you correctly used the word "were" instead of "was" makes me think you should be a history major. It is my first love." And, thus, I became a history major, as I breezed through registration assisted by Dr. Welling's hints. I returned to the room and proceeded to share my new-found wisdom with Natale, and he went back to register with a major in math. By the time our Thanksgiving fiasco had come and gone, we were well into academics.

Eventually, I took more than 40 hours of classes from the erudite Dr. John Welling. I reveled in his World History, History of the Ancient Greeks, History of the Middle Ages and much more. Dr. Welling was the college edition of my Ray Granfield, as I continued to be blessed by mentors who took me under their wings. I was saddened to hear of his passing not long after my graduation. I can still recall him strolling across the campus with his hands thrust into his pockets and a Pall Mall dangling from his lips. His 6-foot 2-inch frame topped by a shock of pure white, wavy hair made him look like he was from central casting. He is owed a sincere, if tardy, posthumous thank you.

Natale and I were making enough money so that we could draw less from our accounts and think about investing in a car. I say "investing," because I figured that if we signed up three other East Coasters and provided them with car service to their homes over the Christmas holiday and the summer break, we could make money on the trips and the car would pay for itself. I was orchestrating another win-win; I was always thinking. We purchased a 1949 boat-tailed Buick, with a fresh coat of paint that could best be described as coral. You might recognize it today as the Mary Kay Cosmetics car color. It was a shade that sparked comment, and perhaps that is why we were able to make the purchase for only $245. It was a great car, and we were able to sign up three passengers, as planned, for the highly anticipated trek east. These were the days before Interstates, and we were not sure precisely what routes to take; but we calculated that, stopping only for gas, the trip would take 36 hours. We were confident of success. As it turned out, the ride did not require directions or 36 hours, because we finished it by train.

We started out okay, with a full load that included a partially open trunk that had to be tied down, and we made it out of Colorado without difficulty. We were just beginning to bond as a unit, singing 99 bottles of beer on the wall and such, when a rod blew through the engine block, with resulting smoke that nearly asphyxiated us. We were just approaching Salina, Kansas when we were stranded by this mishap, before a kind stranger in a pickup dropped us and our belongings at a nearby train station. Frantic calls to a salvage yard yielded $50 for the abandoned coral Buick, and, after returning the $25-per-person fee to our passengers, Natale and I had enough left to get us to Chicago. The next call, to my Mom to explain our dilemma, resulted in the additional $80 being sent via Western Union to the Chicago Union Station. We missed nary a beat, and we were tracking it to Camden, able to return home just 10 hours after my original ETA. It was not exactly the win-win I had hoped for, but, all things considered, it was a win nonetheless.

The first Christmas break was the model for every Christmas hiatus thereafter, although, like most repetitive events, the first was perhaps the best. Janis and I were developing a deeper relationship, and I was finding a new father figure in her dad, Joe, as well as an adoptive parent of sorts in her mother, Mary. As a result of the relationship to the Zeccola family, I hit the ground running in the job department. Jan's Uncle Al was the manager of a busy liquor store on Broadway, whose owners were reputed to be connected to the underworld. But that was no cause for concern in those days, and Uncle Al hired me. Because I was not yet 21, he arranged for me to get a special license to handle, but not sell, the goods. I loved the job of filling the racks, keeping the place neat and listening to the constant banter, as Uncle Al handled the clientele. He was a master.

I was also entrusted with making surreptitious deliveries of great quantities of booze to Philadelphia. These deliveries were illegal because of the evasion of taxes, and that made the activity all the more exciting. In addition, I made major deliveries to Brownie's, the black brothel, three blocks away, exciting for different reasons. I had to traverse the entire house to stack the cases in the back kitchen. The trip from the front porch to the kitchen was a burlesque show, live porn act and sex education class all combined. Each delivery required multiple trips through the house, and I did not object when Uncle Al was looking for a volunteer to deliver to Brownie's House.

The first college break was important for other reasons. I received my first-quarter grades about a week after I came home. Confident that I had passed everything, I was still curious as to how the final exams I had taken had impacted my grades. I opened the envelope with some trepidation but I was delighted to find only one C, in ROTC, and B's in all of the academic subjects, and in P.E. I had achieved a 3.96 on a 5.00 scale—and, still, I had mixed emotions. My mom was thrilled and proud, and Uncle Mike, Joe Mazzarella, Joe Vitagliano, my dad and the Zeccolas shared Mom's emotions. Of course, Mom set the various means of communication into action, and, as I made the usual obligatory rounds of Christmas visits, I was lauded at each stop with appropriate "atta boys."

I saw that this scholarly achievement, however, was a two-edged sword. The good news was that I had proven I could succeed in college. The bad news was that I no longer had an excuse to fail. Those grades marked the end of automatic sympathy and meant that the days of "broken home" and street kid appellations were past. I was on my own, with no falling back on some built-in excuse for failure. The pressure was on, and I continued running scared.

Following the three-week break, I was ready to get back to academia. I really had fallen in love with learning. I loved the basic philosophy classes and psychology and astronomy, as well as geography and all manner of History courses. I loved the debates I started with Aunt Lydia on the nature of God, and I found that she too had a deep interest in learning. She even wanted copies of my humanities textbooks to study on her own. In physical education, I took fencing and tennis in order to expose myself to new things. In sum, college didn't just teach me—it opened up a whole new world of intellectual curiosity. Natale did not fare so well. He was a hard worker, but, except for math, none of it came as easily for him. He returned with me for the second quarter, only to fall short of meeting the requirements to keep up his probationary status. At the conclusion of the quarter, he returned to Camden to prepare for another try in the fall. I missed my buddy; we had been through combat together, and now my tie to Camden was gone.

I had to look for another place to live, since I couldn't afford to stay in the room alone. I needed another guardian angel, and I needed to supplement my income beyond the little convenience store job. So, I responded to a posting on a bulletin board: "Servants Wanted for Dinner at Tri Delta." I called the number and was told to report at 5:00 p.m. to prepare to serve the 6 o'clock meal. The pay was $5 for the night as well as a free dinner, but I would probably have paid them to be around all those pretty girls. And that was not the best part. My service partner was introduced to me as "Don Allen of Alpha Kappa Lambda." And he would turn out to be my angel. As we shared a cigarette break, I told him I was looking for a place to stay, and he quickly informed me that he and his Guamanian frat brother were looking for a roomie to split the cost of a basement apartment. I agreed on the spot. My curiosity prompted me to inquire, "What in the hell is a Guamanian?" He grinned, "A guy from Guam, of course." At that moment, the "cellar dwellers" were thus born, and, from that day to this, Don and I share a special bond that only certain fraternity brothers enjoy.

The Cellar Dwellers was what Don Allen cleverly dubbed those of us who shared the little basement apartment across 8th Avenue from the campus. The apartment, an exaggerated word for what was an efficiency dwelling, had a rear entrance at the bottom of four steps. Upon entry, you found yourself in an 11 by 15 room, with a ceiling that couldn't have been more than 7 feet high. The room contained a kitchenette and a living area, with a small bathroom and a shower at the kitchen end of the room. At the other end was a 9 by 9 room with a trundle bed and a hutch that had three drawers, one for each of us. Don and I slept in the trundle beds, and Gordon slept on the sofa in the living area. We were quite an eclectic lot—a street kid from the East Coast, a whitebread from the mountain states and a Navy brat of Asian ancestry, of late from Guam. I noticed at least one of our differences on the first day when I spied a 25-pound bag of rice under the sink in the kitchen. That was Gordon's staple, while mine was Campbell's beans, and Don's was PB&J sandwiches. Despite our differences, or maybe because of them, we bonded instantly. Fraternity life was to dominate my non-academic existence for the next two years.

Greek life at Colorado State College was a force on the campus, and I was flattered to have Don's fraternity, Alpha Kappa Lambda, "rush" me at his suggestion. Rushing me meant that they would invite me to gatherings and try to get me to make a decision to join them versus other potential fraternity houses. The truth was that no other fraternity had shown an interest in me, so it did not take too much urging to get me to "pledge." I went through a six-week pledge period and did all the silly things that pledges were forced to do during the initiation, as we went on scavenger hunts and made panty raids on sorority houses and generally acted like fools. I was voted the president of my pledge class, another resume builder, and we all made it through without a blackball. On the night of voting "yea" or "nay," one would cast a vote by placing a white or black ball into a covered box. When all of the members had cast a ballot, the box would be opened, and if any black ball appeared you were not invited to be a member. With all the white balls to prove it, I was now an AKL and proud of it.

The sad truth dawned as I discovered what Don already knew: Alpha Kappa Lambda was made up of a bunch of misfits that commanded little respect on campus and that were held together by small cliques that were satisfied to share a common location called the Fraternity House. We had a clique of nerds, a clique of Hawaiians, a clique of music majors, a small group of jocks and a clique of independent guys like Don, Gordon and me. It was a ragtag bunch that reminded me of the crew of the Caine in "The Caine Mutiny" before Captain Queeg took over. That was soon to change.

Don had been in AKL for over a year and was frustrated with the lack of leadership and direction. One of the most talented and creative minds I have ever encountered, Brother Don was then working on the school newspaper and was an editor on the annual comedy magazine. He had helped me become assimilated into the fraternity, and he now wanted me to help him to move it in a different direction. We both knew that the answer was to recruit more accomplished pledge classes, but neither of us knew how to go about this, except by personal effort. But I was committed to rapidly changing the reputation of the organization, and this was too slow for me. We needed a perception transplant, and fast. We were perceived as what we were, a motley crew of third-tier players. The TKE's Jocks and the Sigma Chi's campus leaders were all class, but AKL was classless and nondescript.

I got elected to the position of Social Director in the fall of my sophomore year, and my first big event was to throw a mountain party with a sorority of similar ilk. If leadership and athletics were the claims of other fraternities, then we would become the party frat. I figured that freshman would be searching for a fraternity that they could "contribute" to, and, if they weren't jocks or PBMOC's (potential big men on campus), they all would like to party.

The mountain party was a great success for two reasons— because everybody had a good time and spread the word and

IN SEARCH OF A NICHE

because it was against the college rules. This was no ordinary party, mind you, it was an overnight party, and overnight parties were verboten. The campus was abuzz when we retuned to classes on the Monday following the weekend party. Students looked at us with envy, and, yes, even respect. On Tuesday morning, I got a message from Dean Opelt, Dean of Student Affairs, requesting me to report to his office at 4 p.m. He asked me all the relevant questions, and I answered each in the affirmative: Had we stayed at the Estes Park camp overnight? Yes. Were there girls in attendance? Yes. Was there consumption of alcohol, besides 3.2 beer? Yes. Was I aware of the prohibition of overnights? Yes. Did I realize that he had no option except to put the fraternity on social probation for the remainder of the quarter and me personally on social probation for one additional quarter? Yes. The announcement came in the next week's school paper headlines: "Alpha Kappa Lambda: Social Probation." The subtitle of the piece read, "A raucous co-ed overnight leads to punishment."

Here I was, the new Social Director of the fraternity, and already we were on social probation and I was twice punished. I was elated! Mission accomplished, my work here was done. For the first time, we were the talk of the campus. Wherever we went, guys wanted to know the details of the party. The TKE's were on the defensive, telling people that they had overnights too but weren't dumb enough to admit to it. I was thinking, "We're dumb alright, were so dumb that we got the headlines and the buzz while they were relegated to one-on-one word of mouth. Our spring pledge class was sharper, cooler and the best we had ever had. Freshmen were coming to us to become AKL's. The following year, one in which I was elected President, we won the Greek Choral Group competition and, thanks to the genius of Cecil Moreno, one of the new cool guys, we took first place in the float contest in the

Thanksgiving Parade. As a result of these two huge campus Greek events, our reputation was transformed and now included being a winner. I was very lucky to be part of this turnaround team. I meant it when I had declared that "my work here is done." At the end of my junior year, I declared myself "inactive"; I would only be an emeritus member. I had other plans for my Senior year. I was on the run, a little scared, and failure wasn't going to catch me.

12

Aunt Lola

Aunt Lola and Uncle Mil with Tommy and Jimmy.

It was fitting that the photo was taken by a professional photographer; both Tom and Jim would later have pictures taken atop a pony in full cowboy regalia.

Aunt Lola

"There was no apology, none was needed; she was protecting her young and her family. We understood, because we were taught to do the same. Aunt Lola was beautiful."

AUNT LOLA WAS THE FIRST OF THE MONARCAS to be born beautiful, and she and her little sister Marie would vie for the Miss Monarca title for many years. Because she had not damaged her lovely complexion by smoking and was always careful about her figure, the consensus is that she was the ultimate winner of the title. The attractive face of this third female born to Teresa and Mario Monarca was only one aspect of her beauty; the outer beauty was even exceeded by the inner. By the time Lola was born in Jamesville, life had fallen into a hardened routine. Given the chores meted out by her two older sisters, she became the one to wait on her brothers at mealtime and tend to her father.

While her sisters had been part of the great adventure that brought the family to America, and her brothers had been able to carve out their own adventures in Jamesville, Lola's early life was unremarkable. By order of birth, she was a follower and more apt to accept her situation as her due, and she did what she was told, fitting into her surroundings without complaint. By all accounts, she was ever pleasant, a joy to be around who took on all the most laudable characteristics of her older siblings. In many ways, she was content to be a lesser version of her predecessors—she was nearly as deliberate as Anna, nearly as wise as Louise, nearly as steady as Phil and nearly as charming as Mike. As she matured, though, she rounded the harder edges of her older siblings—she was never as self-righteous as Anna or as caustic as Louise or as distant as Phil or as crude as Mike. She became an amalgamation of the best the Monarcas had to offer.

Lola continued to mimic her older siblings when the family moved to Camden. By then, she had assumed other duties, because there were now Giacomo, Dora, Milena and Marie to be tended to. She took all her responsibilities seriously and was an unheralded contributor to the maturation of her younger siblings. Of all of the Monarcas, hers was the quiet voice, soothing and with a unique timbre that gave a certain quality of earthiness to the sounds she emitted. She sounded, when she spoke, like a cross between Tallulah Bankhead and Lauren Bacall, the result of an operation that affected her vocal chords. There exists an audiotape of many of the Monarcas in a telephone conversation that was recorded by Uncle Mid, most likely in the 1980s, and on it one can identify the distinctive voices of the various family members; but none of the voices was more distinctive than Lola's. Listening to this recording, I was haunted by her responding to Uncle Mike, at some point in the raucous cross talk, "I love you Mikey." The sincerity of the single comment and the depth of the emotion that prompted it are unmistakable for anyone listening. And sincerity is a trait that epitomized Lola.

The time after the arrival at 734 found Mario working hard at the chemical plant during the week and gardening on the 10th Street "farm'" on weekends. Teresa, meanwhile, was tending to the brood, doing occasional midwife chores and entering contests offered by soap and soup companies as time permitted. She was also adding to the education of the offspring through lessons illustrated by the stories she told. The older siblings were beginning to date and pair off with potential life partners soon after the arrival at 734, fueled by their growing levels of testosterone and estrogen.

John Iannetta began to court Aunt Anna and soon became a familiar face at 734. While he was quite taken with Anna, he couldn't help but notice the lovely younger sister Lola, and he was convinced that she would be perfect for his younger brother, Emilio. In this, Uncle John was right. As for Lola, what better way to continue to emulate her older sister than to be associated with the same family in courtship?

Emilio Iannetta himself would be a contender for the title of the most handsome of the spouses that joined the Monarcas through marriage. He was slight of stature, but his features were more chiseled than those of rounder-faced brother John. Despite his diminutive size, he was possessed of a considerable amount of athletic prowess; and Uncle Mil, as he became known, combined these physical skills with a considerable intellectual capacity that he modestly hid in keeping with his reserved style. He applied both skills at Camden High School, where he excelled as the offensive end on the talented football squad and graduated with a coveted high school diploma. Uncle Mil went on to become an accomplished electrician at the New York Shipbuilding Corporation, where both he and his brother John labored for many years.

Lola and Mil took in the wedding of Anna and John and soon followed suit. The two quiet brothers began an uninterrupted love life with the two Monarca girls, one strong-willed and the other less so; but in one thing the sisters were completely equal, and that was in their unconditional love of their Iannetta men. Not only did Lola emulate her sibling Anna in her selection of a husband, but the closeness continued in Lola and Mil's selection of a family home at 935 Vine Street, just next door to her sister Louise at 933 and seven doors from the 921 residence of her brother Mike.

All the houses had identical physical dimensions, and Lola and Mil's was the mirror image of the other two that were described in the chapter on Aunt Louise. The contents of the basements did, however, differ somewhat. The barber shop replica at 933 and the tools and stored goods at 921 were quite unlike the multitude of electrical paraphernalia at 935. Uncle Mil loved to tinker with radios and old TV sets and became the one that others in the family called upon when their TVs were on the fritz. He had the tube tester and various tubes that he had taken from several old sets and provided his services without receiving pay or giving any complaint. This quiet largesse, a characteristic that was shared by Aunt Lola, was his trademark.

Every member of the family likely has a tale of the silent generosity of the family at 935. When Aunt Lydia was a teenager, she was wrongly diagnosed by Dr. Principato with a pregnancy, after mother Teresa had taken her to the family physician for some complaint or other, only to be shocked by his pronouncement. Having been unsuccessful in her attempts to get Lydia to confess to her indiscretion, Teresa turned the interrogation over to the older sisters, and their various approaches to the task and the style of the sisters' inquiries says much about them. Aunt Louise was relentless in her badgering and coaxing, alternately using gentle persuasion and caustic threats, but to no avail. Aunt Anna tried to shame Lydia into admission, naming particular boys that Lydia might identify as the culprit.

When these methods failed, Anna lost her patience and slapped Lydia across the face, demanding immediate capitulation, but still no confession was forthcoming. Lola, by contrast, having quietly listened to Lydia's protestations and unequivocal denials, offered a rational and generous solution. She told Lydia that she would pay to obtain a second opinion, and the entire incident could be laid to rest. Without fanfare, with no further announcements, Lola made good on her word, and the solution proved the veracity of Lydia's story. No more was ever made of the incident that came to be regarded as the signature event of Aunt Lola's style.

My sister Elaine, who had grave problems in her first marriage, has her own memories of this noteworthy style. When her husband Pooky went to prison for armed robbery, Elaine was left to raise the couple's three sons with the help of welfare and some occasional support from friends and relatives. It was Aunt Lola and Uncle Mil who would arrive at her door on High Street with packages of food on various holidays, and these and other acts of kindness were performed with characteristic silence, never mentioned even among the family's inner circle.

This Iannetta couple was blessed with two sons, Thomas and James, who were gifts given to the two only a couple of years apart. I can remember Johnny and I going to 935 to play with the boys on frequent occasions. I am sure that we enjoyed going there for more than the love of our little cousins, and I say this because both John and I liked to teach the boys to play a war in which they would be designated as the "Japs" or the "Krauts," while we were the Yanks. At this house, we were the older cousins that were looked up to, but Aunt Lola, although patient, was still protective of her home and her boys. She would invite us in with the as-yet unwarranted admonishment, "You can come in, but no roughhousing and no teasing." We hadn't even come through the front door, but, she was full of wisdom and no stranger to our antics.

Uncle Mil rarely raised his voice above a conversational tone, and the most that could be heard from him was an occasional, "Okay, cut that out." He would always ask us to give him an update on how things were going at school or pepper us with questions about local sports. He was an expert on all things sport and was the only member of the family that tried to keep Cousin Joey grounded when his head was being swollen by adulation.

When everyone else was thinking that Joe's performance on a given night was flawless, it would be Uncle Mil who said, "You know your defense was lacking tonight, and you fouled too much; you need to pay attention at both ends of the court." Uncle Mil was knowledgeable about other things as well, and I was on his sofa on May 5, 1954, when the announcement was broadcast concerning the Supreme Court decision in *Brown v. Board of Education*, that ended legal segregation of the races. It was Uncle Mil that opined to me that our country would never be the same and that it was a good decision. I was 13, and he spoke to me like an adult.

Their offspring, like those of all the Monarcas, became the center of their lives. In the case of Aunt Lola and Uncle Mil, Tommy and Jimmy gave them much for which they could be grateful. Both boys were appealing, but in dissimilar ways; with the best of both parents' looks, Tommy is the hands-down choice for the most handsome of his generation, while Jimmy, with a great resemblance to Uncle Mike, is the most rambunctious and carefree. With all their differences, they both made successful careers—Tom as a sales executive with Sunoco and Jim as a chiropractor who practices in Maine—after attending Western Kentucky University, where, on more than one occasion, Tom had to bail Jim out of a scrape. Both now have great families of their own, and Jim is as doting a father as Uncle Mil ever was.

Tom carries on the tradition of his mother's gentle and unpretentious generosity; he lives in Pittsburgh and is hundreds of miles away from the family roots, but he never fails to visit all of the aunts on his semi-annual visits to the area. Sadly, there are only two aunts left to visit, Lydia and Dora, my mother, who 13 years ago suffered a massive stroke that left her unable to walk or talk or even demonstrate much rational thought, although she always seems to recognize all of her family. Tom always goes to see her, alone and unannounced, the only evidence of his visits his signature in the sign-in book and the chocolates he kindly leaves behind. He is his mother's son.

John and I did once have occasion to witness a side of Aunt Lola that few have seen. Tom was being married in 1972 in a suburb of St. Louis, and both John and I had been invited to be part of the bridal party. We, of course, agreed and dutifully set about getting our plane tickets and tuxedoes. The plan to meet at the Philadelphia airport and fly together to St. Louis went off without a hitch, and you could sense the excitement of the entire group. When we arrived in St. Louis, there was an hellacious snow storm that had not delayed our arrival but had sidetracked the ride we were supposed to have been provided by the bride's family—no one was there to pick us up. There were no cell phones to help, so various messages were left at the bride's home, until, finally, contact was made. But we would have to wait for three hours.

In an effort to stay out of the way of all of the frantic activity around us, John and I proceeded to sit in a small café and have a beer and a sandwich. When the ride finally showed up, we got in to see a visibly angry and cold Aunt Lola. We had a two-hour ride to the bride's home and tried to make conversation, but we got no response. John and I shared quizzical looks, each thinking to himself, "What the hell happened to her?" We asked to stop at a gas station to use the facilities. when we were given a hint by her reply. "If you two had not started drinking, you wouldn't have to stop," came the icy statement from the gentle Aunt Lola, who spit out her next words with slow elongated precision: "Thanks a lot!"

It was only after the wedding, as we were leaving the reception of cake and punch, that she was returning to her warm self. By this time, of course, John and I were the ones feeling a bit miffed; we were grown men who had taken the time and resources to make the trip halfway across the country, only to be treated like visitors to 735 getting the "no roughhousing" lecture. Mutual rapprochement was achieved after we asked her what we had done to initially upset her, and she replied by saying, "I thought you guys had started drinking and would act up and embarrass the family." She continued, "I just wanted those people to know what a great family they were getting with my Tommy, and I thought you might spoil that." She told us that she was proud of how we conducted ourselves at the reception and how everyone loved us. There was no apology, none was needed; she was protecting her young and her family. We understood, because we were taught to do the same. Aunt Lola was beautiful.

13

In Search of Comfort

Uncle Mike DiSibio with Aunt Lena in front of 233 Berkley Street, the DiSibio headquarters.

The two boys joined them later, and together they were my surrogate family.

In Search of Comfort

"I went to 530 to get some driving lessons, to get some help in trying to land summer work at Campbell Soup and to watch The Three Stooges with my little cousins, who made me feel important."

T HE MONARCAS ARE THE THREAD THAT HELD THE CLOTH of my maturation, indeed my life, together. Without them I would have had unmended gaps, rips and tears that could have left me unfinished as a man. Uncle Mike DiSibio's family represents a large piece of the fabric that the Monarca family thread held in place.

Mike DiSibio was the second son born to Raffaello and Domenica DiSibio at 233 Berkley Street in South Camden. Like his brother and sisters born before him and those born after him, he was abused by the tyrannical Raffaello. He took his share of beatings, witnessed his mother being humiliated and slapped about and obediently turned over his earnings to his thug of a father. World War II was his ticket out.

Mike was a good looking young man with charm and affability. He isn't as handsome as Tony, although he would dispute that, nor as gentle as Joseph, since a tender touch might have impeded the tough reputation he was seeking to cultivate. In place of Tony's wide smile, Mike bore an impish grin. He hung out on the corner at Frieda's candy store and engaged in all of the iniquitous pastimes of young men during the Great Depression. In the tradition of the family, he also worked hard, and he rarely complained about the difficulties of life. He shared a bed first with his big brother, Tony, whom he looked up to, and later with his little brother, Joe, one of many things about the DiSibio house at 233 that could have provided grounds to complain if one were inclined to do so. There was the old man, of course, the nearly constant bickering of Mike's whining sisters and the chiding of his older brother, to say nothing of the nagging of the younger brother.

When the Second World War erupted, Tony was married, had had daughter Elaine and was soon to be the father of son Ralph, all of which precluded his drafting. Uncle Mike, on the other hand, would have been a prime target for the Selective Service, but there was no need for the Draft Board to seek Mike out; he was more than willing to do battle. He didn't want to lend his expertise to some marginal outfits, like the Army or the Navy, but rather wanted to be a Marine, the toughest of the tough.

When he returned after a Parris Island boot camp, Mike cut quite a figure in his dress blues, a wiry and muscled Marine on leave to visit his mom and see his girl. The picture of Uncle Mike standing in front of 233 in his uniform, with his arm around the demure and beautiful Lena Perno, is something I value greatly. Assuming his prototypical stance with one hip below the other and looking nonchalant, it is clear that he was nonetheless ready to go to war.

Mike served in the Pacific Theater and saw combat in the Marine landings and occupation of a string of islands in the middle of nowhere, Iwo Jima and Okinawa, that were among the experiences he keeps hidden in his memory. Recently (in 2006), he shared some of those details with his sons when he turned over to them a Japanese war relic that he had kept all these years. He had taken the rifle from a dead enemy soldier and never relinquished it until more than 50 years later.

Mike returned from war to find that the War Bonds he had sent home to his mother, for safekeeping or emergency use, had been squandered by his sisters. They had conned Domenica out of the bonds for frivolous things, and Mike was furious at this turn of events, the first of many incidents that would eventually lead to his estrangement from several of his siblings. It was at this time that he took a bayonet to his father's throat, after witnessing the old man striking Mike's mother in the face with a high-topped shoe. He grabbed his cowardly father and put him against a wall with a force that lifted the bully off the floor. Mike put the knife to his throat and cried out, "Old man, if you ever lay a hand on her again, I'll kill you, so help me God!" Domenica would now be safe, but this confrontation did not stop the old man from continuing to abuse the other siblings.

Mike eventually married Lena Perno, his pre-war sweetheart, a resident of the 300 block of Berkley Street, where her brother, Joe, still resides over the protest of his nephews. For the rest of her life, Lena was the quintessential Italian wife, filling her husband's every imaginable need. She waited on him, did all the domestic chores, bore and raised two great boys and was in all ways a perfect mate. When modernity led to the growing independence of other wives, she simply said, "He wears the pants in this family." Maybe that's why her pet name for him was "Drawers." When "All in The Family" was a hit TV show, everyone who knew Mike and Lena thought the script could have been about them. Both sons, Michael and Joseph, began to refer to their parents as Archie and Edith.

After living with us at 523 for a short time, Uncle Mike purchased a little house, smaller even than ours, across the street at 530 N. 8th Street. After climbing three steps to the entrance, you found yourself on a porch that could not have been bigger than 4 by 9 feet. When the front door was opened, it struck the arm of the sofa that kept it from swinging against the wall. Once you made your way into the living room, where the sofa took up the entire north wall, you also found an overstuffed chair that sat catty-corner, with one side against the south wall and the other against the small front window that looked onto the porch. Looking straight ahead, you could see the TV set that filled a wall made short to accommodate the staircase that led upstairs. The entire room was about 9 by 9. Sliding between the sofa and the TV, you could either head upstairs or go into the dining area that provided a place to sit for meals and space for the Kelvinator refrigerator. The door at the far end of the eating area led to a tiny kitchen, maybe 7 by 6 if that, that housed the sink, stove and refrigerator; and a door on the northeast corner of the room led to a small yard.

A mirror image of the first floor, the upstairs had a master bedroom of sorts over the living room; the room over the eating area was the kids' room; and the room over the kitchen was the bath. You are picturing this all correctly if you figured out that Uncle Mike or Aunt Lena, or anyone else for that matter, would have to walk through the kids' room to get to the bathroom. This 530 was no estate.

Though no mansion, 530 was my other home through all of the years I spent growing up. It was the first place I would go if I was hungry or when 523 was a little short of food, and it was the place I would make my first stop when I arrived home from college after a 36-hour drive from Greeley looking for breakfast. I went there to get some driving lessons, to get some help in trying to land summer work at Campbell Soup and to watch "The Three Stooges" with my little cousins, who made me feel important. It was also the destination of choice for sharing my manly stories about girls and sports with an attentive Uncle Mike or Aunt Lena. At 530, like nowhere else, I felt like I was with family. I respected the house on Elm, the houses on Vine and Grant and Willard were all important, but I loved the house at 530 as none of the others. I didn't have to knock on the door, and I didn't have to wait to be invited to lunch or dinner. No one scolded me there or looked down on me or gave me unsolicited symphony. I felt like another son, because that's the way I was treated.

As a surrogate father, Uncle Mike did not always set the best examples, but you were never unsure of how he felt. He loved cars, and, while remaining in his very modest residence, got a new Buick every couple of years; the '53 blue Roadmaster was the car that Elaine and I learned how to drive. He was not gentle in his tutelage, but he was faithful to his efforts to teach us. Even with the windows up, someone a block away in the neighborhood might hear him bellow, "Yo! Yo! The brake, *the brake*," as we headed into a right turn at 25 miles per hour, giving no indication of being aware that braking technology had been invented.

There was a pattern to my returns to Camden from college. I would be dropped off with my duffel bag in front of 523 at the break of dawn, and I would cross the street to where Uncle Mike was getting ready for work and walk through the front door. He would look up with a smile and an inquiry, "When did you get in?" "Just now," I would say, "I haven't been home yet." His next words would be to Aunt Lena, who was in the kitchen making coffee in an all-glass percolator. "Make your nephew some breakfast, he must be hungry." Without blinking an eye, Aunt Lena would start the eggs and bacon while we watched the show put on by the brewing coffee. When breakfast had been made, I would regale my aunt and uncle with tales of my college exploits, while eating the hot and delicious food. That was the level of comfort afforded me at 530.

Uncle Mike and Aunt Lena had two wonderful boys, Michael and Joseph, born a couple of years apart. I was Joseph's senior by ten years, and, although we grew up living only 50 feet from one other, the age difference was like miles of separation. I remember these cousins as little guys who had to be dragged, as if kicking and screaming, to the DiSibio house on Berkley on major holidays.

Uncle Mike was often in some major dispute with one or another of his sisters, and the holiday get-together could be cold as ice. But Uncle Mike was drawn by tradition to pay these visits, and, on these occasions, he would put his family in the Buick, fill the trunk with the accordion, the music stand and music that had come with Michael's lessons and head off to 233. He would begin the obligatory call on the relatives by marching into the house, without much more than a terse "Merry Christmas," sitting Michael in a dining room chair and putting up the stand and the music. He would command Michael to, "Play that new song you learned." Michael would comply with the command, and, at the conclusion of the performance, Uncle Mike would pack up everything, including his family, and say his brusque goodbyes with the Buick's engine still warm. You never wondered what Uncle Mike was thinking. He could be a best friend, but he could be your worst enemy with equal facility.

As I grew into adulthood, his boys and I grew closer and closer. By 1969, Uncle Mike had realized his dream of building his new brick house in Cherry Hill, into which he moved the family. As time went on, Michael and Joseph evolved from great kids into great men, who have experienced great successes as husbands and parents. Michael is a military veteran, an accomplished master plumber and all-around expert with all manner of tools, whose current job at a county hospital caps an enviable career of uninterrupted labor. Joseph followed my own early path and has become a leader in the education world, a revered teacher and coach for more than three decades at the Gloucester City Public Schools. Both Michael and Joseph are prized by many as husbands, fathers, friends and, certainly by me, as my cousins and "brothers."

Unfortunately, Uncle Mike's temper and long memory for slights, real and imagined, cost him many years of contentment and joy. For nearly 10 years, he refused to speak to my father, his beloved brother, because of some perceived affront. This same treatment was afforded every one of his siblings at various times over his lifetime. His need to avenge some insult even caused him to absent himself from his sister Lucy's funeral, a defection almost unheard of in Italian families, regardless of the wrong committed by the deceased. After Dad and Uncle Mike had spent almost a decade apart, I succeeded in bringing them back together, and we had many a fine hour of family pool matches and holiday events as a result of their reconciliation.

Uncle Mike coveted his reputation as a hard man, and I believe he artificially enhanced it. In an example of this, one that demonstrated that he had gone to the Tony DiSibio school of dentistry, he sat across from me at his kitchen table, complaining of a tooth ache. With no fanfare, he got up, went to a drawer, lifted a pair of pliers and removed the offending tooth, spitting the resulting blood into the sink with a satisfied, "There, that's better." We continued our conversation as if nothing had happened. He was a tough man, and the culmination of his toughness came when he banished his sons from his presence, causing a rift in the relationship that was to continue for many years. The estrangement can perhaps be explained, if not justified, by the fact that it followed the death of his loving Lena after her heart-wrenching loss to a bout with brain cancer.

At this writing, father and sons are back together, but the years of joy that might have flowed from watching his grandchildren grow and mature were relinquished by him as a result of his own stubbornness. In many ways, he became a caricature of himself. And yet, none of this behavior, however outrageous, detracts from the value he added to the life of the nephew who lived across the street from 530.

14
Uncle Jim

Uncle Jim and Grandpop Monarca, taken from across Birch Street, with Joe's Meal Market as a backdrop.

Uncle Jim

'The references to Jim were always expressed with reverence and pride. He was tall, dark and handsome, with a look unlike the thick-bodied masculine type that his brothers personified."

UNCLE JIM WAS A SAINT, OR SO I'M INCLINED TO THINK, because no one can recall him ever doing anything untoward or unkind. Giacomo, known to us as Jim, was born the third and last son of Teresa and Mario Monarca in Jamesville. He had the best of all worlds. As the youngest, he was spared the heavy chores of his elder siblings, and, as a boy, he was waited on by his sisters. His brothers treated him like a mascot when he tagged along to their games.

Of all of the Monarcas, it is Uncle Jim of whom I have the most opaque memories. In fact, my earliest recollection is of Aunt Pat awakening us at 523 with the news of his death that followed his courageous battle with heart disease. I was groggy and thought the screams I heard were in a dream. When I ran towards my mother's room, she was hanging out the second-story window, and I made out Aunt Pat's tortured howls, "Jim is dead, Jim is dead." This tragic and shocking news was announced within weeks of the burial of the patriarch Mario; barely had the family dried the tears of grief from their faces when a new flood began.

All of my life, I have heard of the man who only lived for 32 years. Though his life was short, the references to Jim were always expressed with reverence and pride. He was tall, dark and handsome, with a look unlike the thick-bodied masculine type that his brothers personified. Rather, he seemed to have taken on the best of the physical assets of both males and females in the family. While Phil and Mike had dark straight hair, Jim's was black, wavy and full of ringlets. While his brothers were oval of face, his countenance was longer, and he was finer of feature. His nose had a distinct Roman look, while his brothers had pug-like nostrils. He was a full two inches taller then either of his male siblings, but at only about 5 foot 6 or 7, he was by no means tall by today's standards. Nevertheless, it is with a deep sense of respect, nearing worship, that he is unfailingly referred to as "quite tall and devastatingly handsome."

Uncle Jim also seems to have been the most intelligent of the three boys. Unlike Phil and Mike, he cultivated learning, and Lydia vividly recalls the "brain teasers" he would present to her; he would rarely be in her company without challenging her to spell a difficult word or requesting the definition of another. He also had a sunny disposition that is always included in descriptions of him, and it is likely that he had the most sophisticated and finely tuned sense of humor of the clan as well. There is little doubt that he was the most vain of the boys, and certainly topped his sister Dora in that regard, and many of the girls remember waiting to enter the single bathroom at 734, while Jim took an inordinate amount of time to ensure that every curl was in place and every orifice was cleansed. He was dapper in his clothing and unquestionably set the family standard for male attire. He was known well only by Cousin Joe, who, although often critical of everyone around him, never uttered a negative word about the saint-like Jim.

The beneficiary of all of Jim's fine qualities was the fair Josephine of Bridgeton. Uncle Jim often paid visits to his cousins of the Morroni family, who had settled in that farming community, and it was in Bridgeton that he met the woman who would become his wife, the future Aunt Josephine. She was a tiny beauty of Italian descent with a wonderful disposition; I have never met a gentler and more constantly pleasant soul. Uncle Jim and Aunt Josephine could have served as the models for the bride and groom that adorn the top tier of wedding cakes. After their own wedding, they moved into a pleasant single-family home which was as charming as they were. He was a valued employee in the offices of the Birdseye Company that dominated the community, and the home he shared with his bride was practically within walking distance of the plant.

I do not remember visiting the little white house while Uncle Jim was alive, but we often visited Aunt Josephine and the fruit of her union with Jim, Teresa, after his demise. Terry, as we called her, was the perfect product of the perfect pair. She was tiny, bright and effervescent and was blessed with her father's bright outlook and demeanor. And did I mention that she was beautiful? And so it was that little Aunt Josephine lived in the little house with her little daughter and her little mother. I clearly remember my aunt's Italian-speaking mother, even tinier than Josephine herself and possessed of the most unusual voice. It had such a high pitch that I fancied that it could be heard by all of the dogs in the neighborhood. To this day, I smile when I recall, in my mind's eye, this cute little lady rattling off a long string of Italian words in that odd pitch of hers.

Aunt Josephine was widowed by the time she was 30, but she was able before her death to start the process of raising her daughter to be a lovely woman, who is cherished by friends and family. She also cared for her aging mother into senility. Undaunted by the sacrifice of having to make the 80-mile round trip, Aunt Josephine rarely missed a Monarca wedding, a funeral or a special event for decades after she buried Uncle Jim; she would have made him proud. Having never married again, Aunt Josephine denied some lucky man the pleasure of her loving nature.

I am positive that Saint Jim is observing the events of the half century since his death and nodding approvingly at the progress the family has made. He made a contribution while he was with us and must be pleased with how his bride and daughter turned out. He is likely surrounded by the Monarcas who have followed him since he was taken from us. The mystery of what Jim would have become allows us to continue to cling to his memory with our own imaginations.

15

In Search of a Mate

The Zeccola family taken in Cherry Hill on Fulton Avenue. The entire clan was present and included Vito's offspring, Danny, Joey and MaryKay as well as Aunt Codi and Aunt Josie and Uncle Bill. Dean has his arm around Pop-Pop and Doreen is hugging MaryKay.

In Search of a Mate

"I was convinced, of course, that Janis was rich; how else could they afford to have ginger ale delivered by the case every two weeks?"

I NEVER REALLY RETURNED HOME TO 523 once I departed the North Philadelphia station in September of 1959, using 523 only as a place to occasionally sleep and to store my stuff. Elaine was gone and was a full-time mother to my nephew Billy. Mom had developed a relationship with a neighborhood bachelor, John Keller, who lived with his mother just five doors north of 523 on 8th Street; he was a handsome man of German extraction and treated Mom well. She still took great pride in my success at college but knew that we had both carved out new lives for ourselves. Mom worked at Magnetic Metals on the factory floor and spent her spare hours with Johnny, while I was working every spare hour, when I wasn't at my girl's house or across the street at Uncle Mike's.

Dad had settled just three blocks away on Cedar Street and, together with Eleanor, had a son, little Tony. Anthony James DiSibio was born to the couple late in life, and neither of them was any more suited to parenthood than they had been when they had their first children. She was an alcoholic, and Dad was more than occasionally abusive to his newest son. Despite all of this, Dad and I had developed a positive relationship that was continuing to grow.

On my first summer home, between my freshman and sophomore years, I walked to his Cedar Street home to pay a visit, only to find him washing an unfamiliar automobile. It was a

1948 Mercury 4-door sedan. He smiled as I approached and asked, "What do you think?" gesturing toward the brown hulk. "Neat," I replied, "when did you get this?" His smiled broadened, and he announced with some pride, "It's yours; I picked it up for a hundred bucks and thought you could use it to get around." I was thrilled on a number of levels. For the first time, my father had given me a gift from his heart, without an agenda or an obligatory holiday. After spending a little time, I left in my Mercury. That car lasted most of the summer, as Cousin Johnny and I drove it all over town, looking for work, before it too blew a rod and was salvaged by Pooky.

Many of the miles put on the Mercury before its demise were on the drive to 3425 Westfield Avenue in East Camden, the business and home of the Joseph and Mary Zeccolas. Mary and Joseph were mother and father to a son, Vito, the same age as my sister, and a daughter, Janis, 10 months my junior. Since the day she introduced herself to me in the halls of WWHS, our affection for each other had grown, taking us into dating, then going steady, and, later, it would take us into engagement and marriage, although our marriage was still a couple of years away.

Westfield Avenue was primarily a commercial street, stretching from the confluence of South and North Camden to Route 130, which formed the border with Pennsauken. The property at 3425 was one of only two structures on the entire block between 33rd and 34th Streets on the north side. The south side of the street was the home of many little stores, including a hardware store, a tavern, and an ice cream parlor. The north side had a bakery on the 33rd Street corner and a Gulf gas station on the 34th Street corner. In between the two, right at 3425, was Joe's Barber Shop. The only other structures on the block were two huge billboards, which hid an empty lot between the bakery and Joe's Shop. The building seemed out of place in the neighborhood, with brick that appeared more modern than its surroundings and a rich-looking wrought iron gate, that provided an entry to the side residence. It was a building that Joe had designed and constructed, and it stood in the midst of structures that were older by decades. Entrance to the shop was on the right side of the 12-foot wide, stand-alone structure, with its front highlighted by a large picture window and the red, white and blue barber pole, constantly in motion, positioned like a sentinel next to the large evergreen.

Upon entering, you faced a traditional barber shop setup. The four chrome chairs, decked out in their green plastic seats, sat on the right, just beyond the door, barely allowing for the door to swing away to the wall, and beyond the chairs was the entry to the living quarters. To one's left was the first of two old style barber chairs, and only four feet to the right was the second chair, identical to the first. The entire wall opposite the green chairs was dominated by large mirrors, starting about waist-high and extending nearly to the ceiling. There were three four-drawer chests, which added symmetry to the wall by keeping the first chair centered between the first and second chest and the other chair centered between the second and third chest. The first chest held the National cash register that was manually operated by selecting the proper number of keys that, in sum, totaled the amount of the sale. The tops of the other chests held various items of the trade, such as clippers, combs, brushes and hand-held mirrors.

You could reach the residence either by going through the iron gate on the side of the house or by climbing the two stairs inside the shop that led to a door. No matter which way you entered, you would find yourself standing in the living room, a small space, but adequate nonetheless for a love seat, three side chairs, one console TV and a marble-topped table. The furniture was well-made and expensive, purchased at Menchell and McDonald, and it complemented the lush, dark green, wall-to-wall carpeting. The back wall of the room was fully taken up by a wood-stained staircase, and the area beyond the living area was occupied by the efficiently laid out kitchen. Across one wall was all the kitchen counters and appliances, and the rest of the room was filled by a large kitchen set with six chrome chairs. The back wall had an exit door which led to a very large rear yard.

The upper level had three bedrooms and a small bath. At the top of the stairs on the left were the bath and a tiny bedroom that could accommodate only a small single bed and a three-drawer chest. To the right of the landing was a hall leading to a small bedroom on the right and a generous master bedroom at the end of the hall.

Back downstairs, the basement was entered through a door that you came to just before you entered the kitchen. At the bottom of the steps was a laundry room to the right and a sitting room to the left. In the sitting room were an old sofa and two other doors, the first of which led to a step down that took you into a low-ceilinged room used for tools and other storage. The "room" behind the other door was unique, revealing, when opened, a space no wider than the door, with two steps up to the item that was the main purpose of the room: a toilet. That's right, a toilet, a white toilet to be precise, poised at the top of two steps, resembling a throne. The space was so tiny that you had to literally keep the door open to turn around, and only then could you close the door and be seated on the "throne." You would be right to chuckle at the unusual picture this presents, but the odd height I've described was as a consequence of having to get plumbing above the sewer line that ran about a foot above the concrete floor. This "second facility" was quite a convenience, as well as a conversation piece. Such was the ingenuity of Joe the Barber.

Joe had been a barber since his youth. While the other guys, including his brother, Carman "Bon Bon" Zeccola, were gambling and drinking and the like, Joe was building a trade and a career. He married the fair Mary Del Fico for many reasons, not the least of which was her resemblance to Mary Pickford. Once Vito and Janis started school, their mother augmented the family income by working in the sweatshops in Philadelphia. In the beginning, Joe further supplemented the cash flow by taking bets and numbers— what was sometimes called "bookmaking"—with the support of Bon Bon. By the time I had entered the scene, the bookmaking activities were history, and life for the Zeccolas was good, certainly by my standards.

I was a soon-to-be high school graduate with an acceptance to Colorado State College in hand. I was Italian. My people were from South and North Camden. And I was not unattractive. In sum, I was a potential catch. Westfield Avenue was home to a bus stop on nearly every corner, and when I did not have my own car, I would use the bus to go to see my girl, Janis, at her house. On more than one occasion, Mr. Zeccola would drive me home on a Sunday afternoon and ask about my family history and my ambitions along the way.

He could tell by my house that we were not people of means, but he seemed to like me well enough, and Mrs. Zeccola was even warmer in her interactions with me. I didn't see much of Vito at that time, because he was away at Furman University, but I knew of him by virtue of his reputation as a tough guy who was hanging out while I was doing the same. He had stature as a tough kid who, despite his diminutive size, backed down from no one before he turned his aggression into a football career of note in high school and college. Janis could often be heard telling some wise guy that,

"You keep that up, and my brother will beat the crap out of you." So, Vito's standing was further enhanced by Janis' threats.

As Janis and I became more of "an item," her family began to treat me as part of it. I would invariably have a traditional Sunday dinner there, spending my spare time on the living room floor, lying on the soft carpet and watching TV with Jan. I was convinced, of course, that she was rich; how else could they afford to have ginger ale delivered by the case every two weeks? And if that was not enough, there was more support for my conclusion all around me—the wall-to-wall carpets, two toilets, rear and side yards and a washer and dryer. The evidence was crystal clear.

In addition to the time spent at the Zeccolas, we were soon visiting Jan's Aunt Codi and Uncle Al and Aunt Josie and Uncle Bill as well, the sisters and brothers-in-law of Mrs. Zeccola. Uncle Al promised me work over my Christmas break, and I was developing relationships with other members of the family, like Jan's grandmother, who welcomed me with a fresh cup of coffee. I was becoming part of a wonderful and seemingly normal family. I was a happy young man. The feeling of normalcy just kept going, and my happiness grew. While I was planning to start college, Janis was planning to follow in her Aunt Codi's footsteps and become a cosmetologist. She had already gone to modeling school and now needed only to complete high school and special training and she would become a licensed hairdresser. We began to talk of a future together.

The home at 3425 was to become more than my home away from home. On at least two separate occasions, Janis and I took up residence, first as a married couple and then as a family of three. This attractive unattached home, with the throne-like toilet room and a barber shop front, had all of the warmth and comfort of the stable family I had only experienced on rare occasions outside of my own imaginings. At 3425, I was respected and admired for my work ethic, my manners and my dreams. The people at 3425 had expectations of me, but, most importantly perhaps, never had sympathy for me or any cause to feel sympathy. On occasion, they would even ask me my opinion. I felt comfortable in their home, where I was always welcome without an agenda. The Zeccolas, like the Monarcas, the Molotskys, the DiSibios and the Mazzarellas, contributed to my maturation and development. I felt at home in many houses during the years that I was growing into a man, but the only two places I ever called home were 523 N. 8th Street and 3425 Westfield Avenue.

Aunt Pat

Aunt Pat is resplendent in her beautiful wedding gown. Grandpop Mario never looked so handsome as he escorted her down the steps of 734 Vine Street.

Aunt Pat

"Aunt Pat could be outrageous; she could be charming; she could be warm; and she could be a lioness when protecting her family."

AUNT PAT WAS BORN MILENA, the last of the children born to Teresa and Mario Monarca in Jamesville. She would turn out to be the most fashionable of all of the girls and, always ahead of her time, would remain so for the rest of her life. For a while the youngest, she had duties that others didn't want to do handed down to her, just like the younger ones before her. The practice of passing along unwanted assignments was not new, but, unlike all the rest, she did not accept them as obediently or without question. She was not Lola, who bordered on naïve, nor was she as demanding as Anna or as direct as Louise; she was not just the combined characteristics of her sisters.

Her pre-teen years were not particularly remarkable, except that she went further in school then her predecessors, although this distinction would prove to be short-lived when Lydia eclipsed them all. But no one would eclipse Pat in the style department. She was the first to attend dances without escort, the first to go horseback riding and the first to take up sports. My memories are reflected in the eulogy I delivered at her funeral, and I include it here.

On the occasion of the funeral of Aunt Pat - May 7, 1997

Every family should be blessed with a Milena, a Mildred, a Pat. Beloved wife, mother, sister, aunt, cousin, friend—loyalty was among her most endearing attributes. I could remind us of a whole series of those kinds of qualities that we all have observed over these many years. But when I was told of her passing, I was struck by many emotions and thoughts. I want to share them with you. I want to share my impressions of a woman I knew the whole of my life.

Those thoughts came triggered by words, words that helped to describe her. Flamboyant. Elegant. Obstinate. Resolute. Generous. Kind. And unconditionally loyal!

She could be charmingly flamboyant. When the rest were driving Fords, she was sporting a Packard convertible. When everyone was buying American, she was setting trends by owning not one, but two, Simkas.

When the average were wearing headscarves, she toted a pillbox with a veil. And when others were hatless, only she could don a beret! A legitimate trendsetter.

Elegant. I hope you have had the opportunity to see a series of pictures taken on her wedding day. They personify elegance. As she descended the steps at 734 Vine Street, with that gentle man Mario Monarca, they made the house look like St. Patrick's Cathedral.

Perhaps the most perfect picture which epitomized her elegance, her dreams and her self esteem is my favorite. Picture this humble girl, perhaps in her late teens, fresh from the asphalt and row houses of North Camden, here she is in a complete riding outfit: high leather riding boots, riding britches and riding crop. Looking very rich and self-possessed, standing next to, and holding the reins of, a large stallion. To all the world, she looked like she was manor born and bred. Liz Taylor and Black Beauty would be green with jealously!

Obstinate. From the beginning she showed that she was different from the previous Monarca clan. She stayed out later. She challenged her big brothers and tested the limits. She was the leader of the younger sisters who were awed by her pluck and watched as she walked the high wire without a net. But always, she had her own moral compass and her obstinance was a tool that helped her make tough decisions like marrying the first non-Italian, not an easy thing in those days, and yet it may be the most important contribution she ever made to the family. How he grieves for her today.

Resolute. What strength of conviction she always displayed. Whether striking out from Willard Street to Erie Street or packing up and trekking all the way to Marlton with her buddy Dolly. The family felt like we had to pack a lunch in order to visit. The boys had done it, but not the girls.

Who can know the pain and terror of having your very lifeblood stricken with the dreaded polio. She stuck out her chin and resolved that this too would be beaten, and, with the strength of her husband and the courage of her stricken son, her resolve was rewarded.

Kindness, generosity. These are well documented traits. There are few among those present who have not been the recipient of her largesse. You recall the Packard I spoke of earlier? She gave it to me when I found myself in the market for a car and in need of the funds to purchase it. She said, "It does not run well, but you can use it to trade for a better car." By the way, she did this when I was living with her and Uncle Bob because I was home for the summer and in need of room and board. No big thing to them. It was so typical; you need a car, a place to stay, a ride home, extra cash, need to drop the kids off for a couple of weeks while you and your wife go to Italy, need a house sitter? She was always there.

If you were ill or near death and you needed to have an in-house nurse, waitress and cleaning woman, call Pat. Her motto was "Have overnight bag, will travel" It got so normal that Joe Tag begged her (in jest) not to visit because it would spell the beginning of the end. Yes, her kindness has been shared by many. And, most importantly, never once did she ever speak of it or refer to it again, never once. She was a real Good Samaritan.

How can we put her to rest without reference to her fierce loyalty to family and passionate love of her husband and lioness protectiveness of her son and his family. Her own ambitions seemed to give way to supporting and urging her men to succeed. She was there every step of the way, from Thule, Greenland and London and home again. Uncle Bob was the glint in her heart's eye. From Bishop Eustus through Medical School, with hardly a nod toward polio, Bobby was always the fire in her soul. Each event and success bigger than the previous. What joy and satisfaction she experienced.

And then on a dark day a shadow was cast upon her world, and she would never be quite the same. A little of the fire was gone, but still enough for most mortals. We thank the Lord for at least two blessings. She was not made to suffer the indignities of the infirm which she could not tolerate. And we know that she can rekindle the fire which was dimmed, as she joins Kerry in joyful reunion. May the Lord enfold you in His warmth as you enfolded us.

In her wedding dress, Aunt Pat had a movie star quality; her black hair and hourglass figure gave her a Jane Russell appearance when she confirmed her selection of Robert Jamison as a spouse. Uncle Bob, the adoptive son of Irish/English parents, was a handsome whitebread, who was reluctantly accepted into this previously all-Italian family. Together, they began their married life with us at 523. My mother tells of the grief she got from my dad after Aunt Pat and Uncle Bob began their married life with us at 523, because both of them enjoyed sleeping in. My father, who had an exceptional work ethic, could not understand how his in-laws could be so lackadaisical, wasting time and not looking for work from sunup until sundown. Mom explained that it was a disease of the young. Eventually, they both found work and moved into a home on Willard Street.

Willard Street was a block from sisters Anna and Dora and just two blocks from sisters Lola and Louise and brother Mike. The street was even narrower than Birch, with cars unable to park and still leave enough room for others to traverse the street, and their house sat in the center of the block on the east side of the street. Just as the street was smaller even than Birch, the house was smaller even than the Mike DiSibio house at 530 N. 8th.You entered the home, with no porch or vestibule, after climbing two and a half steps. A tiny living area was separated from the eating area by an enclosed staircase leading up to two tiny bedrooms and a bath that was tinier still. There was a miniscule kitchen with a range, sink and refrigerator on the first level. Upstairs, you had to go through the back bedroom, as you did at Uncle Mike's, to reach the bath.

My mother often went to Willard Street, because there she was the older sister. Even at that, she would still seek the help of her little sister to spy on Tony or to figure out how to discipline me in an innovative way. On one such occasion, after I had taken to playing with matches, I had been caught lighting a fire in our dirt cellar. Not knowing my mother had shared the frightening experience with Aunt Pat, I came in to look for my Mom. Aunt Pat snatched me up and dragged me to her gas range. "You like to play with fire?" she asked. As she pulled my shaking hand toward an open flame, she warned, "I'm going to show you what will happen the next time you play with matches." She held my hand over the flame until I was screaming for her to let go. In reality, it was only a second or two; but the length of time, however short, was just long enough to break a bad habit. She could be a tough cookie.

The little house of the Jamison's was a happy house. Aunt Pat was proud of her choice of a mate, who went right to the head of the line as the most handsome, if you didn't count the green-eyed Tony. Uncle Bob also fit the mold of the other male in-laws, again save for Tony, in that he was subservient to his wife. He was always a gentleman, and his mild demeanor belied his intelligence. On many occasions, he could have challenged various conclusions reached by his wife or her siblings, but, as often as not, he chose to just listen. His early work history was sporadic, but after their son was born, he was diligent as the breadwinner of the family.

Uncle Bob worked as an electrician at RCA Victor, the government contractor chosen to erect the Defense Early Warning System. The DEW line, as it was called, consisted of a series of special radar facilities strategically placed in some of the most remote sites, close to the North Pole. No sooner had Aunt Pat learned of the double pay that would be awarded to those who provided service for 18 full months than Uncle Bob was on his way to Thule, Greenland. Later, he would take a long-term assignment in the United Kingdom, where Aunt Pat joined him for a time. Such was his temperament and his love of family.

Their son, Robert Jamison, Jr., arrived in 1946, and he would change their lives forever. He had the prominent head and the looks of his handsome father generally but with the softer features of his mother. He was a contemporary of Tommy and a great complement to his older cousins, Johnny and me. He was not immune from the excesses of his doting parents and, in fact, as was her nature, Aunt Pat showered him with an overabundance of affection. Bobby, like most of the neighborhood kids, played in the empty lots on the block and in the tiny street. As he matured, he attended Holy Name School and tried to emulate his older cousins. He had some athletic ability and followed our lead by going out for the midget football team. He was small for his age, and many were surprised when he became the starting center of the squad. But his normal maturation was to be interrupted by the first family tragedy. Before his teen years, he was struck with polio meningitis, the scourge of the times. Bob would be handicapped by an atrophied left leg for life but otherwise undeterred in his pursuits.

The discovery that this horrific disease had struck our little Bobby was devastating to the whole family. I remember my mother taking the bus to Veteran's Memorial Junior High School to await Elaine and me as we came through the exits, crying out to us, through a vale of tears, "Bobbie has polio!" Of course, Elaine and I thought that he was thus condemned to death. Everyone was panicked.

The incident changed Bobby, not only from a physical perspective, but psychologically as well. From that day forward, he received attention from the family that rivaled that bestowed on the athletic hero Joey. While everyone ministered to him and gave him special care, he displayed great courage in battling the dreaded illness. He even returned to the midget football field, on crutches but in full uniform, to cheer the team on from the bench. On these occasions, he would be applauded, like someone who had made the winning touchdown in the Super Bowl. He enjoyed the attention, and it spurred him to do even more extraordinary things.

During this period, Aunt Pat was fulfilling her considerable ambitions. She was the first to move from the initial residence she shared with Uncle Bob for reasons of vanity; she was "movin' on up." She always was convinced that she deserved more: more house, more cars, more stuff, more of everything—just more. And I would have to say that there's a little of Aunt Pat in me. Aunt Pat had her eye on a beautiful home that looked onto Pyne Point Park. The Erie Street address rivaled the Vine Street homes of Mike, Lola and Louise, and once Pat's eye was fixed on this property, it was destined to be hers. No one in the family could be unimpressed with the new standard she set in home acquisition.

The enclosed front porch was reached after ascending five steps. The house was set high to accommodate a full basement, with oversized windows no less. The porch was like a veranda and acted as another room. Through another interior door lay the expansive living room and a large dining room with an elaborate staircase. The kitchen was the most massive of any of the family homes, with a rear exit that led to a large rear yard and a yard on the side. The home was a veritable park across from the park—and there was more. The second level had three generous bedrooms, with the front one reserved for the master bedroom and the rear one for Bobby; the middle bedroom was left for a new member of the family.

Uncle Bob's mother, Mrs. Jamison to one and all, moved in with Aunt Pat, Uncle Bob and Bobby. She was a wonderful woman, of diminutive stature but with great warmth. Her demeanor was constant and pleasant. She was a great addition to the Jamison nuclear family and to the Monarcas in general and was immediately integrated into every activity. To say that she was a great help to Aunt Pat would be a gross understatement. She cleaned the house, cooked most of the meals, entertained and waited on Bobby as he slowly recovered his ability to walk, with a pronounced limp but sans crutches. Her charge would go on to become a stellar performer on the Bishop Eustis High School football squad and be a charming and intelligent young man. Because he was, however, his mother's son, he was prone to extravagance and had a finely tuned sense of privilege.

During his convalescence, I spent as much time with Bobby, as any of the cousins, although my reasons were not just altruistic. I was treated generously by Mrs. Jamison when it came to candy or other food, and I added the Erie Street home to Uncle Mike's at 530 as one of the places I could pop in for a meal without invitation. I was like the big brother Bobby didn't have, and he and I became close. I sponsored him at his confirmation in the Catholic Church, making me his second godfather. It reminded me of the same event in my own life at which Aunt Pat and Pippi Galasso were my godparents for baptism and Cousin Joey was, of course, my confirmation godfather. As the years went by, Bobby and I continued our close relationship. When I was in college and Janis was in need of an escort to her senior prom, Bob was our choice. Bob had been a regular on American Bandstand, and the family was glued to the TV sets during his appearances to catch a glimpse of him as he tripped the light fantastic to the records of Dick Clark. Bob had the dramatic flare of his mother and was the perfect prom date.

When it came time for a bride, he was perfect once again in his choice of Judy Zimmerman, the eldest daughter of Sam and Helen. Like his mother before him, he broke another invisible—but strong—ethnic barrier by choosing a Jewess as a mate, but what a fabulous addition to the Monarca clan she was. The couple visited Janis and me often during their courtship and after they married, and we always enjoyed those times. Bob had gone off to Parsons College in Iowa and didn't quite finish his degree. Seemingly somewhat spoiled by all of the attention he had always received, his work habits were erratic. His bouncing from job to job seemed to reflect his lack of discipline, and he did not appear to have any focus.

One day he and Judy came by our home in Woodstream to ask for my advice about the possibility of Bob entering the University of Texas to finish his B.S. degree before going on to Medical School. I was flabbergasted and responded by asking him how he intended to pay for this effort, since he and Judy now had a beautiful girl, Kerry, and would have no means of support. Judy said she would work to help pay his way, and they would be entitled to government support as well. They were both resolute in their approach to the endeavor. I said I would, of course, support such a great ambition; but, inside, I was doubtful of his ability to stick to such a rigorous program and all that would be required. I was wrong on all counts. With the aid of his parents and the unrelenting support and sacrifice of Judy, little Bobby became Dr. Robert Jamison.

Together, the couple gave Aunt Pat and Uncle Bob four lovely grandchildren, Kerry, Lisa, Kristen, my goddaughter, and Bobby.

The young couple enjoyed the fruits of Bob's labors in the medical profession, and Bob, true to his mother's traditions, was given to drama and continued to display a bit of extravagance. He also suffered from bouts of unreliability, caused no doubt by a history of having others do for him. Family was important to him, however, and having no family on his father's side, he tended to lean heavily on the Monarcas for tradition and heritage, and some would say he was more Italian then those with pure bloodlines. He acted the "Don Roberto" when inviting one and all to poolside gatherings at his home on Partridge Lane, entertaining while Judy cleaned up.

He had early fits of brilliance in the medical practice, but eventually settled into a routine family practice before two events that were to have a dramatic impact on his life. When Kerry was just 23, she suffered a fatal asthma attack in the family home only 20 feet from her doctor father. He was unable to save her, and the entire family suffered a devastating loss, but none worse than Bob, Judy and Aunt Pat. No one of them would ever be the same. Judy was the rock of the three and dealt with the loss as well as any mother under the circumstances. Aunt Pat lost her sparkle and over time deteriorated into poor health, aided by too much alcohol. Bob's proclivity to approach his practice haphazardly became more pronounced, and he eventually lost his license to practice, as well as his marriage. The downward spiral continued until he suffered a major stroke that has left him without speech and barely ambulatory. He resides in a nursing facility in a condition similar to that of my mother. It was fortunate that Aunt Pat and Uncle Bob were not witness to this last tragic occurrence. Cousin Bob is barely 60 as I write this, and I cherish the memories on a grand scale that he has provided all of us.

Long before all this misfortune, I had had the distinct pleasure of living with Aunt Pat and Uncle Bob during my last summer of bachelorhood in 1962. Both of them welcomed me to the Erie Street home when my mother and Johnny got married, leaving me looking for a place to bunk. They were their typical generous selves, and I could not have found a more congenial atmosphere to prepare for my wedding, while continuing to earn money at different jobs during the summer. The height of their largesse was when Aunt Pat called me into the kitchen and told me that they would like to give me the 1955 Packard that had gone unused for several months. She explained that since they had two other cars they would have no use for it. She said that she knew it wasn't worth much, but I could drive it until it died or use it as a trade for something else. There was no fanfare or expectation of payment; it was a gift of love and I never forgot it as a symbol of who they were as people. They were generous to a fault; they were the life of every party; and they were adventuresome and innovative.

As they were the first to move within the neighborhood, they were also the first to move away from Camden. It came as quite a shock when Aunt Pat announced that both she and her next door neighbor and best friend, Dolly, were moving to Marlton. Marlton was a full 10 miles to the east of the Camden city limits, and many in the family couldn't find it on a map. Only Uncle Jim had moved farther away. A visit to Aunt Pat and Uncle Bob became the new adventure, enhanced by the fact that they were the first to move into a brand new house. It even had more than one bathroom. Until then, only Uncle Phil had such a luxury.

Aunt Pat could be outrageous; she could be charming; she could be warm; and she could be a lioness when protecting her family. Pat was her chosen name; some say glamour was her middle name; and Milena was her given name. But I think of her as elegant. Above all, Aunt Pat was elegant.

In Search of Independence

Natale was obviously impressed with my military bearing as we posed in front of our modest digs across from the girls' dormitories.

Natale later joined Janis and me for a grand Thanksgiving meal at P-108 in the married student housing area.

In Search of Independence

"We sat at a beautiful table and I, as the man of the house, began carving the bird. I wasn't sure if it was my technique or the knife, but it was not artful."

IN MAY OF 1962, I RETURNED TO CAMDEN, but not to 523. Mom and Johnny had gotten married after making sure that I had no objections and could find a place to stay for the summer. I certainly did not object; in fact I was thrilled and delighted at the thought of Mom finally being able to enjoy a normal life, enriched by mutual love and respect. She and John moved into an apartment on 32nd Street, with family ties as close as sister Lydia, who lived just upstairs on the second floor. Their choice of a place to live was also important to me, because it was just three blocks from the Zeccolas. I chose Aunt Pat's and Uncle Bob's large home on Erie Street, described earlier in the chapter on Aunt Pat, as the place to spend my summer. And it was a special summer for a variety of reasons.

I worked at the Wood Conversion Company, empting boxcars full of fiberglass insulation, while awaiting the onset of the tomato season and my promised job at Campbell Soup with Uncle Mike. The previous summer had been split between The New York Shipbuilding Corporation and Campbell's, and my time at the shipyard validated my decision to go to college. I knew I did not want to spend my life traipsing about robot-like and dirty and looking forward to a Friday paycheck. I was, however, proud of having worked on two great ships there, the USS Kittyhawk, the world's largest nonnuclear aircraft carrier, and the NS Savannah, the world's only atomic cargo ship. Cousin Johnny and I made good money for continuing education expenses from our work at the yard.

Campbell Soup was another story. It was a place full of pride, not least because you could see the product of your labor on the shelves at Joe's Meat Market and everywhere else. My Uncle Mike was a leader in the union and renowned for the massive checks he brought home by putting in record numbers of double shifts when the tomato trucks were backed up for blocks on Second Street awaiting delivery to the plant. So, at Campbell's, the mention of my last name got me special treatment and respect. I liked the work and took after my uncle by putting in as much overtime as was offered.

The Wood Conversion job was unremarkable, except for the check that was enhanced by an additional 10 percent for my second- and third-shift assignments. As for the time at my summer home, Aunt Pat was a gracious and disinterested landlady who never monitored my comings and goings. Not that I was up to anything improper. My activities were centered on the jobs I was able to secure for the summer and on visits to 3425 Westfield Avenue. It was there that plans were being developed for the coming event of the season. On September 8, 1962, the honor of the presence of the family and friends of the Zeccolas and DiSibios was requested to celebrate the union of Ralph and Janis. The event would be held at the Holly House Restaurant in Pennsauken, attended by more than 400 guests.

The planning process was typical for the time—it was all about the bride. Janis' mom was all atwitter, and she and her sisters, Aunt Codi and Aunt Josie, were up to their eyeballs in the planning of the festivities. I had little input into any aspect of the grand event, save for picking the men in the wedding party. Of course, Natale would be the best man, and Cousin John, Larry Carroll and Vito filled the rest of the team. The women included Aunt Codi as the matron of honor, with my sister Elaine as well as Janis's cousin Nicky and her friend Mary as bridesmaids. The decision was made to have two separate outfits for the men, formal morning tails for the religious ceremony at the church and white dinner jackets for the reception that would follow a four-hour break for changing and pictures. With all of the folderol—the selection of alter boys (Cousin Joseph and the son of Aunt Pat's friend Dolly), the choice of extravagant flowers and the open bar selections—nothing proved to be more difficult than the seating arrangements.

There was one joint meeting held at 3425 Westfield Avenue, where my mother and father were invited to discuss "the arrangements." My father-in-law-to-be was not enamored of my father because of his past indiscretions and abandonments, and the barber, irrespective of his ability to pay 100 percent of the cost of his daughter's wedding, as was the Italian custom, was determined to extract whatever he could from my dad. I had delivered a message to my father to the effect that, if he wanted to have half of the invitees he would have to chip in $1000; otherwise, "my side" would be limited to 100 attendees, and Joe Zeccola would pay for everything. To his credit, my dad sent back word that he would provide the $1000. This was not a small sum in 1962, but Dad was about to go on the shakedown cruise of the NS Savannah where he would earn double pay for several weeks. In response to his commitment to put up half of the money, he received an hellacious response from an alcoholic and vitriolic wife, but he kept his word. The meeting on seating followed the financial agreement and was generally very cordial; Joe was cool to my father, but Dad behaved in his usual charming way. There was some discussion about the decisions that had already been made, and the rest of the night was spent on deciding who would sit where.

The dilemma surrounding this aspect of the planning was largely the result of old family feuds involving Uncle Mike DiSibio and my dad, Uncle Mike DiSibio and others, and, of course, Dad and Eleanor and Mom and Johnny. They would all come to the wedding, but we had to employ care and strategy in figuring out how the chairs would face and which tables would face which other tables. I am positive that the arrangement for seating on the Battleship Missouri in Tokyo Harbor for the signing of the Japanese surrender was far easier and concluded with fewer changes. Where was Douglas MacArthur when I needed him?

To make matters worse, I exhibited a Mike DiSibio stubbornness when I informed my father that I would not be providing Eleanor with any flowers, traditionally given to women of honor associated with the family. He was visibly hurt by my position on the matter, but I told him with resoluteness that I had no intention of doing anything that would take away from my own mother's moment on that special day. This, of course, was an absurd position on my part, but I was playing the role of an adult making my own choices; and he accepted my dictum without challenge. I have always regretted that decision that put him under even more strain than he already endured in his fragile household. It does not lessen my regret that I had already insisted that he buy both formal suits, even though his role in the ceremony was nonexistent; he thought that it was a waste of needed money, but he acquiesced nonetheless. To cap things off, Eleanor refused to come to the wedding, and Dad was made conspicuous by her absence. The only satisfaction I attained from my ill-advised decisions was a valued picture of my sister and my dad in his formal morning coat outfit, the only time he was ever captured on film in that attire.

I was used to weddings being held at the Italian-American club or in a fire house, raucous affairs with a live trio, a long table with Anisette cookies and biscotti alongside the wedding cake, and a few bottles of Seagram 7 and Anisette of the liquid variety as well. To get your food, you went to a small window, beyond which was the kitchen, and waited your turn to order a sandwich—meatballs, sausage, roast beef or roast pork—and the requested sandwich would be delivered to you wrapped in waxed paper. Beer or wine was served at another window or at a table manned by a relative of the groom. The young would serve the elderly, and the elderly could be seen stuffing their oversized pocketbooks with sandwiches or biscotti for a later snack or their husband's lunch. The kids would start the night neat and tidy but by the end of the evening would look like ragamuffins. Cousin Johnny and I got more than one scolding for "acting up" at these simple but joyous celebrations.

The Zeccola/DiSibio union was quite a gala in contrast to what was common to me. We had a large band, a sit-down dinner and, even though the table seatings were a hassle, they were lovely with their flowers and expensive china. This was all due to Janis' vision becoming a reality, and the already beautiful wedding was made even more so by the spectacular wedding dress that Janis picked out. She looked elegant and virginal, and rightly so. Together, we had thought of everything, and a wonderful time was had by all. My brothers-in-law, Vito and Pooky, were successful as guardians of the entrances to ensure against crashers, while my dad made certain that drinks were offered to his many friends and family members. He hobnobbed with his old in-laws and, in general, seemed to enjoy his investment. Mom was proud as a peacock with her new husband and newly married son. My in-laws were reserved and accepted the thank-yous of all of the guests with supreme grace. I was the only one who was too concerned about the wellbeing of everyone to enjoy myself. Aunt Anna insightfully remarked to me, "Ralph, sit with your wife and enjoy yourself, and stop worrying about everyone." But, as someone who still feared failure, it just wasn't in my nature to relax at a time like this.

After spending the night at the exclusive Cherry Hill Inn, my new bride and I packed up my newly-acquired '57 Chrysler New Yorker the very next day and headed to the P-108 married student housing unit in Greeley, Colorado. We left from the front of my mom's apartment, with my mother waving and wiping away a flood of tears, while sobbing, "You take good care of her, Ralphie." I felt comfortable for the first time in months. I was in control, with Janis depending on me for everything for the foreseeable future. We were exactly what two young people should be under those romantic circumstances. More than happy, we were joyous—right up until we pulled up to P-108.

We learned that the "P" stood literally for prison. The married student housing was a series of barracks-like, single-story wooden structures that were originally constructed to house interred Japanese-American citizens who lived quite legally in California, except for having committed the offense of being of Japanese descent. Sadly, it was one of the low points in American history, when the decision was made to force these people from their homes and inter them inland, in what were euphemistically called "camps"; in fact, they were virtual prisons and the people in them prisoners. My bride and I would start life in this hovel. Good-humored on the outside about this turn of events, Janis may well have been thinking, "I didn't think when I vowed for better or worse that the worse would start so soon."

The wooden structure was entered by climbing three steps to a tiny landing. Once inside, you were in a small room that appeared to be two rooms, because in the middle was a freestanding metal space heater with a stove pipe exiting through the low ceiling. On the other side of the heater were a gas range/oven and refrigerator. There were sparse furnishings, including a sofa and small chair in the front portion of the room and an old wooden table and four chairs next to the rear door. To the right were two doors, one protecting a tiny bathroom and the other a small bedroom. When we entered that room, we were both quite taken aback—these furnishings were as sparse as the rest, but, what was worse, there were two tiny, cot-sized beds that were the cause of our alarm. This would not do for newlyweds. So, we emptied the car of all our worldly possessions, and I was dispatched to find a suitable bed.

I had no difficulty in finding precisely what we needed, a double bed frame, a mattress and an old-fashioned spring, that I managed to tie efficiently to the roof of the white and blue Chrysler. The Salvation Army store was an old haunt of the Cellar Dwellers, so the trip was not complicated. But I had one other item on my short list—wire hangers, since P-108 was bereft of hangers of any kind; and I have often thought that I was the only person in North America to have ever actually purchased wire coat hangers. As poor as we were at 523, we never had to buy hangers. But married life was going to have many firsts, and this was the first of the firsts.

While I was gone, Janis was performing magic in our own little cell. She had unpacked a number of our shower and wedding gifts, including a tablecloth that now hid the ugly wooden kitchen table. We had left most of our booty stored in the basement at 3425, but we had transported the items we knew we would need.

Most of our wedding gifts came in the form of cash, as is the Italian tradition, and both sets of parents required us to list the name of the gift-giver and the amount rendered. The lists were to serve two purposes: they would provide a gauge by which future gifts were measured and also provided a basis for comparison to what the parents had given to the givers' children at similar ceremonies. The exercise yielded another piece of information, as I learned that Janis' side gave between $20 and $100, while my side gave between $10 and $25. I did not feel sheepish at this revelation, because I also knew my people gave from the heart and gifted all they could afford. Mostly, I was warmed by the notion that nearly everyone that was invited came. And the end result was that we had a considerable nest egg of $2500, a tribute to our combined families.

P-108 was 25 feet from the cross-country railroad track and two miles from Monford's cattle feed lot, and all of our senses were tested to the limits every day. The train came barreling through twice a day, at 4 p.m. and 4 a.m., trumpeted by a wailing whistle that announced its arrival and tested our sense of hearing, while P-108 and its neighbors literally shook. Meanwhile, the southerly winds would waft the aroma of cow manure from the thousands of beasts being fattened for slaughter at Monford's, testing our sense of smell. We became accustomed to all of the offenses to our senses and to the circumstances of our living conditions, because they took a back seat to our awe at being on our own and being in love. From my perspective, this was far better then 523. Here I had love provided every day in the form of food and attention, all delivered in a rodent-free environment at that. I competed with no one for unconditional love. Life was good.

As good as life was, we both missed holidays with our families, and Thanksgiving was the first test of our commitment to one another without familial support. By this time, Natale had returned to Colorado, but not to Greeley. He was at Sterling Junior College, some 50 miles north of my campus, and the three of us needed one another on that first holiday. Janis made extravagant preparations for our first formal dinner guest, and a special one at that, by putting together an opulent repast. While we could not afford all the fixings—a turkey was not in our budget, so she got the biggest chicken she could find—we had almost everything.

We sat at a beautiful table and I, as the man of the house, began carving the bird. I wasn't sure if it was my technique or the knife, but it was not artful. When we simultaneously took our first bite, the toughness led us to believe that we had sunk our teeth into the leather in my father's shop. It turned out that it was a stewing chicken that Janis had purchased for such a low price, and we have laughed about it ever since.

We could not afford to go home for Christmas, but we made do with presents sent from Camden and the solace of numerous phone calls. The first time Mom and Dad Zeccola called, the train went by with the accompanying blast of noise, as the room shook around us. Mom said, "What is that awful noise?" And Janis nonchalantly replied, "What noise?" She reminded me of Elaine and the rats in the ceiling. We had settled in to our own little home, such as it was.

As the spring approached, we began to discuss my career future. Colorado State College had a great reputation for developing teachers, and the graduates were recruited to opportunities all over the world. Having decided together that we would not limit my job possibilities to the East Coast, I accepted interviews from American Samoa, Hawaii, California, Alaska and New Mexico. Since it was a seller's market of sorts, I knew I could secure a teaching position near home if we changed our minds. After all, I had maintained a 4.0 out of 5.0 average, had been a fraternity president, had been the cadet of the quarter in Air Force ROTC and had carried a dual major in History and Speech.

All of the interviews went well, and I was looking forward to the next. The interview with the Carlsbad Public Schools in New

Mexico, where they were in search of a U.S. history teacher, proved to be the most intriguing and looked like the ideal opportunity for me. It turned out to hold even more intrigue than had at first been apparent. The interviewer visited and did the interview with the obligatory questions: where was I from, why did I choose CSC and the like. When I mentioned Camden, he lit up. "How about that," he exclaimed, "one of our teachers used to teach in Camden." Of course, I was excited to know that teacher's identity. "Ray Granfield," he told me, with no idea how astounding I would find this revelation. I was flabbergasted.

For the previous two years, every time I visited WWHS, I tried to discern the whereabouts of Mr. Granfield. The first year I attended CSC, I had kept in touch with him, each time expressing my extreme thanks and utter satisfaction with the college. He was always pleased to see me and very satisfied, I think, with the positive influence he had on me and on Natale. At the end of my second year, I discovered that my guardian angel had left for greener educational grasses, but, without Google, there was no way to find him. Serendipitously, I had found him in the middle of an interview in Carlsbad, New Mexico. After sharing my story with the interviewer, he assured me that Mr. Granfield would contact me in Greeley. And indeed he did, in a long and pleasant letter in which he invited Janis and me to use his home for a visit to Carlsbad, while he and his wife were off to Cincinnati. He advised me in the letter that Carlsbad might not be to a Camden kid's liking and that a visit of a week or so might help me decide. He, of course, was right about me once again.

We did not take him up on his generous offer to stay in his home, but I took the opportunity, in a lengthy telephone call, to express my deep gratitude for his having helped to turn my life around. He gave his modest thanks for the praise—and we were not to speak again for 30 years. With the assistance of Google and Jesse Vitagliano, I found him again recently, but not one year of that 30 went by without my relating the Ray Granfield story to my friends, employees or associates. Mr. Granfield was truly someone who made a difference in my life.

Meanwhile, as graduation was approaching, the romance of Samoa and Alaska had worn off, as our homesickness reached epidemic proportions. The pull of our roots was palpable, and we were ready to go home. It had been a great nine months, full of adventure, but it was time to return to Camden. Mom and Dad Zeccola and Mom and Johnny came out to see me graduate, all of them bursting with pride. So were Janis and I. We picked the Zeccolas up at Denver's Stapleton Airport in our new Volvo, having made a deal for this exotic Swedish beauty the week before with nothing but my Chrysler, a bank loan and a degree. On the eve of graduation, Pop Zeccola picked up the tab for the six of us at Branca's Little Italy, one of our special-occasion restaurants. If I could save time in a bottle, as the song goes, that would be one of the times that I would save.

Janis had displayed an inordinate amount of courage. She had left her nest and traveled cross-country with only me. She had spent her first Thanksgiving, as well as Christmas and Easter, without her family. She never complained and never really got any credit, while I was getting all the credit from everyone, including the Zeccolas. It was pretty much all about me—my education, my career, my decisions. The seeds of Janis' discontent—living in my shadow, despite her own accomplishments and support—were sown in Greeley and would take root, then continue to grow unabated for two decades. Thus began a pattern and a trend that would color our entire life together.

We returned to Camden, and Janis and I accepted the invitation to live at 3425 until my job situation was settled. It was a learning experience for me, living in a totally healthy family environment; while it was sometimes confining, it was, on balance, positive. I had a job at Campbell Soup, thanks to Uncle Mike, and Janis was "doing heads" in the basement to earn a couple of extra bucks. I had applied to Gloucester City, Pennsauken and Wildwood public schools. I got offers from all three and needed to make a decision. As I sat with my father-in-law, he offered me an opportunity that was impossible to refuse.

18
Aunt Lydia

Aunt Lydia, the Monarca Poet Laureate, in all her glory. The inset is a rare photo of Aunt Lee, her beauty intact, with her two sons Joey and Melvin.

Aunt Lydia

"Mel was sullen in the passenger seat... I surprised him by telling him that I thought he was essentially a bum... I explained that our destination was the U.S. Army recruiting office at the Camden City Hall."

LYDIA WAS THE PENULTIMATE BIRTH IN THE HOUSEHOLD of Teresa and Mario Monarca, and, as the first child to be born in Camden, she marked a new era. She would like the word "penultimate" being used in her context, because it will send many readers to the dictionary; if you asked her, she would take pleasure in explaining that "penultimate" does not mean the highest but rather denotes the next to the last. She would react as I describe, because she fancies herself the most intelligent of the Monarcas. In usual fashion, she is likely right.

Lydia was a precocious child. Having been spared the harshness of Jamesville, she knew only Camden and Delair. She was even more recalcitrant than her older sister Pat, with whom she shared many secrets that were kept from the others, because the others were seen as old-fashioned when compared to Pat's sharper attire and style. Pat passed her modern attitude onto her little sister. At the same time, Louise, Anna and Lola were looked up to by Lydia and were often the subject of her incessant curiosity. She questioned everything and everybody, a habit I believe my ever-questioning sister learned from Aunt Lydia. But Lydia was the only one whose inquisitiveness led her to create questions designed to educate and gather information. She might, for example, ask her mother, "How did you and Pop meet?" Although she was nearly the youngest, it was Lydia to whom others would go late in life to gain clarity on particular family issues or long forgotten events.

Her intellect and her questioning nature often gave Lydia the air of a skeptic. In truth, her approach was borne less of skepticism than it was her ability to ferret out a subterfuge. In other words, she had a good nose for sniffing out bull; it was hard to get one over on Lydia. She could never be described as naïve, and you were discouraged by her strength from deeming her worthy of sympathy. She set high standards for herself and others. In her personal habits, she was always fashionable and was more inclined than Lola—but less so than Pat—to "make up." Her figure was always a point in her favor, and she spent time and effort to keep herself fit and attractive in the eyes of men and women alike. Her confident air often, unintentionally, exhibited an abrasive tone. I took on one of her traits: "Often wrong, but never in doubt." She would dole out advice, advising her older sister, Dora, on ways to keep her man and counseling her younger sister, Marie, to be more sophisticated. Her sharp wit is often exceeded by her sharp tongue, but the wellspring of all of these characteristics was love, love of family.

She followed Aunt Pat's lead by falling in love with and marrying a whitebread, Melvin Mathews, a virtual Donald O'Conner look-alike. He had a twinkle in his eye and a little boy countenance that made you like him. If Tony was handsome, then Mel got the award for being the cutest of the in-laws. He contributed a fine family of his own, including a younger brother, Ronnie. Mel was witty and possessed of an intelligence that enabled his career to culminate in important positions of trust in the accounting world. Uncle Mel had no rivals when it came to clothes, with the possible exception of nephew Joey; in fact, it was Uncle Mel that taught Joey a good deal about quality and style.

Aunt Lydia and Uncle Mel moved into a house at 827 Grant Street; in keeping with the tradition of staying close to the rest of the family, it was within blocks of the Monarca hub. This house had a grand front porch that was reached by climbing two steps. Once inside, you were in the living room, which reminded you of Aunt Louise's house with its fine staircase on the left just before you reached the dining room. Beyond the dining room was a generous kitchen, and upstairs were three bedrooms and a bath. Grant Street was about the size of Birch Street and half the width of Elm and Vine, and although there was nothing remarkable about the structure, it was more than adequate for what would become a family of three.

Not surprisingly, given Aunt Lydia's flair for modernity, the couple was contemporary in every way. They were a little hipper than their elders, and Uncle Mel was every bit as exciting as Lydia, sometimes more so. While her sister Pat had to lead her husband Bob in the direction of adventure and fun, Aunt Lydia sometimes had trouble keeping up with Uncle Mel in the whimsy department. He had a lighter charm than my dad, but he shared with Dad an attraction to the ladies and they to him. He was the type that did not have to be cajoled into wearing a giant diaper at the family New Year's Eve fete. He could be the life of the party with a quip, a joke or by playing the xylophone, which he did with great facility. Together, Lydia and Mel were quite dapper and "cut a mean rug" on the dance floor. Uninhibited would be an apt description of this good-looking couple.

The child produced by Aunt Lydia and Uncle Mel was handsome, as expected. Melvin was the name given to this baby boy, and "Little Mel" was the apple of their eyes and was very special to the entire Mathews family as well. I often babysat for this little fellow, as well as for Judy Vitagliano, and remember them both as being happy babies, not prone to whining. I was never close to the younger Melvin in his early years due to the difference in our ages, but later I would be called upon to infuse some discipline. Although not malicious or cruel, Cousin Melvin did not meet his mother's lofty standards. When he showed a distinct lack of interest in high school and began to disrespect Aunt Lydia, I went to reason with the handsome 17-year old. By the time I got there, Aunt Lydia had grown completely exasperated and frustrated at his lack of motivation and backtalk. I smacked him lightly on the back of his head and told him to wait for me in my car.

I pulled away from the house and headed off in the direction of Camden. Mel was sullen in the passenger seat, and I let him stew for awhile. Finally, I began to unveil my plan. I surprised him by telling him that I thought he was essentially a bum, and I assured him that he fit the definition: he didn't earn any money, he didn't work in school, and he sponged off others for food and clothing. Thus, he was a bum.

I told him I had lost respect for him but had come up with a solution to his problem. I explained that our destination was the U.S. Army recruiting office at the Camden City Hall. I would sign him up and, finally, he would have the means to earn his way. He was dumbstruck and finally murmured his objection, "You can't do that, you're not my father." "Watch me," I said with confidence. With Camden City Hall looming in the distance, I was hoping he would crack—and finally he did. On the verge of tears, he promised me he would straighten out and buckle down. He said he didn't want to go in the Army and would I please take him home so he could apologize to his mom. It was not just Melvin who was saved but me as well; and, without a word, I made a U-turn in the middle of Market Street and made the transition into normal cousin-to-cousin talk until I dropped him off. He was a good kid with a good heart who had little interest in academics. He has grown to be a great husband and father and continues to be close to his dad and provides him much support in his elder years. He also continues to demonstrate unconditional love for his mom, and he often calls her from his home in North Carolina, where Aunt Lydia goes to visit her grandchildren and great-grandchildren.

Upon one of our evictions from 523, we were taken in by Aunt Lydia and Uncle Mel. They had available bedrooms and were generous in helping us survive. Although I was only 7, I can remember that stay. Elaine was nearly 9 at the time and was un-remitting in her need to play "Daddy's Little Girl" on a little 45 rpm record player, all with great dramatic effect. This was Elaine's way of mourning my father's multiple abandonments, but Aunt Lydia finally lost patience after the 24th continuous rendition at full volume. She came to the top of the staircase and screamed at Elaine, "If you play that song one more time I'm going to break it in a thousand pieces." Silence reigned until bed time. When Elaine and I went to bed, we were moaning about that mean Aunt Lydia, and we were exchanging some choice descriptions of our aunt, when we were interrupted by a voice on the other side of the wall shared by our room with the master bedroom. "I can hear every word, you two, now go to sleep or else." Once again, silence reigned.

One evening my dad attempted to visit us, and Aunt Lydia allowed him to come into her home, but told him to wait on the sofa and said she would send us down from our bedroom. We beamed when she told us of our father's presence. Just as I got to the top of the stairs, however, Uncle Mike Monarca burst through the front door and confronted my father, threatening to "break his back" if he didn't start supporting us. My father did not dare challenge him in Lydia's house, besides which Uncle Mike would likely have made good on his threat. I hated both Aunt Lydia and Uncle

Mike that night for making my father look cowardly, even though Aunt Lydia had nothing to do with it. All I knew was that we didn't get to visit with dad, and the next day "Daddy's Little Girl" started all over again. I observed my eighth birthday on Grant Street, complete with a birthday party organized by Aunt Lydia. There was a lot of compassion under that tough exterior.

Aunt Lydia and Uncle Mel divorced not many years after my mom and dad. The reasons were largely, but not entirely, different. Uncle Mel could not stay away from women, and that was the primary cause for the dissolution of their marriage; but, unlike my mother, Lydia kept an adequate home, was exceptional in her appearance and had few discernible bad habits. While Tony felt superior to Dora, it's probably safe to say that the relationship was reversed in the Mathews home, where, it is likely that Uncle Mel felt intellectually inferior to the ambitious Lydia. They may have been equals in the financial arena, but few contemporaries could compete with her in matters of the mind. Uncle Melvin ended up in Statesville, North Carolina, and Lydia returned to Camden.

No one provided a better foil for me when I was in college than Aunt Lydia. She was someone with whom I could spend hours discussing Plato or Lincoln of any number of other things. She had original thoughts and shared them liberally. She challenged me to do better and to excel. Her interest was not feigned, but was rooted in her own curiosity and a love of learning. Sometimes I thought that she was going to college vicariously through me. I was always stimulated by her company in my school years and beyond. She allowed me to test my notions and also experience the delight of sharing my knowledge with her. I learned a lot from her, and she made an enormous contribution to my development as a student and a person, and I am indebted.

There is little question that Uncle Mel had been unable to keep up with her drive and ambition, but there was a match out there somewhere, and Aunt Lydia met her match when she met Joseph Cini. Joe was an entrepreneurial businessman in the clothing manufacturing business, outspoken, often brash and possessed of mental prowess that belied his lack of formal education. In the ways of business, he had flashes of downright brilliance. Where the mixing of Lola and Emilio induced a warm glow, the Lydia and Joe mixture produced sparks bordering on lightning. I can remember being at a coffee and cake event at Aunt Anna's when we first met Joe Cini, who arrived with Aunt Lydia. He was in top form, questioning everyone about everything from the ingredients in the cookies to how much did they pay for the house, it was quintessential Joseph Cini. He enjoyed verbal combat like Pooky enjoyed a fist fight, and they were both good at what they did. Within months, this animated man would become Uncle Joe.

Joseph Cini was a short man with a tall vision of himself. He was generous, quick of wit and tongue, insightful, streetsmart, and not given to cons. He did not suffer fools gladly and was blindly loyal to those who were loyal to him. He could teeter on the brink of cockiness but be as compassionate as any Monarca. He came from Italian stock out of South Philadelphia and was a first cousin of Al Cini, who became Al Martino of "Spanish Eyes" and "Godfather" fame. Uncle Joe was the owner of several sweatshops in Philadelphia and had had Aunt Lee (before his marriage to her), Aunt Mary, Mary Zeccola, my mother and me in his employ. He was taken with Aunt Lydia and finally won her heart. They were fire and ice, oil and water, and butter on a burn; but, somehow, the union worked. It was as though she was the flux to his torch, causing them to bond like parts held together by a weld seam.

I had observed Aunt Lydia's generosity at age 7, and I observed it much later from afar as she and Uncle Joe hosted Bobby when he attended medical school. Uncle Joe waited on Bobby as though he was a respected elder; even Aunt Lydia would bridle when Uncle Joe would shush her because Bobby was studying. I saw this outpouring of warmth when I visited them while Bob was there, and it was a sight to see. There was this street tough kind of guy making the aspiring young physician a pot of tea and watching him, over the rims of his bifocals, as if he could learn from looking. I came to understand why Aunt Lydia had fallen in love with Uncle Joe.

When Carol and I met Aunt Lydia and Uncle Joe in Las Vegas, he was beginning to fail in health. He wasn't too frail to shoot some craps, however, while Carol and Aunt Lee tried their hands—and arms—at some slots. Uncle Joe noted, at one point, that I had stopped betting, and I told him that I had lost enough. He asked, "How much have you lost?" I told him about $100. Thereupon, he pulled a $100 bill from his pocket and put it on the "Don't Pass" line on the table. When the shooter rolled craps on the next throw of the dice, Uncle Joe picked up the $200 from the table, handed it to me and said, "You can't be here and not gamble; it's un-American." That was Uncle Joe.

I always stayed in close touch with them both as they moved from Camden to Anniston, Alabama, and then to Dania, Florida. A month would not go by without phone contact, and at least twice a year we would see each other in person, always a memorable occasion. We strode the streets of Las Vegas and San Francisco with a certain style that only Uncle Joe, comfortable in any environment, could display. Together, they were great and stimulating company. When we lost Uncle Joe, we lost a star; and I commemorated the event by having a star named after him. It was only fitting.

The union of Lydia and Joe produced Joseph Cini, Jr., known as Joey, who was born to the couple late in life and was thought of as a blessing. Joey was as precocious as his mother in her time and could be as quarrelsome as his father, and he brought them both great joy. Joey had an extraordinary mind that the parents were determined to cultivate, and they sent him to a Montessori school at an early age. While he never finished college, which left their ambitions for him unfulfilled, he found his niche in the world of computers and technology. He has traveled to many countries to apply his unique capabilities and to search for opportunities. Most importantly, he has been a loving son who brought his father peace in his last years and who recently resigned a management position in Florida to make haste for New Jersey to tend to his ailing mother. He has sacrificed much to act on the sense of responsibility instilled in him by his parents. His mother continues to be justly proud.

Today, Aunt Lydia is the only one of the Monarcas remaining who is able to share the tales of the family and to impart continuing wisdom to the young. She suffers from the disease of the elderly, by often expecting too much from those whose love for her is beyond question. She still sets the bar high when it comes to family loyalty and the accompanying expectation of excellence. She can still be combative, but now there is no Uncle Joe to offer retort and to put her in her place. We, however, know her place, and it is at the head of the family Monarca. She has assumed the role of offering the wisdom of Louise, the deliberateness of Anna, the gentleness of Lola, the grit of Dora, the style of Pat and the steadfast family loyalty of Marie. She now has become all of them, and we love her.

19
Those Wildwood Days

I always assumed that Dean would be President one day,
and I wanted him to study up on what it would take.

Those Wildwood Days

"The teaching life was exhilarating in every regard. Here I was, literally a new man. It was as if I had no background as a street kid, as an abandoned child or a target of ridicule or sympathy..."

THE ZECCOLAS HAD A LITTLE RENTAL PROPERTY in North Wildwood, New Jersey, a seaside resort community that was the destination of tens of thousands of sun-seekers from all over the mid-Atlantic. This property was a two unit rental just three blocks from one of the finest beaches in the world. The building was a flat-topped, one-story structure measuring 20 by 40 feet. The units were self-contained, but attached, each measuring 20 by 20 feet, and they split the building precisely in half. The side entry opened into one L-shaped room containing a kitchen-living room combination; the other portion, a reverse L, held two 9 by 9 bedrooms on the long end of the L and a bath on the short end.

All the spaces were miniaturized to accommodate sleeping arrangements for six, two in each bedroom and two on the fold-out sofa. The units were modern, attractive and always spotlessly maintained by the Zeccola owners, who would come down on Saturday to clean for the next week's renters. Commanding $100 per week, these rentals were a good investment. This property would also turn out to be an opportunity I could not—and would not—refuse.

Pop said he would let us use one of the units gratis through the winter and beyond, until we had an opportunity to get the lay of the land and save some money. This was a great and generous offer, notwithstanding the catch: as great as the property was in the summer, it was not winterized for seasonal living. Pop said that he and I would make the needed modifications during summer weeks when the unit was not rented, so the summer of 1963 was dedicated to working at Campbell's and spending spare Sundays winterizing at the shore. The process included insulating the floors, putting in triple-track storm and screen windows and a storm door, putting in a wall-unit space heater and, most importantly, erecting a TV antenna. All of the chores were learning experiences for me and, although Pop could be a bit snappy at times, he was generally a good teacher.

The biggest challenge was the TV antenna. We were 90 miles from the transmitting stations in Philadelphia, and without satellites or cable one had to have an antenna large enough and erected high enough to "catch" the signal from the source. It was like a Keystone Cops episode as the one of us tried to steady the 20-foot-high pole, atop which was an unwieldy eight-foot antenna, while the other "cop" tried to attach and adjust the guy wires to the four corners of the roof.

The challenge lasted an entire Sunday. After several attempts over many hours, we finally steadied a slightly bent antenna, a bit damaged because of the many wind-blown attempts that had failed; and we were now ready for testing. Pop would go down, turn on Channel 3, 6 or 10, and I would holler down, "How's it look?" He might say, "Snowy, but I got a picture." I would then ask him to try Channel 6 and, again, ask how it looked. Every time there was a "No good" response, I would make adjustments to the direction the antenna was facing. Often one channel would improve but another would take a turn for the worse, so to speak.

Becoming more like an Abbott and Costello skit, this routine went on for most of the day, with my efforts often punctuated by the entire contraption toppling to the roof because of my clumsy manipulations. Finally, we switched places, and after a mere seven hours of additional work, we could see, not quite clearly, three channels. We declared it "close enough for jazz." Never once did my new father-in-law curse at me or lose his temper, and this alone was a new experience for me. Janis and I moved into the now cozy place, where she once again made a little box a home.

I had taken the job offered to teach one 11th-grade history class and a half-day of "self-contained" seventh grade. The latter part of my job description meant teaching English, science, history and math to 26 seventh-graders. I didn't care, because I was at the top of my profession. Teaching, as a matter of fact, is one of very few professions where you are at the top as soon as you finish college and are state-certified. When you close the door of that classroom, you are in complete, unsupervised, control of all that you survey. It is a heady and heavy realization. On the first day of teacher orientation, I met the other "rookies" who would become Wildwood High teachers; Bill Carr, Bernie McCracken, the irrepressible Jay Craven, my new guardian angel, Frank Caterini, and I would soon form a new clique. The classroom, the extracurricular activities and our completely unencumbered lives made the first year special.

I learned a lot in the first year of teaching. For one thing, kids were not always naïve, nor were they always honest, and the same could be said for their parents. James Harper was often late or absent, and one day, after a three-day absence that required a signed parental excuse, James strolled in and dropped the note on my desk on his way to his seat. I looked up as I was opening the envelope and spoke to James, saying, "Well, welcome back, James, what was wrong with you?" He met my gaze and replied, "I don't know, I didn't read the note." I also found my charges to be clever on occasion. Robert Mulwinny was challenged to use the word "frugal, meaning to save," in a sentence.

Robert hesitated and grinned as he said, "Jane fell in the lake and was drowning when Billy jumped in and frugaled her." Clever kid, that Robert. But I kept a straight face, since I always tried hard to be in control, following the counsel of my old history professor, Dr. John Welling, who opined, "When you first walk into a classroom, if the windows are open, close them; if the lights are on, turn them off. Take command!" His advice often served me well.

Teaching and married life were as good as it got on the seven-mile-long island made up of Wildwood Crest, Wildwood, and North Wildwood. Janis worked her usual magic in making the 20 by 20 square at 310 10th Avenue a warm home. Given that the interior walls were the same green stucco as the exterior, the ceilings were less than 8 feet high and the floors were linoleum squares selected for price and not beauty, she did a remarkable job. Of course, she had practiced at the college prison site, and this time she was aided in her task by the additional shower and wedding gifts that she unpacked. Our social life was filled with members of my new-found clique of teachers, and we shared an interest in high school sports. We attended most games, with the usual fervor of biased home fans, and taunted the opponents at away games, in fraternity fashion. When the games concluded, we proceeded, en masse, to the Anchor Inn for huge bar sandwiches and copious quantities of beer. The ladies often experimented with Black Russians or some such exotic drink to display their sophistication.

The teaching life was exhilarating in every regard. Here I was, literally a new man. It was as if I had no background as a street kid, as an abandoned child or a target of ridicule or sympathy; I was a fully certified professional teacher, someone to be respected and admired, and my future was up to me. I thanked my lucky stars—and my guardian angels—for the contentment. Of course, I wanted more, and to get it I cultivated the attributes that had gotten me here in the first place. I aligned myself with "my guys," I was a good friend, I sought to be creative in the classroom, I took on extra assignments, I immersed myself in my mission to be the best at whatever I did. In short, I put myself under pressure; and if I wasn't running scared, I was beginning to trot in that direction.

Our little clique was uproariously funny, or let's just say we thought so, behaving on occasion like fraternity brothers. This frat behavior frequently involved taunting other less enlightened colleagues or the administrators or pulling pranks. No one was immune from our sophomoric high-jinks, and we were proud of our ingenuity. An easy target was the rotund band director, Harris Rosselli, whom Craven would greet with a pithy comment like, "So, Harris, what do you go around the girth there?" Harris, who commuted 80 miles roundtrip from his home in Bridgeton, bragged incessantly about the great gas mileage he was getting on his new Ford and would arrive in the morning, beaming with pride, with a new report like, "I'm getting 20 miles to the gallon on this new beauty." He was asking for it, and we had an elaborate plan

We secretly added a gallon of gas to his car every other day for several weeks. Each week, he would tell the stories of his impressive mileage, and each week, of course, his bragging became more pronounced. We would always egg him on and tell him he should write to Ford or even "Ripley's Believe It or Not" because of his now-claimed 60-miles-per-gallon average. He was telling everyone about his magic car and about his laudable expertise behind the wheel. Enter the next phase of the sting. We began to siphon gas from his tank on the same every-other-day schedule that we had used to add it, escalating the amount weekly. The scheme was diabolical and required patience.

Suddenly, Harris's bragging ceased, and he began to avoid the teacher's lounge. Needless to say, we sought him out to inquire about the magic car and his latest driving exploits. The reader can conjure up how we played the "mark," Harris, for all he was worth. Before it was over, Harris had the car back to the dealer every week to try and diagnose the mystery. Eventually, we stopped manipulating the amount of gas and allowed the mileage to return to normal; and after a month or two of his threatening letters to Ford headquarters demanding some solution, we unveiled the secret to Harris. He was a good sport about our little game and related it to everyone. Like the John Ryan fight in North Camden, this episode distinguished Frank, Jay and I as men to be respected, even feared a little. People wouldn't want to get on the wrong side of such creative pranksters.

Frank and I were willing contributors every step of the way, but Jay was the ringleader. He was a local boy and was one of the brightest and most charismatic guys I ever met. He had a Joe Vitagliano quality about him that was magnetic. He was quick of wit and was never stuck for a quip. When the waitress brought our order of beer, Jay would invariably say, "Way to go, this gal is up for the waitress of the year award." When she would then set the beer down, Jay, timing the next line just right would say, "Unfortunately, the year was 1958." Even the server would laugh along with us. Jay got me a job at the local recreation center and got me into the varsity club and into coaching, all of which made my acceptance at WHS a breeze. Jay's wife, Toni, and all of us along with her, suffered when we lost Jay to cancer when he was just 42 years old. All who knew him felt the loss; those whom he never met were deprived of the pleasure of his company.

My long-term guardian angel was Frank Caterini. Janis and I were childless newlyweds, while the Cravens, the Carrs and the McCrackens all had kids. Frank had no wife, and so we naturally gravitated toward one another. Frank, a local whose family was prominent in the business community, lived with his mother, father and three sisters above the Riptide Nightclub that they owned. They also owned Johnny's Bar on the west side of town. The Nightclub was the best on the island, and every act that was popular with the younger set appeared there during the raucous summers, when the tourists would cause the island to swell almost to bursting. Johnny's was a neighborhood spot with an associated liquor store and sandwich service. I would come to know both establishments intimately over the next couple of years. I would come to know Frank for decades to come as our friendship grew to mirror the love of brothers.

Frank was the school's history teacher. He and I had both majored in history and had a love of the subject that gave us a natural affinity from the start. In addition to my attraction to his interest in history, he reminded me of David Molotsky. Frank possessed a great deal of gray matter and intellectual curiosity; he was as thoughtful and deliberate as I was sharp and quick. He had an interest in jazz and classical music, while I enjoyed the emerging rock and roll and doo-wop. We shared an interest in sports, in education and in politics. The bond that was slowly being formed between us was solidified on November 22nd of 1963.

Like everyone of my generation, I know exactly where I was when I heard that President Kennedy had been shot—I was teaching at Wildwood High. When his death was announced over the loudspeaker, I was teaching a civics class. After a tearful moment of silence, I immediately launched into a lesson on the succession of power at the passing of a President. At the same time, I could recall sitting in the living room of my fraternity house, listening to JFK speak to the nation about the threat posed by the Russian missiles in Cuba and warning of a potential war. My fraternity brothers and I vowed to quit school and sign up if such an event transpired. Such was the charisma of the now fallen President.

After a long discussion with Janis, she agreed with my decision to go to Washington, D.C. to participate in some way in the unfolding history. After dinner, in what was a sort of reprise of my recruitment of Natale to go to Colorado, I went to the Riptide to recruit Frank to go with me to D.C. The massive apartment home of the Caterinis was the second floor of the entire nightclub. It had the size and comfort of any large home, but for the fact that it was on only one floor and shook when a big band played below. When I arrived, everyone was, of course, glued to the beginnings of what would be the constant coverage of the assassination, the arrest of the killer and the tentative schedule of coming events. I said solemnly to my friend, "Frank, we are history teachers; we can't stay here when history is being made just 200 miles away." Frank was deliberate in his response. "Let's see what the arrangements are and see if we can get there and back without missing school." I replied gravely, "To hell with school, we've got to go, period." He nodded in his wise way, and we started to make plans. He called his friend Nate Cohen, who he knew had similar interests and passions, and the three of us made our way to our nation's capital in Mr. Caterini's new Cadillac convertible. The final funeral plans had not been made, but we knew Kennedy would be laid out for public viewing in the rotunda of the Capitol Building. We arrived before dawn.

We weren't sure how the process would work or where the tens of thousands of people would line up to view the casket or where they would be allowed to enter. As the morning wore on, we kept trying to gather intelligence on these important matters. Finally, I had a chat with a friendly Capitol policeman, and he told me where the line would form. I shared the information with Nate and Frank, and we began our vigil that would last for the next several hours. We started by planting ourselves on the curbing where we thought the line might start. The area was a beehive of activity as masses of humanity were pouring in from every direction, literally surrounding the Capitol grounds. Barricades were being erected, and ropes cordoned off various areas as gaggles of men in uniform traversed the area. Every military service was in evidence, along with Capitol police, District police, police on horseback, and motorcycle cops, and all of them seemed to have a mission. Lines were beginning to form in several locations, but we were resolute in our decision to stay where we were, believing as we did in the accuracy of what we had been told.

It was now early afternoon, and, except for bathroom breaks, we had stood the entire time in the sunny, but chilly, location where we had started. Rumors abounded, with a number of different notions of how the process of public viewing would commence. Dignitaries could be seen arriving, then being swallowed up in the huge building as they entered for their privileged opportunity to pay last respects. Some in the line behind us had portable radios, and the news crackled over them that Oswald had been shot in Dallas. To this point, the massive crowd had been eerily quiet, although it is hard to imagine such a huge collection of people being so reserved out of respect. But the Oswald news sent waves of murmurs through the crowd, and an occasional, "Good, I hope the bastard dies!" could be heard.

Finally, a cordon of uniforms presented themselves right in front of us and began to link arms in two parallel lines about 6 feet across from each other. The linked men that began to our front stretched across the courtyard and up the Capitol steps. We were ecstatic when the tall uniformed man at our end counted off the first 25 and told us to proceed into history. Yes, indeed, we were among the first 25 members of the public to view the flag-draped coffin containing the lost leader of a grieving nation. Later, the practice of small groups was abandoned, and just one continuous line filed by the President. The circle of velvet ropes was eventually extended from 5 feet to 25 feet from the casket, so we were lucky to have been among those permitted to stop and kneel in homage just five feet from JFK.

We emerged, in tears, on the rear portico of the Capitol, looking down to the Washington Monument and the Lincoln Memorial beyond, fully aware of the historic importance of what we were experiencing. At that moment, I loved my country to a greater depth than ever before or since. We headed to the car but didn't get more than five miles out of the District before I asked Frank to pull over. Overwhelmed by the events of the previous 24 hours, I leaned out the window and vomited. We returned to Wildwood immediately, changed men. We had bonded forever.

I believe that we grew up at an accelerated pace after that day, a little more serious and thoughtful than we had been before. I wrote a piece for our school newspaper describing our experience and reflecting on the death of the President and its impact on our nation. Frank and I were both starting to think about graduate school, and I was getting ready to start a family. Frank was also facing the prospect of going to Viet Nam. With all of the changes, many Wildwood days were left, but they would be different than what had gone before.

My contract at Wildwood paid the generous sum of $4,600 per year, and that meant two things: I was clearing about $80 a week, and I was going to have to find part-time work if I hoped to "get on my feet," as my father-in-law had described the goal in our deal for the living quarters. Janis and I had ambitions of buying a home, and we agreed that graduate school was a prerequisite for advancing in the world of education. Jay Craven got me an assignment to referee basketball games at the recreation center, and I put in a lot of hours just monitoring the general activities. I worked a full daytime teaching schedule, two evenings at "the rec" and applied for the job as head baseball coach to boot, although "applied" might not be the correct word. Because baseball was a spring sport, many of the potential players were helping their parents ready their tourist businesses for the influx of summer business; therefore, baseball was less than a third-tier sport. As a result, they were desperate for a coach, a sacrificial lamb of sorts to head up the program. I needed the $300 extra, I loved baseball and I could always use the addition to my resume.

Indeed, by this time my resume was building. I was already a liquor store maven, a butcher, a cobbler's helper, a factory work-er, a union card holder (shipyard boilermaker), a referee, a coffee shop manager (thanks to the previous summer's three-week stint) and now a head coach. I was practically ready to head the United Nations. Excepting for occasional overnight visits to Camden, we were locked onto the island because of my work commitments. Summer was rapidly approaching, and Janis was heavy with child. Before Dean was to change our lives forever, I had to get a job in the job-rich environment of this summer tourist community.

Still watching over me, Frank made me an offer I couldn't refuse. He and his father saw some management potential in me and were totally secure in their assessment of me as honest and loyal, so I was offered a job at the Riptide Nightclub as manager of waitresses and service bartender. Not only would this be a great job, but it would once again expand my resume. My responsibilities included assigning tables to waitresses based on three important factors: the proven ability of the particular waitress to handle the number and locations of certain tables, the anticipated draw of the act that was playing (which impacted the complexity of the assignment) and, lastly, how respectfully the assignee treated me when she brought orders to the service bar. There was one other factor that was not spoken about, and that was whether bachelor Frank was hustling her or not.

The service bar was the hub of any nightclub business, and there was no other bar at the Riptide, since it was a table service business. Waitresses would bring orders to me in the large back room next to the "stars'" dressing room. I would have all the fixings and mix all the drinks, put them on a narrow counter in front of me, and off the girls would go to make the delivery. It was fast-paced, full of stress, like the job of a short-order cook at a busy diner, and great fun. I loved everything about it. I played my role to the hilt and took it seriously. I made process improvements and generally performed fine. Frank and John Caterini were very satisfied, and I was grateful.

Just imagine being 22 and not only entrusted with huge responsibility, but able to see all of the acts up close and personal. The summers of 1964 and 1965 were fantastic, the pinnacle of the Riptide. We had just about every hot act in show business. The small stage was graced with Fats Domino, Lloyd Price, Little Anthony and the Imperials, Frankie Lyman, The Shirelles, The Platters, Mel Torme, Wayne Newton and last, but not least, The Supremes. Fats Domino would always have me line up four shots of Scotch on my bar, which he downed one after another in machine gun fashion just before he was introduced. He would finish the last, turn to me and grin, "Ralph, ma man, you the best."

Diana Ross would want a good luck hug before she went on stage, and I obliged with pleasure. Wayne Newton patted Janis' belly, guessed it would be a boy, and said so on the 8 by 10 photo he autographed for her and Dean. I could not even begin to wonder what more a man could want, but, indeed, there would be more.

We had been looking for opportunities to buy a home on the island, knowing full well that the summer was an opportunity for the Zeccolas to make good on the investment at 310. There was no pressure being applied, but I was putting pressure on myself, that patience thing rearing its ugly head again. Then, a new development in Wildwood Crest provided the ideal opportunity, and 107 Pittsburgh Avenue became our new address. Pop and Mom Z lent us $300, which we added to the $700 we had saved to make the $1,000 down payment toward the purchase price of $12,400. We applied to Howard Savings and got our first mortgage, and for the large sum of $99.50 per month we had our piece of the American dream. The house was still under construction, and so was Dean. Dean was born at Burdette Tomlin Memorial Hospital in Cape May Court House on September 30, 1964, and we had all moved into 107 by the end of October. I continued to ask myself, "What more could a man want?" And I would continue to find out.

On the five-mile drive to the hospital for Dean's delivery by Dr. Fath in the pre-dawn hours, the Volvo interior was almost unable to contain our glorious anticipation. Our dreams were coming increasingly true as the miles ticked off. As was the practice of the day, I put Janis in the hands of a nurse upon our arrival and was told that, by the looks of things, I would have to wait awhile. I went to the Craven residence and awakened Toni with the news of the impending birth. The three of us enjoyed a breakfast together and, after my third call to the hospital, I announced the wonderful news that the first son of the first son of the first son of the DiSibios was born. Tears of joy welled in my eyes as I silently counted my blessings. I have ascended to the heights of corporate America; I have met Presidents and Princes and been in the presence of a Pope; I have won championships, had the adrenalin rush of motorcycling and skydiving; and I have beheld many momentous historical sites and moments. However, there is no elation that can compete with the feelings I had at that moment. None.

I went back to the hospital as sunlight was blanketing the island. Janis was angelic as she held our new son, this 18-inch, 7 pound, 15-1/2 ounce infant that gave true meaning to the phrase "bundle of joy." Janis gave me the assignment of making the obligatory phone calls to the many people awaiting the news, and I left the hospital to complete my first fatherly duties with the full realization that this would be the first day of a lifetime of new responsibilities. Dean forever changed everything about our lives.

Every holiday thereafter included packing up the portable crib and traipsing up to Camden; every meal centered on his habits; every extracurricular activity entailed the making of proper arrangements before and after for the new master of the house; every night was spent listening for his breathing and arranging him in a comfortable sleeping position. In sum, he dominated our lives. And we loved it.

My extended family was growing. Events around 3425 Westfield Avenue took on a routine. Vito had married the lovely Lynn Harkins and had beaten Janis and me by presenting Joe and Mary with a namesake, Joseph Zeccola. Joey was the first of three, followed by Danny and MaryKay. The lives of others were developing as well. Elaine had her hands full with the birth of Steven, while Pooky was turning out as many predicted, which is to say, not husband material. My mom and Johnny were enjoying marriage and had purchased a cute little white cottage on 42nd Street, just eight blocks from the Zeccola's. Johnny was moving up in the State Department of Transportation, as supervisor of signs, and Mom was still at Magnetic Metals. My dad had borrowed some cash from his lifelong pal, Sam Romano, and bought a fixer-upper in Somerdale, a suburb of Camden.

Dad was driving a huge dump truck for my godfather, the Italian contractor Pippi Galasso. Pippi had been in and out of my life and never really fulfilled his duties to step in, in the absence of my father, but he was always quick to offer my mother ludicrous advice about my upbringing: "The boy is out of control, you need to send him to Valley Forge Military Academy, they'll put some discipline into him." That was like telling a street bum that all he needed to do was to buy a new suit of clothes, get an education and get a job. Thanks for the help, godfather. Dad enjoyed the job working for Pippi, however, for a number of reasons, among them his ability to purloin materials for fixing up his fixer-upper.

The residences of Janis' parents, my father and my mother formed the triangle the Ralph DiSibios would travel for the next several years on our visits to Camden. From our headquarters at 3425, we would religiously visit the other parents, then make many visits to all of the relatives on both sides of our families. We loved to keep the ties close and were always warmly welcomed. We were surrounded with love.

Once again, Janis worked wonders with the new Wildwood Crest home. It was the same overall size of the 310 apartments combined, but we lived in the entire 20- by 40-foot home. It consisted of a small living room, a small kitchen, a tiny laundry room, three bedrooms and a bath. None of the bedrooms was more than 9 by 9, but we were used to that. I had made some modifications as the house was being constructed, including placement of the windows in the two back bedrooms directly in the corners of the building to allow for more uninterrupted wall space to accommodate furniture and the addition of custom bookshelves in the living room. These kinds of modifications—and many others—would be my hallmark in the many homes I was to purchase or build over the years. One problem remained with the Wildwood Crest residence in that the house, unlike 310, had no outside shed to hold any tools or garden items. My dad would soon remedy that deficit.

When I shared with my father my tale about the lack of a shed, he jumped at the chance to provide help, in one of the few ways he could. He told me he would come down the following Saturday morning and stay until the shed was finished on Sunday. He planned for a whirlwind construction schedule and assigned me the task of procuring the asbestos shingles and roofing shingles that would match the originals; he promised he would supply the rest of the required materials.

In addition to completing my assigned task, I ordered an 8 by 8 concrete pad to be laid in the center of the rear of the house and recruited Frank Caterini (again) to be a helper. Frank was highly challenged in the use of tools, a challenge which to this day has never been overcome; he was eager to lend a hand. While we shared a cup of coffee, Janis was preparing breakfast for the maiden visit of her father-in-law. We all heard the clatter of the big red truck as it turned the corner of Pittsburgh and Atlantic Avenues. The truck was bursting at the seams with all manner of materials; Frank and I were not surprised by the amount of material, but were shocked at the proportion of the items. Dad had "secured" a dozen sheets of four by eight plywood and studs for ceilings and walls, but all of these materials were designed for a huge warehouse, not for a house shed. The four-by-eights were three quarters of an inch thick, and the studs were all four-by-fours, instead of the quarter-inch plywood and two-by-four studs that could have been expected. We all had a laugh as Dad proudly remarked, "This baby will be standing after a hurricane knocks down the rest of the house."

The three of us worked on the task at hand like a well-oiled machine as the framing went up. The openings for the used 2-foot by 2-foot windows dad had brought to the job matched the ones I had designed for the house, and the massiveness of the studs made it look as though we were constructing a bomb shelter. That night, Jan made a great spaghetti dinner, and Dad honored her by downing about a half a pound of pasta, much to Frank's amazement. Exhausted, we agreed to take up tools again at 7 a.m. Frank left, and Dad engaged, uncomfortably, with his new grandson. I would say, "Dean, say 'hello' to Grandpop," and Dad would invariably respond, "Call me Uncle Tony." Dad didn't want the ladies to think him old enough to be a grandfather. That night, Dad was put in the middle bedroom on a fold-out sofa that we had salvaged from the curb a few weeks earlier. As I climbed into bed, I called out, "Goodnight, Pop," and I heard something I had longed for my whole life: "Good night, Butch." My father was here, and I wasn't scared.

Dad left Frank and me to finish the siding and roofing when he left about 2 p.m. on Sunday. He had shared with me his concern that Eleanor would get drunk in his absence and continue the fight that they had started when he told her of his plans to come down to help. This would mark the beginning of a shift in our relationship, as I moved from my role in our father-son relationship into becoming someone he could lean on for support. It also marked the last time we would share the same house together in slumber. I was 23, and he was 50, and he would have only six years left to live.

Together, Frank and I reached the conclusion that we should go on to get our Master's Degrees. Glassboro State College was 60 miles of back roads away and presented a challenge, but, undaunted, we enrolled in our first night class in the second semester beginning in January of 1965. This would mark an unbroken expanse of my continuing education that would last through 1974 with the bestowing of my doctorate. At times, it was a hassle and a burden, but, on balance, it was enjoyable, made the more so by Frank's company. Every trip to Glassboro seemed to have a story associated with it. Frank always reminds me of a driving maneuver that I executed to avoid a careening dump truck, and he counts this as a time I saved his life. I allow him to believe that, but, in truth, it was only a defensive reaction borne out of the survival instinct.

Of course, it was Janis who had to make the real sacrifice of doing without so that I could have tuition money and having me absent during the commutes and classes. I was oblivious to this, because it was all about me, a notion that was confirmed by everyone in both families, including Janis, as they heaped praise on me for my sacrifice and dedication. For now, Janis was comfortable in my shadow, sharing in my glory.

Life was good, Dean was healthy, Wildwood High was terrific, my part-time jobs were very enjoyable and Glassboro State gave me a mission. Frank and I continued to bond as we spent more time together. He would go to dinner with us, and we would learn much about gourmet foods and good wines. I was introduced to Rob Roy, not the Scot but the Scotch drink. Frank and I both signed up to direct the school plays, another resume builder, with a small monetary reward. We coached midget football, at no charge, and were all-around contributors to the youth of the community. At the time, I could not imagine ever leaving the island. As it turned out, not only did I finally imagine leaving, but I actively sought to make it happen.

Dominick Mancia became the Principal of our high school at the end of our second year of teaching. Dominick had been the Assistant Principal in charge of student discipline and had done a fine job in that role; but in his new position, he gave me my first real taste of "The Peter Principle" (or, perhaps, in this case, "The Peter Principal"). This principle holds to the theory that over time every employee will rise to his level of incompetence. And, sure enough, when Mancia was made Principal, he had fulfilled the prophecy.

This was also the genesis of several lessons in leadership that I later chronicled. The same talents that made Dominick a good assistant made him atrocious as a principal: he treated the teachers just the way he treated students, with the same distrust, condescension and disdain; he was ever suspicious and wary of the motivations of, first, the students and, then, the teachers. Teacher morale plummeted, a general pall fell over the school, and it was no longer exciting and stimulating to come to work. It became a job instead of a calling or a passion. Frank and I attempted to use the proper channels for initiating change, but to little avail, and I began to think about leaving the district; I could feel my impatience tugging at my sleeve. I was doing well in grad school, and my eyes were being opened to numerous opportunities in education, but outside of the classroom. Meanwhile, things were going from bad to worse at Wildwood High School.

I had witnessed Mancia take Polaroid pictures of the graffiti in the boy's room in an effort to find the culprits through careful handwriting comparisons. I considered sending him two steel ball bearings, al la Captain Queeg, but thought better of it. The tipping point occurred with an incident involving not me, but Frank. Frank was the faculty sponsor of a school yearbook that included several captions, some with clever double-entendres under teacher's pictures. These were not edited out and Mancia was furious. He berated Frank for his failure to catch the indiscretions and went on to tell Frank that next year he, Mancia, would personally approve every caption. To Frank's credit, he stood up and announced his resignation from the extracurricular post. Mancia demanded a reason, and Frank made a profound statement that I have always admired and often quoted: "I demand the right to make a mistake, and you have taken that away from me." Unfortunately Mancia did not understand the subtlety. From that day to this, I always gave employees the right to make a mistake. Today, it's called empowerment.

I wasn't a quitter. I decided to promote myself out of WHS and began to apply for graduate fellowships and assistantships all around the East Coast. There was no internet in those days, so I was limited to research at Glassboro and the ads in the New York Times. Finally, I chanced upon an ad for an internship for a Media Specialist at John Carroll University. John Carroll had a fine reputation, and I thought I could compete for the slot. There was only one problem: I didn't know what a media specialist was. I did some research and found that this was an up-and-coming specialty in the multimedia approach to education. It combined the library, the audio-visual department, the explosive expansion of TV news and fledging computer technology. I, of course, thought, "How tough can that be?" I constructed an exaggerated resume highlighting my play directorship, my experience showing films and film clips to my history classes and every other possibly relevant thing that might make me attractive. I was surprised to receive a letter of appointment, and I announced to the world that I was honored to get this scholarship, which would lead to a Master's Degree in Educational Media. I promoted myself out of Mancialand.

Frank chose to stick it out, for the next 30 years until he retired from Wildwood High School as the Director of Special Services, only to be called back as Acting Principal in 2004. He made a lasting contribution. I, on the other hand, did not have the patience. The truth was, I had no idea of how the next year at John Carroll would go or how to answer a variety of questions that Janis asked. Mom and Pop Zeccola were once again proud of me, and they invited us to live with them over the summer so I could earn the additional funds necessary to supplement the meager stipend I had been awarded by John Carroll. We rented the house to cover the mortgage and made our way once again to 3425, this time in preparation for a September move to Cleveland and the University.

However, the Fellowship was not to be. As fate would have it, I fell from scaffolding while installing asbestos on the USS New Jersey at the New York Shipyard, where I had gotten a summer job. Many days in traction in the West Jersey Hospital depleted my modest supply of cash and forced me to put in applications for teaching in the Camden area. Gloucester City, here I come. Running scared, but coming.

20
Aunt Marie

*Aunt Marie and Uncle Mid were a classic couple,
as this picture portrays; the union of the two would result
in an enviable family within a family.*

Aunt Marie

"Marie did not have an easy life for the first couple of decades of marriage. As Aunt Anna took in father Mario, so Aunt Marie took in both of the elder Marianis, giving her duties that lasted for over a decade."

AUNT MARIE, OR MARIA, WAS THE LAST of the 10 children born to Teresa and Mario Monarca. While Lola was beautiful in the 1930's sense, Marie was the undisputed modern beauty, the one who easily held the title of most beautiful of the young girls. As the youngest of the clan, she was going to carve out a different life for herself if she was to be independent, because it was Marie who had to suffer the advice of all of the siblings who came before her. While Anna could be second-guessed, Marie would be second-, third-, fourth-, fifth-... and ninth-guessed by all the older children. As it turned out, Marie would be different from her siblings—and very similar to her parents—in the decisions she made and the lifestyle she chose.

Her first three sisters married men who were happy to relinquish leadership. The two sisters closest to her in age married "modern" American boys of fair skin. Marie would be different from all of that. All of the sisters established homes within shouting distance of the Monarca headquarters at 734; Marie would be different. All of her siblings would stop having children after one or two offspring; Marie would be different. All of her siblings would have bold ambitions to acquire the accoutrements of modern life, including better homes and cars; Marie would be different. All of her siblings would escape the confines of Camden, as the neighborhoods began to be dominated by people of color; Marie would

RUNNING SCARED • RALPH DISIBIO

be different. Her siblings paid partial attention to Catholicism, by going to Mass and sending their children to parochial schools; Marie would be different. Her siblings' offspring would flee the nest, seek adventure and often avoid family traditions; Marie's offspring would be different.

The Monarca family left Jamesville to seek a better life in industrial Camden, living for a time on 3rd Street in South Camden before settling at 734. Marie returned to 3rd Street with her husband, and they remained for decades. The youngest and most modern of the Monarcas found her mate in a polar opposite, Emidio Mariani, who was decidedly of the old school. While born in America of Southern Italian parents, much of the traditions and culture of the motherland were transferred to him. He may have seemed at first blush an unlikely match for the tiny, modern Marie; in truth, however, it was a match made, if not in heaven, then in Italy.

Emidio, aka Mid, was rustically handsome, with his deep black curly hair and a smile that could charm even the coldest heart. He had a swagger about him when he walked and a husky timbre to his voice when he spoke. He was a man's man. It was hard for Aunt Marie not to fall in love with his appealing combination of rugged good looks and boyish charm. In his strength and confidence, he reminded her of her beloved brother Phil, while his warmth and charm were reminiscent of her brother Mike. While the sisters born earlier married men who reminded them of father Mario, and still others rebelled against the Italian image, only she and Dora would be attracted to men with the attributes of their brothers.

Emidio Mariani won the hand of Maria Monarca after a whirlwind courtship. The older females in the family whispered to one another that Mid might turn out to be another Tony, recognizing that he was not of the same ilk as an Iannetta or a Vitagliano.

In fact, he was already showing signs of being the dominant member of that family, and it wasn't to their liking. But family attitudes had no impact on Maria; she loved Mid and, while she respected her sisters, she also saw how well her brothers got along with Mid. And, after all, she always knew that she was different. The wedding itself was celebrated at a gala formal affair. The DiSibios were represented, not only by my father and mother, but also by Uncle Mike and Aunt Lena, because the pretty Marie had been part of their wedding party years earlier.

Married life began on 3rd Street in South Camden, and, thus, Marie became the only girl not to live in North Camden near 734 headquarters. In this, once again, she was different. Aunt Marie became pregnant soon after the couple was joined in matrimony, and it seemed to some that she stayed in that condition for the next several years. Donna was the first of the Mariani children to be born to the veritable newlyweds, and she was followed by Teresa, Debbie, Emelia, Dominic and Emidio. In this too, Marie was different.

In looks, the firstborn, Donna, resembled both parents, and I have often said that at maturity she resembled Kim Novak. She had a sexy, raspy voice that made you think of Uncle Mid, but she was as sweet as Aunt Marie at her sweetest. Teresa has an Aunt Lola quality about her. While she can appear to lean towards naiveté, she can be profound in her insights of people. Debbie is, by solid consensus, the beauty of the group, with a political bent in the tradition of her mother. Emelia has an even raspier voice than Donna's, but not to the same extent as Uncle Mid. Nonetheless, Emelia is her father's daughter in her soft interior that often causes her to weep; like her dad, she can be brought to tears by a memory or a smile. Dominic was born after four girls, and that probably tells you much of what you need to know about him. His gender alone caused him to be idolized, as was Uncle Phil before him, and it is fortunate that he has led a life deserving of the adulation. Young Mid is the youngest, just like his mother was. And, like her, he has a special wisdom and portrays a definite style in his approach to life.

Each of Mariani offspring has been blessed with a spouse that accepts the uniqueness of the entire Mariani clan, and all of the kids now have kids of their own. With such a prolific group, it is not unusual to hear the annual Monarca picnic referred to as an offshoot of the Mariani picnic. I was never really close to the kids as they were growing up because of physical distance; like most of the cousins, I only saw the clan on holidays and at special events. Our love for one another, however, has not suffered as a consequence. I have even gotten to know some of the spouses; but I confess that I have a tough time remembering the names of all of the younger children, and when I do, I don't always keep the names of the parents straight. My love and loyalty for all of them is not diminished by these lapses.

Only Donna's husband, Sammy, has been incorporated into the activities of the cousins because of his age and relationship to Dr. Bob. Sammy, Bobby, Peppe, another friend of both of them, and I have shared some special times together. Bob always wanted to be Sammy when he grew up; Sammy is that kind of guy. There are those who might be put off by Sammy's flamboyance, but anyone who could see him alone with Dr. Bob, mentally and physically disabled by his stroke, could never question his generosity of spirit or loyalty. For his support of Bob, as well as other actions, Sammy will always have my respect. As for the spouses of all of the Marianis, I know every one is blessed with a special nature—after all, they all married well. Choosing these wonderful cousins as life partners shows they are smart, and lucky as well.

Marie did not have an easy life for the first couple decades of marriage. Handling six children would have been enough of a task, but there were additional burdens as well, since, almost from the outset, she was responsible for Uncle Mid's parents. As Aunt Anna took in father Mario, so Aunt Marie took in both of the elder Marianis, giving her duties that lasted for over a decade. When the elder Dominic Mariani died, the obligation for his care was replaced by the necessity of caring for the sister of the elder Mrs. Mariani. Thus, Aunt Marie had two of her in-laws for charges for many years.

Caring for these additional family members might not have been overwhelming, if it were not for the little Marianis being delivered with regularity and without respite. And if that were not enough, Marie was in a situation that required her to conduct herself like an old-fashioned Italian wife. She did not have the benefit of having married a man who would share the household duties, and, by necessity and by choice, she was as close as a modern wife could be to the Teresa of Jamesville.

Uncle Mid was not a cruel man, far from it. He was a loving son, a loving husband and a loving and devoted father; but, he was firm in his stubborn adherence to the culture of the old country. In that world, and later in his own, the woman was expected to take on responsibilities that a man was not to assume. It was the woman who not only bore the children, but tended to them, tended to her husband, cared for the elders who required such care, cooked the meals and served them, and generally handled everything that needed to be done inside the home. The man's role was to provide for the family outside the home. He brought his paycheck home, doled out allowances for family needs and made decisions.

Aunt Marie accepted her position without question and performed her role with little complaint. Still, even a casual observer would conclude that she had a hard life. Uncle Mid would help with his parents, also out of tradition, and played with the children and helped to keep them occupied from time to time, but that was about the extent of his assistance in the house. As the girls grew, they helped in minor ways, but they did not provide the relief that the Aunts had provided mother Teresa. While in Jamesville, there was little else to do; in South Camden, the streets offered the Mariani girls many distractions and attractions that had them finding excuses to escape the responsibilities of their mother. Despite the difficulties of Aunt Marie's life, however, it was full of love.

One thing she could look forward to were the visits from clan members from North Camden who came calling on occasion; but those visits became less frequent as the South Camden area turned more and more "colored." The change taking place in the neighborhood extended to 3rd Street, and the relatives from the north, more used to a segregated environment, were nervous parking out of sight of the Mariani home. But this cultural change in South Camden did not ruffle Uncle Mid, and I never heard the kids complain.

Uncle Mid had a moving business which gave him a living adequate to provide for his family. I was always awed by the size of Uncle Mid's hands, looking as they did like hands that belonged to a much larger man. With these huge appendages, he would apply his considerable strength to lift heavy pieces of furniture onto his large moving truck. And it was not just for his business that he did this; that truck and the strength of Uncle Mid to load it enabled him to carry scores of goods for Cousin Joey, my family and many more Monarcas, when desire or necessity prompted a move. He was a loyal and generous brother-in-law and uncle, often hiring Joey or others to help him out in an effort to allow them to earn some much-needed extra money. Few of the helpers would return for a second day of the hard labor that Uncle Mid, tireless provider that he was, endured every day.

Eventually, Uncle Mid made the decision to extricate the family from what was an increasingly hostile environment in South Camden. The rest of the Monarca clan had often given Uncle Mid the unsolicited advice that this was what he should do, but he didn't make the decision until he was ready. The Marianis moved to a large home on the White Horse Pike in Collingswood, just one mile from the Camden city limits, the first that they themselves, as opposed to the in-laws, owned. The home was not in perfect condition, but was repairable, and it would be under repair for several years. Cousin Joe likened it to the constant construction on Admiral Wilson Boulevard. Uncle Mid had his own pace, but, in time, this headquarters for the Marianis was complete.

By the time the Marianis arrived in Collingswood, the moving was no longer the primary source of income. As if she had time to spare, Aunt Marie had become a political operative, relentless in ensuring the election of many local politicians. For these efforts, she was rewarded with cushy jobs in City Hall, and Uncle Mid became a toll collector on the Ben Franklin Bridge, a coveted political plum.

For the first time in her adult life, Aunt Marie was freed from many of the tasks that had come from being surrounded by offspring and in-laws, and she and Uncle Mid settled into a life of mutual respect. The sons and daughters, all hardworking and kind, grew into adults worthy of the Mariani/Monarca bloodlines. Not one among the six could be described as lazy, brash or cruel. No description of this family unit would be complete without mentioning the fact that they displayed an inordinate amount of love for one another and great respect for their parents, and there was no event that better captured this than the obligatory Sunday spaghetti meal at home base.

Every Sunday, for as long as Aunt Marie and Uncle Mid were together on the White Horse Pike, automobiles would pull into the long driveway on the side of the house that fronted the Pike in a seemingly unending stream. The activity began soon after the 11:00 mass concluded, as the kids, accompanied by their spouses or dates, and all the grandchildren arrived amidst a flurry of hugs, kisses and greetings. Conversation always centered around inquiries about health, pregnancies, schools and the events of the past week.

Uncle Mid would invariably have established himself at the south end of a huge dining room table that had been purchased for events just like these. In his usual Sunday attire, a sleeveless undershirt and black slacks and white socks, he would already have had a glass or two of Chianti that would hasten his tears when his grandchildren came to hug him. Aunt Marie would be perspiring over the gravy in the small kitchen, stirring the meatballs and sausage. The boys would gravitate to the portable TV that sat atop the unworkable console TV in the living room to watch the NFL game. The girls, of course, set the table and tended the kids. It was a scene full of love and respect that was repeated every Sunday. Relatives, along with occasional strangers, would arrive without invitation and be treated without ceremony, but as members of the inner family. This ritual was the embodiment of "family," and the rest of the Monarcas looked upon it with curiosity and envy.

As I reflect on the Marianis, I cannot help but liken them to the original Monarca clan, even with all of Marie's individual differences. She was different, not only because she was famous for saying aloud what others only thought, but for many other reasons as well. Deeply religious, she cared little for luxuries and cared even less what others thought of her attire or her sometimes outrageous behavior—that very same behavior that never failed to bring laughter to her uncommunicative sister Dora in the nursing home. She was also different in knowing her strengths and weaknesses, and she was comfortable with them. She was different because she became more like her mother than any of the rest.

Teresa kept her children close to her, and Marie kept her children close to her, as well. Teresa had 10 children, when those around her were having fewer; Marie had six children, while none of her nine siblings ever had more than two. Teresa tended to her family with no assistance, save a paycheck, from Mario; Marie went beyond Teresa in this regard by adding the in-laws to the coterie that needed to be cared for. Teresa was relentless in teaching her children the morals and values that were part of a civilized society; Marie was equally diligent in passing her values on to her children. Teresa was consistent in the example she set with a life modestly lived; Marie was consistent in setting all manner of examples for her children to follow. There is not much doubt that Marie was most like Teresa.

The result of all of this is that the Marianis are most like the original Monarcas. Devoted to their parents, respectful of their elders, loving and protective of one another, bound to and by tradition, they remain close to the nest and to each other, taking true enjoyment in one another's company. Each has no apparent jealousy of the successes of others; indeed, they all grieve the tribulations of the others. The six of them are like the 10 Monarcas, full of love and commitment to family devotion. God was wise when he waited until the last of the original Monarcas to plant the seeds of the new Monarcas. Marie was different because she was the same.

21

12,500 Archie Bunkers

*I loved teaching and the automatic respect it provided. I was
serious about having an impact on my students.*

12,500 Archie Bunkers

"That night, as I was sitting at the kitchen table at 3425 with pencil and paper, analyzing the figures and the down payment requirements, Mom sat quietly next to me with her little jewelry box."

W E MOVED BACK INTO THE MIDDLE BEDROOM at 3425 Westfield Avenue, where Dean took up the tiny back bedroom next to the bath. Mom and Dad Z didn't blink an eye; I, for my part, had reached an accommodation, without compunction, to pay $200 a month room and board. As the summer drew to a close and I received offers from both Pennsauken and Gloucester City to join their staffs, I settled on Gloucester City. In my last year at Greeley, I had received an NDEA loan from Uncle Sam, thanks to Joe the Barber's having read about this possibility in U.S. News and World Report. The terms allowed for the loan to be repaid by giving teaching service to a disadvantaged school district; since Gloucester met the criteria and Pennsauken did not—and since I was always thinking—I knew what to do. Jan and I needed more space, so we began to search for a new home, as I was taking on a new job.

With Mom and Johnny living a comfortable life on 42nd Street, I was delighted that she was finally being treated as an equal by her siblings; you could almost feel her satisfaction at no longer being the object of sympathy. Regrettably, Elaine had assumed that unwelcome role, as her life with the ne'er-do-well Pooky had taken on a dark side of large proportions. The Binders were living in the projects, and Pooky was engaging in nefarious activities with his brother, Chicky, while Elaine played the parts of a lioness protecting her young and a long-suffering wife trying to change her man. These adversities never diminished her big heart or her unqualified loyalty to family and friends, but they did make her wary as a deer in hunting season when it came to all others. While others were prospering, she was struggling, and it was yet to get worse. Whereas others spoke of the silver lining behind the dark cloud, Elaine was coming to learn that "behind every dark cloud there is...a lot of rain."

Dad, Eleanor and, now, little Tony were living in Somerdale. Dad was doing magical things to his tiny house, and his family swelled by yet one more when none of the other siblings would take Grandmom DiSibio and she moved in. It was an arrangement that added to the already escalating dysfunction of the household. There was a cycle to it, with Eleanor drinking, Dad exploding, Eleanor drinking, and Dad abusing her; and the beat—and the beatings—went on. Conversations with my father always included the latest details of these sordid battles.

The Monarcas otherwise progressed normally for the era. Johnny had graduated St. Joseph College and had gone on to get his law degree. Cousin Joe was busy expanding his family with Charlotte and was off to Thule, Greenland, to make some of that easy cash that Uncle Bob had made. Bobby was dating the lovely Judy and working for the Camden Health Department, thanks to the growing political connections of Aunt Marie. Tom and Jim were beginning their Western Kentucky years. And Phyllis and Frank had produced Frankie and Angel. Everyone was focusing on their own families, but the Monarca links were maintained and strengthened by the visits during each holiday and at special events and functions, with regular contact facilitated by all the weddings, showers, funerals and christenings. Because of my own accomplishments,

I had no cause to feel inferior and, in fact, along with the rest of the family, derived great joy in the many achievements of the new generation.

The 1966-67 school year started at Gloucester City High School with a cadre of rookies that had me among them. Gloucester City itself was somewhat of an anachronism. Lying at the southern border of Camden and against the Delaware River, the city should have been a hub of industrial activity. Instead Gloucester City served more as a veritable labor pool, as it provided workers to the industrial giant to its north and to Philadelphia across the river. The city clung to its all-white, mostly Irish, population—and continues to do so, long after the disappearance of segregation in the South.

Gloucester City's reputation for bigotry and exclusivity, of sorts, was, thus, well-deserved. It was reserved for the blue-collar, tough-talking, hard-working, lower and lower-middle classes. It prided itself on continuing to be almost incestuous in its institutions and politics, and its inhabitants were distrustful of strangers who dared to continue down Broadway beyond the Camden city limits, particularly if the strangers were of color. And they made no bones about it. Upon institution of the national Martin Luther King holiday, when every school in the region was closed for this new observance, Gloucester remained open. When the Courier-Post called to get this comment on why the school was open, the assistant principal gave them a comment, "Why are we open? It's Tuesday, ain't it? We're always open on Tuesday." This was to be my place of employment for the next decade.

God help me, I grew to love Gloucester City. Ya gotta love 'em, I guess. While the racial attitudes were repugnant and reprehensible, some of the other core values embraced by the citizens, as much an anachronism as the city, were refreshing. They were loyal, compassionate, warm, given to respect for authority, protective, patriotic and loving. I would be remiss if I didn't mention that they could also be cold, crude, combative, unforgiving and clannish. In an era when parents might bring a lawyer to other schools to demand better treatment for a pampered child, things were different in Gloucester. When a Gloucester student was sent home, say because the teacher didn't like the T-shirt the kid was wearing, the student would return with a clean shirt and a lump on his head. What part of Gloucester you got depended on what you gave. I gave her my best.

I maintained the pattern I had established at Wildwood High by associating with a clique of brash and witty fellow rookies that included Jim Kelly, Paul Gibbs, Diane Lusk, Kathy Malan and Ron Pritchett. I loved the classes I taught and the free time spent in the smoke-filled teachers' lounge as well, sharing views with my like-minded circle of co-workers. We all respected our profession and ridiculed teachers who were too lazy to work hard at the job. We were also ever the wise guys. When the New Jersey lottery began, it was the buzz of the day, and when one of the laziest of the corps was asking everyone in the lounge what they would do if they won the multi-million dollar first prize, he got a surprising answer from me: "I would buy the school and fire your ass!" Such was the state of our juvenile humor. But, I continued to engage in extra duties to earn cash, and soon was responsible for the school play and began to help Jim Kelly with the baseball team.

Not long after the school year began, Janis and I found a dream home at 108 Champlain Road in the Woodstream development in Marlton. We had discovered Woodstream on a trip to visit Aunt Pat, who was very content in Marlton and often told us of her satisfaction. Janis and I both fell in love with the development, but not for the first time, we felt we could not afford the huge asking price of $16,900. Still, we could not wait to bring Mom and Dad Z to see what we had found. Pop was, in his usual way, wise in his advice. "If you think you can stretch to barely make the mortgage and you want this house, you should buy it." He went on to give me his logic, explaining that I would continue to make more money, but the mortgage would stay the same. So, the sacrifice would lessen with each passing year and, in the meantime, the home would appreciate as an investment. I would impart the same sage advice to Dean and Doreen many years later.

That night, as I was sitting at the kitchen table at 3425 with pencil and paper, analyzing the figures and the down payment requirements, Mom sat quietly next to me with her little jewelry box. She opened the box and took out a little stack of money. She handed it to me, saying, "Here is the $800 you gave us for room and board. You can use it to help with the down payment. Pop and I want you to have it." There were tears in my eyes then, as there are now as I write this. I thanked her and kissed her on the cheek. She rose and curtly said, "Don't worry about it." And that was the last mention that was made of this generosity. We bit the bullet and, by November, were ensconced in our new home.

Life was glorious in Woodstream, where we lived in our little bi-level that represented the latest in home design. The development offered a two-story, a tri-level and the economy bi-level that barely fit our meager budget. But it was ours. Its name came from the way that the house was laid out, in effect as a single-story home with a full basement, but with the basement above-ground and able to be fully used as part of the home. You entered the home on a landing. If you went up four steps you found yourself in the living room that you could see from the landing through the wrought iron railing; if you went down four steps, you were in a recreation room, with a door leading to a fenceless back yard.

The upper level consisted of a large living room that opened onto a dining room, next to which was a fully equipped eat-in kitchen. Down a hallway were three bedrooms and a full bathroom. On the lower level, off of the rec room, were a powder room, a utility room and a single garage. The upper level was just a little bigger than the Wildwood Crest home, and the lower level was half again as big. To us, the house was humongous. We had never had a garage, a recreation room, extra bathroom or a big back yard. We had died and gone to heaven in Marlton.

We discovered in time that the bricks and mortar that made up the house did not begin to match the permanence of the life-long friends we developed in our new neighborhood. When we looked out, through the rear window, we could see a two-story home directly behind ours and another just to the left of it. These homes were separated from ours by large expanses of lawn, unobstructed by fences. A full 60 feet separated the rear exits of the houses, constituting a vast playground of turf. Whoever said that good fences made good neighbors was wrong. We could not have invented better neighbors.

Jack and Marie Ziegler occupied the house just behind us, and Phil and Naomi Lippincott were just next door to them. Dean made quick friends with the Zieglers' Johnny and the Lippincotts' Grant. Eventually, the families would grow, as the bond between all the adults and the affection they had for one another grew as well. Jack and Marie had two additional sons, David and Robbie, and a daughter, Suzie, while Phil and Naomi added Kevin and Kerry to their own family. The lives of the DiSibios, the Zieglers and the Lippincotts would intertwine for lifetimes, enduring through celebrations, weddings, funerals, moves, divorces, grandchildren, career changes and every other life experience. I have been greatly enriched by the unconditional friendship and love of these fine people.

Back in Gloucester City, I continued to hone my teaching skills. I was also making the weekly trek down to Glassboro State, fulfilling the requirements for a Master's Degree. Thanks to Jim Kelly, I was earning extra money as a basketball referee for the Catholic Youth Organization, and this, combined with holidays at Uncle Al's liquor store and my base pay of $6600 per year and the $300 extra for assuming duties as Kelly's assistant on the baseball team, allowed us to become a two-car family. Janis was now driving a 64 Corvair. All I needed now was a summer job, and an ad in the Courier-Post presented just the opportunity.

Ever since my days in Wildwood, I was in the habit of perusing the want ads, thinking that one day I would find a description of the perfect job just for me. "Wanted: Young Italian-American male for executive assistant to the CEO; duties include handling all manner of exciting problems and supervising others. Must have street smarts, a BA degree, and some graduate work and have extensive experience in dealing with the public. Ability to fight with fists and drive cars fast in reverse is a plus." I didn't find exactly that ad, but I did find one that was close enough: "Wanted: Manager of several swim clubs, experience required, summer only." Okay, so I didn't have any experience, but how tough could this be?

I called my old friend and guardian angel Frank Caterini, whose family now owned a large motel in the heart of Wildwood. The motel had a pool. Problem solved. Frank created a grand letter extolling my virtues as an expert manager of the pool facilities and the staff. He used words with which I was unfamiliar, like backwash and sand filtration system, but I could see that the recommendation was very well written. Armed with his glowing words about my skills, I went for my interview with the owner.

Using my Lake Worth experience, I told him I had training as a Water Safety Instructor, never mind that I had only been 8 years old at the time, and Frank's endorsement of my competencies and my confident banter landed me the position. I became the manager of two apartment pool complexes and a private swim club located in Kresson. I quickly interviewed the returning workers and put the most experienced among them in charge of all of the filtration systems. I now had my first staff, and they preformed well. Of course, I recruited Natale to be my assistant. Again, life was good.

The winning team of Natale and me also propelled me into the management of the Woodstream Swim Club during the following two summers. At Woodstream, Natale was the head of the swim team and pretty much ran the staff, while I handled the board of directors, scheduling and payroll. I got $2000 per season, and I paid Natale $1500. We were enjoying ourselves and were both gaining valuable experience while we were at it. When September rolled around, I was more than ready to get back to the classroom and my winter routine.

Things at 108 Champlain Road were rather idyllic. We were happy, even though I spent much of my time working two jobs and taking classes at Glassboro. Janis continued to contribute by building a small clientele of relatives whose hair she cut and styled. My own mom was happy, although Dad's life was contaminated by his marriage, and his troubles were exacerbated by signs of deteriorating health. I would get calls from him almost nightly complaining of health or relationship issues. I was the only one he could talk to, and I would often interrupt our meals and drive the eight miles to his house to settle him down. As winter deepened, Janis announced she was expecting another child. A new bundle of joy would be delivered in September, and we were overjoyed.

I had been applying for grants so that I could attend graduate school in the summer to accelerate my degree work, plagued once again by my own impatience. Mom and Dad Z were planning a trip to Italy, and Jan had been scheduled to go with them; I had agreed to take care of Dean so she could avail herself of this unique opportunity. The pregnancy meant that there would be no trip for her, so I was free to expand my search for a summer grant. I was accepted at three universities with a small stipend, and one of the offers was unusual, to say the least.

In a fit of fancy, I had applied to the Johns Hopkins University Center for International Studies in Bologna, Italy. The application had a quick turnaround time and a requirement for a letter of recommendation from my department chairperson that would highlight my potential for future advancement and predict how this course in International Relations and Economics would aid in my future. Mrs. Jameson, the head of my department, was on leave during the time I needed to fulfill the recommendation requirement, so, undeterred, I "borrowed" an official piece of school stationery and proceeded to write what I hoped would be her thoughts about me and my value to the program. The result was a somewhat fictionalized, but quite glowing, rendition of what I had already contributed to the school and, of course, what I was likely to contribute in my future as a budding principal or superintendent. The words were prophetic and, in any case, helped to get me accepted.

Once again, this time somewhat reluctantly, Janis agreed that this was an opportunity I should not pass up, notwithstanding the fact that my scheduled return would be just three weeks before the predicted delivery of our child. Once again, I was universally lauded and applauded for this latest honor, and Janis received little notice of her far greater sacrifice. My shadow was getting longer, and perhaps darker.

After visits to my mom, who was bursting with pride, my father, who was fighting a mysterious illness diagnosed as a hiatal hernia, and assorted other relatives, I was Italy-bound. If Colorado was a mystery in 1959, Bologna was a mystery wrapped in an enigma in 1969. But off I went with my usual approach to the challenges that might lie ahead: "How tough can this be?" I arrived in Rome to await the start of classes some eight days hence. My early arrival, as well as my delayed departure eight days after the classes ended, was due to the cheap charter airfare I was able to get. In Rome, I was enthralled—as an Italian, as a student of history and as a human being. I couldn't get enough of it.

While there, I happened upon a ubiquitous street hustler by the name of Lorenzo Fontana, who was to become my Italian guardian angel, and we formed an unusual bond. I ended up staying in Lorenzo's apartment for my last two days, as he regaled me with stories of his exploits as a man who preyed on mostly female tourists, who kept him in the manner to which he had become accustomed. He helped me find the right transportation to Canale Montorano, where Aunt Louise was visiting from the States and where I slept in the same room my great-great-grandmother had slept in. It was wondrous and wonderful. Finally, Lorenzo put me on the train to Bologna, home of the oldest University in the world.

Bologna, a city of incredible beauty and mystique, is also the gastronomic and educational center of Italy. It lies between Venice and Florence in the center of the country, and its porticoed walkways and lavish architecture are world-renowned. Everything grand that can be said about this great city is true. I was in awe of it from my first day, as I made my way from the train station to the University Center occupied by Johns Hopkins, and it was here that I met my next guardian angel. I had made inquiries of the receptionist as to the schedule and such, and as I sat in the small snack bar with a glass of wine, a young man sat next to me and said, "So, have you found a place to stay yet?" I looked in the direction of the guy with the New Jersey accent and replied, "No, what part of Jersey you from." Thus began a friendship that continues to this day.

Ron Verdicchio was one of the 20 students accepted to this elite and rigorous program. He was from Ridgefield, New Jersey, but was finishing up a teaching assignment at the United States Military Schools. At the time of our meeting up, he was teaching in Amsterdam. Ron had a VW and a permanent pass to any post exchange on U.S. military bases in Europe, and he was an all-around cool guy. We hit it off from the get-go, and then hooked up with Irv Hanson, a married teacher in the military schools who was teaching in Germany. I had managed to team up with these two, both Americans but sophisticated in European ways, and I was a quick and grateful student. Instead of a room in a hotel or convent, we lived on the economy. We rented a three-bedroom apartment at #5 Piazza Volta, and the place not only housed us in splendor but became the venue of choice for the parties hosted by the University for visiting dignitaries engaged to speak. We studied hard and never missed a class, but we partied heartily also.

Each week we would visit a different location, to see Italy but also to visit one PX or another to stock up on gin at $3 a bottle and cartons of cigarettes at $2 apiece. We camped out in the tent and with the supplies that Irv had in his Renault station wagon and went to the beaches at Rimini or to San Remo. One weekend, we went to Lake Garda near Verona and attended a performance of the opera Aida with Leontyne Price performing the lead role. The performance was held in the world-famous Verona Amphitheater, which is similar to the Roman Coliseum. We got the best tickets for $3 each, and we followed the lead of the locals, we thought, by bringing wine and snacks to the event. Unfortunately, we were not sitting in the grandstands on the stone steps with the other peons with wine; rather, our $3 had us sitting with operagoers in gowns and tuxedoes and bedecked in jewels. In the beginning, we were embarrassed in our jeans, until the true Italian live-and-let-live tradition took over, as everyone around us accepted our offers to share our wine and cheese. We had a night to remember that was eclipsed by only one other night in Italy, and that was when we watched the brave Americans landing on the moon and planting the Stars and Stripes in the middle of the night of July 20th. I was never more proud to be an American, and not since viewing the JFK casket with Frank had been I more conscious of witnessing history in the making.

The classes ended with a successful final exam, and I still had a week to kill before I would return to my own long-suffering wife and beautiful baby boy. Ron and I decided on a great adventure. We drove the VW to the dark side, traveling into communist Yugoslavia at a time when Americans were the enemy. It all felt very cloak-and-dagger. We visited Rijeka and Split and stayed two nights in Bakar before we had to retrace our steps through Trieste and back to Bologna, where I hopped on a train to Rome. The people in the country were as warm and welcoming as the border guards were cold and menacing. Thirty years later, I would return to build a power plant in Zagreb and tell the tale of my pre-democracy visit, which never failed to foster a conversation.

I easily survived the excruciatingly long flight that arrived at JFK Airport, but I was exhausted and had made no plan as to how I was going to find my way home. I was nervous as I went through Customs and exited the metal doors of the international arrival terminal. Hundreds of people, waving signs to welcome travelers or to identify limousine services, greeted the incoming passengers. Suddenly I heard the cry, "Ralph, Ralph, over here!" An old guardian angel was beaming at his success in catching my attention. I later told him, quite truthfully, that I had never been so happy to see a friend's face in my entire 28 years. Frank Caterini and I embraced, as he helped me with my gear and led me to his 1968 Mercury convertible. He dropped the top, and we departed the lot and headed to Marlton. We were both in good spirits as Frank reminded me that I had written him with my proposed schedule, so he took the chance that he could spot me at the exit. What a guy! We continued to laugh as, now safely through Customs, I emptied my pockets of six switchblade knives and a pistol. My friend Lorenzo had secured the pistol for me; the knives were obtainable in any hardware store, but they were treasured contraband for Vito, my Dad, Natale, Frank and Cousin John. I, of course, still prize the remaining one. Frank and I still laugh at my courage and stupidity.

I got back just three weeks before the blessed event. Doreen Lynn DiSibio was born in the early afternoon of September 11, 1969. If Dean hadn't already changed our lives enough, she was about to fix that. Not merely a bundle of joy, she was a bundle of unbridled joy. While Dean was unusually obedient, she challenged us at every turn. But the timing of the two and their genders could not have been designed with more perfection. I had always thought that it would be ideal to have a boy first, then four to five years later have a girl. My vision was that the boy could help tend to the little nipper, and as he finished high school and college he would guide and protect her by teaching her all of the tricks of survival. Dean was a willing teacher, but Doreen, the student, was often absent, as she was off becoming her own delightful person. At two, she was marching around the table of an Italian restaurant belting out "Me and Mrs. Jones, Mrs. Jones, Mrs. Jones" in a performance worthy of Ethel Merman. Precocious is too tame a word for this little girl. She was, and still is, the life of every party.

In the meantime, Dean was growing into his elementary school self. He was cute beyond words, with his light eyes and bright blonde hair. He tended to pay attention to his elders and was often quite literal in his interpretation of directions. Once, when Janis spied him eying the peach juice remaining in the bottom of a small square Tupperware container, she anticipated what he had in mind and said, "Go ahead, you can drink the rest of it." He smiled and lifted the container, but hesitated as he tried to figure how he could drink from the square without spilling the contents. Once again, Janis answered his unasked question telling him to, "Drink it from the corner." Dean dutifully rose from his chair and headed to the front door with the container. Puzzled, Janis asked him where he was going. Without skipping a beat Dean said, "I'm going down to the corner to drink it." The comment and his naiveté met with uproarious laugher from Jan and me.

Home was not the only place that Dean followed orders. We became concerned when he kept returning his lunch money to us every day and wanted to know why he wasn't having lunch. He said the teacher told him he wasn't allowed to eat lunch, but he could have milk. After much questioning that failed to resolve the situation, Janis visited school at lunch time. As the kids filed into the lunch room, a teacher was at the door to make things more efficient. One line was for the kids who were buying lunch and another for kids who brought lunch from home and only needed milk. The mystery was solved when Janis saw the teacher pointing as she announced to each kid who entered the lunch room, the following, "Milk only, milk only." Every time Dean came into the room, he thought he was being given an instruction. And that is probably one of the reasons he is a Colonel in the United States Army today: All great leaders are first great followers.

Everything in my life was coming up roses, with the exception of Elaine and my dad. Elaine continued to struggle with her marriage and now had three rambunctious boys, Billy, Steven and Brian, to contend with as well. They were cute as buttons, but, without a positive role model around, they were a handful. Pooky had changed residences, having "earned" the chance to be hosted by the State of New Jersey. Thanks to an armed robbery, he and Chicky were each sentenced to eight years in the State Prison at Trenton. I have no idea how Elaine made it through those years, and she has my abiding admiration for her efforts.

Much to my enduring shame, I did little to alleviate her troubles. I was focused on myself and my family and provided little in the way of support. I went with her to visit Pooky, speaking to him over a telephone receiver through a 2-inch-thick glass panel, and occasionally I lectured the boys on good behavior; but I did little else. The boys still provide a dramatic account of the time I reprised my father's performance after breaking his neon sign. I beat the boys with a piece of lumber, having discovered they had stolen a Zippo from a local store. I wept as I whacked them, screaming, "Do you want to go to prison like your father?" I shed tears with Aunt Lydia when Pooky was denied early parole and tried to visit Elaine at her home on High Street as often as possible, but, in truth, I was not much help. Nor was anybody else. Nevertheless, to her great credit, she survived that challenge and more.

The scars inflicted by Pooky's incarceration remain to this day, and each of his sons has dealt with the forced abandonment by their father in different ways. Billy has a personality to be envied, but is engaged in an everlasting search for stability, Brian is serious and reticent in giving love, except to his wife and beautiful daughters; and Steven raises his girls alone with the fervor of two. The story is often told of a time when Billy was in elementary school, and the teacher was asking each pupil to give his or her father's occupation. Billy replied, "My father is a crook." The teacher attempted to correct him, "You mean he's a cook." "No," Billy replied without a smile, "he steals things; he's a crook." Out of the mouths of babes.

The toxicity of Dad's relationship with Eleanor, meanwhile, continued to grow unabated. Contributing to the turmoil, he had gone through several jobs as the industrial base in Camden began to flee to the south and west. The shipyard was great in its time, and Dad got as much from the yard as any man. When he worked in the welding shop as an examiner for testing the skills of would-be welders, he allowed many of his friends to skate by with less than required scores. Due to his performance, I am sure there are ships in our Navy with substandard weld joints. When he applied for a guard's job, he fibbed on the form when he failed to disclose that he had done "time" in prison for bootlegging in the '30s; he figured that the authorities wouldn't need that information. It is the story of the transfer of his records to the new job that has become my favorite tale to illustrate his approach to life.

A little background is required. Once I was in college, he felt me worthy of filling out his tax returns. I would go to his house and ask questions, then fill out the papers. Every year after little Tony was born, he would instruct me to add another dependent to the form. When I warned him of the danger of such a deception, he first said "Just put it down; put Tony and my mother." Then, the follow-ing year, he added Elaine, and then Michael...and so on, never once heeding my warnings. When I told him he could get caught, he re-plied, "What are they going to do, come here and count them?"

So, then the time came for him to take the new job as a guard, which required that all of his records be transferred; he sat at a clerk's desk, as she perused his old records and began to transcribe the information onto new forms. There were the normal questions: Do you still live in Somerdale? Same phone number? She finally said, "I see here where you have eight dependents; will you give me their names?" His face took on a quizzical expression for a moment, and he began, "Well, there is Tony, Elaine, Domenica, Eleanor, Michael, Joseph and me, of course," he concluded with satisfaction. She looked at him, looked at the old records, and looked back at him again. "What happened to Marie?" she queried, as if she had found a discrepancy. He stared back at her and said gravely, with a quivering chin, "Oh, she died." The embarrassed worker intoned, "I'm so sorry." Dad was forgiving when he said, "Oh, that's okay, she is better off." Dad was rarely stuck for an answer.

When I returned from Italy in 1969, I found that my father's health was worse than when I had left. The nightly phone calls became more desperate, and my visits more frequent. After several months of seeking the cause of his maladies, he was finally diagnosed with coronary artery disease and told that the only solution was open-heart surgery. I begged the doctors to allow him to remain in the hospital until the surgery could be done, but the operation was scheduled for three weeks away, so that wasn't possible, and I knew that the constant battles in Somerdale would take their toll on his condition. By this time, he had to take two or three nitroglycerin pills every time he climbed a ladder, which he continued to do in his painting business. I was worried, without really knowing much about what this open-heart stuff was about; but I trusted that the doctors would fix him. In 1970, the bypass was still a relatively new procedure, and Dad was slated to have three of them on June 20th of that year.

I took him to Jefferson Hospital in Philadelphia the day before the operation. He received his brother Joe as his last visitor, then they said a quiet "so long," leaving me alone with my father. I helped him with his shower, followed by two nitro pills. I tucked him into bed, and we chatted a bit. He knew he wouldn't be coming back to this particular room, so he gave me his personal possessions for safekeeping. When he gave me his checkbook, he explained that he had about $5000 in the account and wanted to be sure I did not give the book to Eleanor, because she would "drink up the five grand." We exchanged kisses on the cheek, and I told him I loved him and that I would see him after surgery, which was set to take place at 7 a.m. He said, "I love you too, Butch." He never made it off the operating table. He was dead at age 56.

The nature of the pain over the next several days was something that only those who have had a similar loss can relate to. Words just cannot express the depth of the grief. There was some solace to be had from the huge turnout at his funeral, a testament to the loyalty of his friends. Before we put him in the ground, in the single plot that Eleanor bought, I had made some decisions about the checkbook. I sat in my home on the night of June 20th and forged his signature on three checks that I wrote: one to Larry Carroll for $1500, one to Elaine for $1500 and one to myself for $1000. I told Larry and Elaine that Dad gave me the checks to distribute in the event he didn't make it. The amount represented $500 for each of the grandchildren. Larry only had two, but since his wife, Marge, was pregnant, I added another $500. I then gave Larry the checkbook to give to his mother. She and little Tony kept the '68 Ford, the house in Somerdale and all of my father's belongings. My "inheritance" was used for the central air conditioning I got for our home. I encouraged Elaine to use her share as a partial down payment on a house I had discovered in our neighborhood, a place that would enable her to get the boys out of Camden. She had met Tom Harris and would soon marry him, and they were to share that house in Marlton. I never regretted forging the checks. I never stopped missing Dad.

Elaine followed through on the purchase of the nearby home and came to live around the corner on Cropwell Road. I was the best man when she married Tom Harris, with whom she had Jeffery. Jeffrey was the last or her four boys, each of whom would choose a different path in the future. Eventually, Jeffery was the only one to totally flee the nest, when he settled in California, where he is a budding music artist. He continues to be a caring and loving son.

Back in Gloucester City, I was taking on more responsibilities. I joined the Association for Community Education and eventually became the state president. I became the lead negotiator for the teachers' association, which brought me to the attention of my next guardian angel, Dr. Thomas Sykes. Dr. Sykes was a sophisticated educator from Billerica, Massachusetts, and he had the accent to prove it. He saw something in me that he felt was worthy of cultivation, and he put me in charge of the evening school and the city's fledging community education program. I took advantage of the opportunity and led efforts to garner state grants for our little underprivileged area. We soon made headlines with a visit from Governor Cahill that highlighted my new program. I was riding high. Dr. Sykes made me the Assistant to the Superintendent, and I moved to his headquarters at the Mary Ethel Costello School. As this job was a year-round endeavor, I resigned my baseball job, as well as my summer positions, but I continued to referee basketball. In 1972, I got my Master's Degree, with Janis, Mom, Johnny, Uncle Mike and Aunt Lena, all as proud as could be, looking on.

I wasted no time in entering an experimental Doctorate program at Western Colorado University. I knew it wasn't prestigious, but it presented me with the opportunity to work toward the next degree without leaving my job. Dr. Sykes not only encouraged me, but convinced the Board of Education to pay for my tuition and appointed me the Assistant Superintendent as well. Once again, I was taken under the wing of a guardian angel, one of many mentors who would profoundly influence my life. I was getting accolade after accolade and often believed my own publicity. I was a great provider, but insensitive to Janis' needs and, my obsession with advancement caused me to frequently be away from the kids. Still, Janis was consistent in her support of everything I did. She was also doing a masterful job with Dean and Doreen, and I knew that they deserved more from me. So when we spotted a lot on Tinderbox Terrace, we had visions of home construction and were ready to move on up. It was twice the home we had and at twice the price: $32,500. I was up to the challenge, my family deserved it, and, best of all, the Zieglers and Lippincotts would be but a block away. My shadow was getting longer, and Janis was growing cool in it. But I was oblivious.

In 1974, I had completed my Doctorate, which was celebrated at an embarrassingly huge and lavish reception rivaling any wedding. It came complete with a band, an open bar and full dinner buffet for the 200-plus attendees. It culminated in a short speech by then Congressman, soon-to-be New Jersey governor, James Florio. Mom, who had lost a brave Johnny that year, had pulled out all the stops. Along with Elaine, she was thoroughly proud, she had some money, and she was determined that no one would feel sorry for her again. The resulting event was as much about her as about me, and I was thrilled for both of us. The Monarcas, the Zeccolas and the DiSibios all attended the event, no exceptions. In addition, godparents, close friends and associates marked the occasion with us. It was over the top, but grand.

One person of importance to me who missed the event was Frank the Fruitman. I had met him a couple of years earlier when I helped his daughter make friends at the swim club, and Frank and

I became close. He was the last person I saw before Janis, the kids and I headed to Grand Junction, Colorado to defend my doctoral dissertation and receive my degree. We stopped in the predawn hours at the Philadelphia food distribution center, where Frank owned a fruit importing business. He was reputed to be "connected," and I suppose he deserved the rumors. He slipped $500 into my hand and whispered in my ear, "If them bums don't come across with your degree, let me know, and I'll send out a briefcase full of money." Such was the way of Frank.

Frank died of a massive heart attack while we were gone, and I still miss that Damon Runyon character. I can see him still, sprawled nude across his double bed, where he had demanded my presence. "You been to college, Ralphie. Who invented air conditioning?" Frank loved air conditioning even more than fruit; he kept his central air conditioned house at 68 degrees and had an additional window unit in his bedroom window, all of which made it feel like Joe's cold box. I thought for a minute before I replied to his question. "I don't know for sure, but it was Carrier or George Westinghouse or one of those types. Why do you need to know?" He grinned that great grin he had and said, very slowly, "'Cause I want to kiss his ass." Now you know why I still miss him.

By 1975, I was nearing the end of my contribution to Gloucester and Dr. Sykes. The Governor's visit had made me a star, and I was beginning to pose a threat to the Superintendent's leadership, not by any design, but by circumstance. He had helped to create me, and now it was time for me to spread my own wings and leave the nest. I applied for the Superintendent position at the Northern Burlington Regional Schools in Mansfield, 30 miles from Marlton. I delighted in the interview process and, when I got a call on May 5th. I was with my mom and Janis watching TV at Tinderbox Terrace. The board president informed me of my selection, and, with tears in my eyes, I hung up the phone and shared the news with Jan and Mom. Then, we all wept. I had made it to the top of my profession. On the run again, and with more than a little fear to inspire me, I was about to leave the security of Gloucester City and running scared.

The Pinnacle

STATE OF NEW JERSEY
EXECUTIVE DEPARTMENT

Proclamation

NOW, THEREFORE, I, BRENDAN BYRNE, Governor of the State of New Jersey, do hereby proclaim

MOVEMBER, 1977

as

ENERGY CONSERVATION MONTH

in New Jersey, and urge our citizens to support this effort by practicing energy conservation at home, at work and on the road during this month and throughout the year ahead and those beyond.

GIVEN, under my hand and the Great Seal of the State of New Jersey, this eleventh day of October in the year of Our Lord one thousand nine hundred and seventy-seven and in the Independence of the United States, the two hundred and second.

GOVERNOR

BY THE GOVERNOR:

SECRETARY OF STATE

In Northern Burlington I was determined to bring well-deserved attention to the rural school with an eclectic student body. The construction of a greenhouse in an environmentally sensitive era was the vehicle.

Governor Byrne accepted my invitation to sign his proclamation at the opening of our student-constructed project.

Standing on the far left is Dr. Fred Burke, New Jersey Commissioner of Education; and on the far right is yours truly, checking his watch to ensure that our timing was perfect.

Dr. Burke didn't know that he and I would be peers within six months.

The Pinnacle

"Here, again, I was asking myself, what more could a man want? I was concluding more than two years at NBC and was about to receive tenure, having achieved everything I had envisioned when I started."

THE NORTHERN BURLINGTON REGIONAL SCHOOL superintendency marked my ascendancy to the top of my profession at the local level, and I was thrilled and elated. My commute to Mansfield, a community just three miles off I-295 north of Marlton, was an easy 30 miles, ending in the lush farming area of the region. The school was a complex of modern buildings, made conspicuous by being in the final stages of a major addition. I became only the second superintendent in this relatively new district, which served, in addition to the farming population, the erudite students whose parents were stationed at Maguire Air Force Base. It had a good reputation as a well-run system, despite the aggressiveness of the teachers' union. I was in my glory.

At home, we had settled into our new house at 7 Tinderbox Terrace, and the kids were progressing at a normal pace. The normalcy was due in large part to the supervision of Janis, although I would occasionally be featured in the warning that went, "You just wait 'til your father gets home!" I had resigned all of my extra jobs, because the $32,000 salary was more than adequate for our family, and I was also unable to afford the time for outside activities as I devoted every ounce of my energies to my new, year-around role as Superintendent of Schools. We purchased a 21-foot boat to replace the old one that Vito and I had owned before it sank with Joe Z and Uncle Bill Nace on board and me at the helm. The old boat was aptly named "The Ark," while the new one was chris-tened "Dr. D." We were beginning to harvest the fruits of my labors and degrees and all of Janis' sacrifices. Elaine was just around the corner in her home with Tommy and the kids. My mother lived just at the entrance of Woodstream in an apartment; she had taken a job as a worker in the cafeteria in the local school system and was content. Given all of that and my father's final abandonment, through death, I was left with little to worry about, and Northern Burlington became my new obsession.

There were many challenges at "NBC," no different than any other school district. The junior and senior high schools were on split sessions, because the new addition wouldn't be completed until the fall and the school was hugely overcrowded. This meant that we brought in half the student population in the early morning and dismissed them at one o'clock, when we brought in the rest of the students for an elongated afternoon session. The entire com-munity was anxious for the return to a normal schedule in the fall; and I had the challenge of leading the charge to normalcy.

I did all of the things superintendents are supposed to do, and I did them without any particular difficulty. My years at Gloucester seemed to be serving me well. Before the end of my second month, however, I was confronted by my first challenge. I believed in keeping the lines of communications open in all direc-tions. Toward that end, I sent a questionnaire to all staff members, asking for their opinions on the bell schedule possibilities for the highly anticipated single sessions that would commence in Sep-tember of 1975.

The questionnaires had been in the teachers' mail boxes about 15 minutes, when Lorraine Gower, my executive assistant, informed me that three very angry union reps were demanding an audience. I told her to bring them right on in. The three irate men loomed over my desk for our first confrontation, as one of them threw some papers on my desk. "What's this?" he demanded. I calmly said, "It's what it appears to be, a questionnaire on the bell schedule." "No, it isn't," he bellowed, "it's a negotiation paper, and you can only negotiate with us!" These last words were delivered with a great air of victory and satisfaction, as he went on to say, "We demand you withdraw it." I hesitated for a moment, a pause that he likely took to be fear, and then said quietly, "Okay, I will do it immediately." Though visibly shocked, they said nothing as they left my office.

I called for Lorraine to come in and take some dictation, a note to the teachers that I told her I wanted to be put in every mail box immediately. "Dear Faculty: I regret to have to withdraw my request for your input regarding next year's bell schedule. I thought your insights would be helpful to me in forming my recommendations to the board, since you will be greatly affected by those decisions. Unfortunately, your union representatives don't want me to benefit from your opinions. I am complying with their demand that I do not consider your thoughts. Please accept my apology for my initial desires for your advice."

This communication was not in the mail slots for five minutes before the trio reappeared in my doorway unannounced. "You have to get these out of the mailboxes. It makes us look foolish; you must remove them, now!" I looked up and replied, "Sorry, fellows, but I must maintain the right to communicate with my staff, and please see Mrs. Gower for an appointment before coming in here; it's the courteous thing to do." I concluded with a curt, "Good day, gentlemen." From that day forward, my relationship with the union was mutually respectful.

I reprised the gubernatorial visit to Gloucester when I got Governor Brendan Byrne to come to the school on the occasion of my having procured a grant to build a huge greenhouse with student design and labor. It was during the heyday of the fledging environmental movement, and we were planning to take full advantage of the event, in which I managed to play a leading role, highlighted by the arrival of the Governor's helicopter from the nearby Trenton capital. Part of the fun of the day was having Joe the Barber there, because it was his day off. Once again I was a little star in a big galaxy, but no less a star. Mom continued to build the scrapbooks of my exploits.

Here, again, I was asking myself, what more could a man want? I was concluding more than two years at NBC and was about to receive tenure, having achieved everything I had envisioned when I started. I had a great career, which could continue for the next 30 years, with a very comfortable state pension awaiting me upon my retirement. My family was happy and healthy, Dean was getting into wrestling, thanks to his godfather, Natale, and Doreen was still her irrepressible self, only more so. Janis was developing deep friendships with Marie Ziegler and Naomi Lippincott and the rest of the neighborhood women. We all attended the Sunday football games, where Dean was displaying some considerable skills as an offensive end. Could life have been any better? I thought not, unable to think of a single thing that I desired. Then came the mail.

I opened an envelope impersonally addressed to the "Superintendent of Schools." The contents revealed a brochure soliciting a Superintendent of Public Instruction for the State of Nevada, who, in New Jersey, was called the Commissioner of Education. Whatever the name, the position was that of the highest education official in the state, and there were only 50 of them in the country.

On a whim, I called Lorraine into the office and instructed her to send in my resume, which we had on file. She exclaimed, "You would never leave us." I smiled and replied, "Who knows, I could get an interview and a trip to Nevada."

Janis and I laughed about it over dinner, and that was the end; or so we thought. Two weeks later, I received a call from the Chairman of the State Board in Nevada, informing me that I was being officially invited to interview for the position. Unlike the corresponding department in New Jersey, the State Board of Education in Nevada was an elected body, and the members appointed the State Superintendent. I was informed that the interview, part of a process to decide among the nine finalists, was to be held on the following Friday in Las Vegas and that the Board would make a decision on the Monday after that at a public meeting. I was speechless for an instant, before telling him that I was delighted and would await the promised schedule and a description of procedures.

With the exception of Janis, I didn't tell a soul about the turn of events. While we were both excited about the honor of being a finalist, we were dead sure that I would not get beyond the first interview. I prepared to do my best, however, and began to do some homework on Nevada education. I had never been to Carson City, where the State Department was located, and had only been to Las Vegas once, when I attended a conference with Dr. Sykes. I called some friends in the New Jersey department to see what they could tell me about the search for a chief school officer. In the course of my research, I uncovered the fact that two of the Nevada Board members were also members of the National Association of Community Education; I had been the president of the corresponding state association when I left Gloucester, so at least I had a hook. When I departed 7 Tinderbox, Janis was in the process of painting the dark-stained kitchen cabinets white. She wished me luck on my adventure, and I was off.

I arrived in Las Vegas on a day late in February, and it was 65 degrees. I had secured a bargain airfare and accommodations at the Tropicana by booking from Thursday to Sunday. On Friday morning, I listened as the Chairman explained the process. They would interview me for two hours or less, and by Saturday morning interviews with all of the candidates would be completed. The board would never discuss any candidate outside of the interview process and, in fact, never again after the interviews had taken place until Monday morning, when they would have a public meeting and take a vote. This rather odd approach was their conservative response to the new open meeting laws that were sweeping the nation. The idea behind these new laws was to try and avoid the back room deals that had traditionally taken place out of view of the public.

In any event, I listened to his explanations and then responded to the first series of questions. Following that, I handed out the manila folders I had carried in with me, with the names of each member typed on the front (a product of my research). I proceeded to "interview" the board, using the questions on the papers I had handed out. I wanted to know what their vision for Nevada education was, and what they thought the ideal candidate to fulfill that vision would look like. I had recalled the admonition of Dr. Welling: take command. And I was determined to differentiate myself. As I left, they asked me about my travel plans, and when I said that my flight departed on Sunday, everyone nodded. I thanked them and walked to the door. The Chairman opened the door for me and whispered, "You might want to attend the Monday meeting." I left with the confidence that I had done well and the Chairman might be in my corner. I made my call to Janis, as promised, and told her I was planning on staying until Monday, out of my curiosity to see what would happen. I called Lorraine and told her that I needed to take one more personal day on Monday, but would see her on Tuesday.

On Monday morning, I went to the public meeting. I carried my small suitcase, because my flight left at noon. I saw the familiar faces of the board members, but was surprised to see the large number of other people in attendance as well. There was a large conference table, and several TV cameras and lights were being prepared for the event. Jim Costa, the Assistant Superintendent and a finalist himself, was sitting nearby, and yet another finalist was several seats behind me. At least, I assumed he was a finalist; like me, he held a suitcase. Always thinking.

The Chairman called the meeting to order and announced the agenda and process. John Gamble (no kidding), the retiring Superintendent, would read the names of the finalists, then pass out a first ballot to each board member. They were to cast their votes, and Mr. Gamble would read the results. If a majority was not achieved by one candidate, then a discussion would ensue, a second ballot would take place, and the process would continue. With that, the proceedings began.

John Gamble opened and read each ballot he had collected. To cut to the chase, I won on the first ballot, by a score of nine to two. Flashbulbs erupted all around me, and film cameras and snapshots recorded my look of astonishment. Microphones were thrust in my face, and a flurry of questions was directed my way, "When do you report?" "Will you keep your present staff?" "What are your priorities?" I held my hand up and announced that the Chairman and I had yet to settle on any dates, and I needed to chat with him before I would make any statement, excepting to say that I was gratified by the appointment.

As I was running late for my plane, I asked Jim Costa if he could give me a lift, and he gladly replied in the affirmative, since I was ostensibly his new boss. Hasty plans were made for the Chairman to call me the next evening, and I was out of there. This was too crazy. The first payphone I spotted in the airport was used to call Janis. I said "Hello," and she said, "You got the job didn't you?" I said that I did, but that we would talk as soon as I got off the plane—that I almost didn't catch.

We spent a sleepless, but discussion-filled, night going over our options. We had spent more than a decade in Marlton, and a new exploit seemed to hold some excitement. This latest development put us on an emotional roller coaster ride. We were elated, but full of trepidation, scared, but stimulated, ready for an adventure, but happy where we were. Neither one of us had answers to the questions that would help us to make the final decision. We knew that it represented a $500 a year pay cut and a move to a higher cost of living to boot. There was an element of the unknown for Janis, since she had never been in Nevada. We knew, too, that such an opportunity would never present itself again. If I accepted the position, I would become the youngest chief state school officer in the country. I must admit that I was a little overcome by the whole notion. In the end, Janis was a trooper, as usual, telling me, "You make the decision, and I'll support it."

I walked into my NBC office at 7 a.m., hoping for some time alone so I could gather myself to talk to Lorraine and my board. But that was not to be. As I entered, Lorraine handed me the phone, and, simultaneously, the fresh front page of the Trenton Times with a big, bold headline that read, "LOCAL SUPERINTENDENT PICKED TO HEAD NEVADA'S SCHOOLS."

On the other end of the phone was Mr. Bob Craft, the local board president. "Hello, this is Ralph," I said. He replied with, "Say it isn't so." I told him that I had, indeed, been selected but that I had not made any final decisions and was intending to sit with him before I did. He was magnanimous, when he told me, "Of course, this is an honor for our little district, too. I'll see you later."

Here it was nearly March, and after all the meetings, phone calls, negotiations and announcements, we were committed to being in Carson City on April 1st to begin my new job. I couldn't help but wonder whether the April Fool's start date would prove to be prophetic, but there was little time to think about that. To say that there was a whirlwind of activity does not even begin to describe the tumult that swallowed us up over the next 50 days. It was like dominoes falling, with one thing after another, and the house was the first to go.

We had invited Jack and Marie Ziegler over to break the news of our departure, and following the tears and congratulations that we shared, they said that they wished they could buy our house. I replied, "Done"; and we negotiated a price and concluded a verbal agreement. Cousin John did the paperwork, and settlement was made two days before we left for Nevada. I have never been accused of being slow. The Zieglers lived in that home for many years thereafter, but before they could move in, there were parties, tearful goodbyes and sessions with Dean and Doreen to get through. The kids had accompanied Jan and me to Colorado when I got my doctorate, and we told them that this would be a great escapade. They had serious concerns about being uprooted, but, like their mother, were little troopers. So, we packed and were off. We got into our brand new silver Cadillac that I was able to purchase for $10,800, courtesy of Vito's connections in the auto world, and headed west, the voice of Horace Greeley ringing in my ears.

Janis and I had seen Carson City for the first time a couple of weeks earlier on a house hunting trip, during which we settled on a small rancher on a steep hillside overlooking the city and the road to Lake Tahoe. We were disturbed by the $70,000 price tag, but still starry-eyed enough to take that plunge. The sale of the Tinderbox Terrace home had yielded $58,000, so we were already a little behind the financial curve; but at 37, I thought there would be many more career challenges with corresponding rewards ahead, even though there was no way I could be sure at the time what those challenges would be.

When my appointment was announced in New Jersey, my old friend from our days in Italy called to express his amazement and congratulations. He said, "So, what does a Superintendent of Public Instruction do?" I laughed and replied truthfully, "Hell, Ron, I don't know, but how tough can it be? He's in charge." With that, I was off and running—running scared.

23
Nevada Gamble

2B—Las Vegas Review-Journal—Wednesday, July 9, 1980

R-J Viewpoint

Overruling DiSibio not healthy

Once again, state Human Resources Director Ralph DiSibio has refused to renew a permit for the Nuclear Engineering Co. to dump radioactive waste at a dumpsite near Beatty.

And once again, the company can be expected to appeal the decision to the state Board of Health—which once before overturned DiSibio's recommendation for permanent closure of the dump.

In refusing to renew NECO's license, DiSibio had some harsh words about the burial of nuclear waste in Nevada, calling it a danger to the health of Nevada citizens.

We couldn't agree more.

When the Beatty dump was closed nearly a year ago, it was because radioactive material was leaking from improperly packaged waste.

Although the dump was re-opened, there have been more instances of leaking low-level radioactivity and we can probably expect more of the same as long as the Beatty site remains open.

Nevada, as one of only three nuclear waste storage sites in the country, is already the dumping ground for waste that other states do not want around their homes or children.

Simply ship it off to the desert wilds of Nevada, they figure, and it will be stored without hurting anybody.

Nevada is already heavily involved with dangerous materials, having had the Nevada Test Site for almost three decades and now with the probability of the MX missile system being based here.

Somewhere along the line, the rest of the country has got to realize that Nevada has done its share and doesn't need the wastes and other things people outside the state don't want near them.

We don't see how the state Board of Health can make any decision besides backing up DiSibio's recommendation for closure of the Beatty dump.

Although the board last December decided the dump didn't present a health hazard, that can simply be chalked up to a lack of knowledge of the situation or perhaps pressures from outside the state.

We certainly hope the Board of Health doesn't back down this time and overrule DiSibio again.

If it's the health of Nevadans the board is truly interested in, it won't vote to keep the dumpsite open.

*One day I was sworn in by the Chief Justice of the
Nevada Supreme Court, and the next day
I was immersed in constant controversy.*

I was always quick with a quote and a decision.

Nevada Gamble

" 'Did you say nuclear, you mean like in bomb, nuclear?'
She replied in the affirmative..."

I T WAS BY MY NATURE AND BY NECESSITY that I threw myself into my new job. It was my way to rush headlong into any challenge, but in this case it was necessary as well. My first month's report to the board looked as though it reflected the work of three people: In one month's time I had traveled all across the huge state, visited a dozen legislators, taken stock of the Education Department staff, interviewed candidates for open positions in the department, given six speeches to various organizations and prepared a position paper on my vision for the Department and a strategy for the upcoming legislative session. I wanted to make a good first impression, and I did; but more importantly, I had listened. I absorbed all that I could in those first few weeks so that I could educate myself and fill in the gaps. I now knew what a chief school officer did, and I was prepared to do it.

The kids and Janis were busy with the process of enrolling in school and filling in their own gaps about our new community. As the family of a high-ranking state official, they were treated with some deference, which no doubt eased their challenges. Still, it could not have been an easy transition. They had left the lush surroundings of southern New Jersey for the barren desert of northern Nevada. They had left behind family and friends, only to confront strangers with no discernible accents, a citizenry to whom they had no loyalty. They had left a large two-story home surrounded by caring people, and now resided in a smaller rancher in an area bereft of friendly faces.

The house was approached by driving up to the mailbox for 3321 Conte Drive, where the driveway appeared on the left. At the top of the steep gravel drive, you parked in front of the double garage. Inside the front door was the sunken living room, with a stepped-up dining area on the right, where there was also an entrance to the rec room and kitchen. The hall on the left led to three bedrooms and a hall bath, as well as another bath off the rear master bedroom. All of the rooms were small but cozy. Outside the rear sliding doors leading out of the rec room lay a sagebrush-strewn and steep hillside rising to a beautiful peak. Ours was the highest home on the hill, a house I saw little of over the next several months. We traded in the garish silver Cadillac, because we feared whispers about the Italians from the East not fitting in with the Western mores, and replaced it with a conservative new Monte Carlo and a Chevy blazer, more in line with local customs, but still well-suited to a tenderfoot from New Jersey.

The legislative session was a revelation to me. I had to prepare for endless hours of committee hearings, where I was required to respond to hundreds of questions from ill-informed, part-time legislators, all in public sessions. I would have to say that I enjoyed the learning experience and the repartee, even the mild combat. The legislature in Nevada met for 90 days every two years, and the sessions were necessarily hectic and compact as a result of this schedule. When a reporter asked me what I thought of the system, differing dramatically as it did from New Jersey politics, my quote made small headlines: "Sometimes I think that they should meet every 90 years for two days." This was a reflection on the amount of work that was required when the sessions were held, and everyone got a kick out of my comment.

I had my first brush with controversy over the issue of immigrant children in the schools, an issue, ironically, that is still with us today. Some of the local districts were excluding the children of migrant workers from school, with the rationale that they were not citizens and, therefore, not entitled to the tax-supported schools. I took exception to this logic and contacted the counties in question to inform them that they must admit the students, stirring up a controversy of statewide proportions. I was very emphatic in my demands, and I announced that unless the schools complied, I would recommend that the board withhold all financial support to the offending institutions. The state constitution, I said, referred only to age and was silent on citizenship, nationality or color, and I insisted that, as a result, the state was constitutionally required to provide access to education to every child between the ages of six and 16.

I was shocked to receive a torrent of hate mail and two death threats, but I was undeterred in my stance. In a scathing editorial published by the newspaper in Winnemucca, they railed against my position and labeled me "That tin-horned tyrant from the East." The editorial itself remains my favorite among the scores in which I have been highlighted over my career. Eventually, the schools backed down, when the state board backed up my threat to withhold funding. Things returned to normal, and the controversy went away, taking with it any hopes of keeping a low profile.

The then-State Attorney General was Bob List, who was campaigning for Governor at the time and called me during the hubbub. "Dr. DiSibio, do you want an official, written opinion on this matter from my office?" he inquired. I replied by offering him some advice. "Sir, you may want to remain silent on this, because it can only be a lose/lose." I told him about the threats that had been made and repeated that he should stay out of it and let me take my lumps. He thanked me for my insights, and we would not speak again until he was elected three months later.

I had a successful legislative session. My department fared well in the financial arena, and we did not have any staff cuts. My own kids had started the new school year and appeared to be adjusting well to the new environment. Janis was getting more engaged in the CCD program in the Catholic Church, and we were all beginning to attend church more regularly.

I had settled into a routine, after reorganizing the Department to better advance my vision, and hired the Department's first man of color to be an Assistant Superintendent when things were calm. I had gained a reputation as a good leader who had the courage of his convictions and was building a record of candor with legislators, media and various organizations. I was unafraid of controversy and handled myself with some distinction when speaking extemporaneously. I felt that I had a career ahead of me in state education. Then, Election Day changed that notion.

Governor Bob List was elected on November 4, 1978, just eight months after I had arrived in Nevada with my family, and I received a call from the governor-elect barely a week after the election. It was an invitation to visit his home for coffee and a chat the following evening. I assumed that he wanted a briefing on the shape of education and perhaps my views on what he might do to energize student performance. But, instead, the subject of the meeting—one of only a handful of times that I was completely stupefied by a scheduled meeting—was to further complicate my life.

Not long after I got seated on a comfortable sofa in the private residence of Bob and Kathy List, he surprised me with the purpose of the meeting. He explained to me that he had been observing my conduct in the State Department of Education since I had arrived there; he said he was impressed with how I reorganized it and how I handled controversial issues. He went on to say that he was challenged to fill his cabinet positions and that one, in particular, was troubling him. The Department of Human Resources, the largest in state government with one-third of the state's employees and fully one-third of the state budget as well, was, he said, fraught with controversy and problems. He concluded by saying, "Ralph, I would like you to join my cabinet and run that department." He paused for my reply.

I was dumbstruck for a moment before I could get out, "Well, sir, I am gratified at your comments, and I really don't know what to say." I paused before going on, "Of course, I am flattered and honored, but I have a commitment to education and would like to digest this for a bit and discuss it with my family, if that would be okay." He smiled and said, of course, it would be fine, asking that I contact him the next afternoon with any questions or thoughts I might have on the matter. I beat a quick retreat, after again thanking him for his confidence.

Elated, I returned to Conte Drive on a cloud. I described the meeting for Janis, as I picked up the phone book to look up the Department of Human Resources. I was looking to see what I could discern about the size of the department the Governor had portrayed as so large. I started laughing as I rifled through page after page of phone numbers for the many divisions and offices of this gargantuan bureaucracy. The departments under the main heading included Department of Health Services, Welfare Department, Aging Services, Department of Rehabilitation Services, Mental Health and Mental Retardation, and Department of Health Planning. There were scores of offices and suboffices listed all over the state. I now knew, generally at least, what service this cabinet office was responsible to deliver.

Jan and I couldn't believe that a new guy from New Jersey, with no political clout yet, could get such an appointment. It was an offer no one, let alone a man like me, could refuse. I called List the next day and told him that I humbly accepted his offer. We agreed that neither of us would make a public announcement until I informed my board, privately. The start of my new position was highly anticipated, and, although I realized that controversy was part of the job, I was not fully prepared for what lay ahead. I had not even been in Nevada a year, and, for the second time, I was running scared.

The cabinet announcements and the Inaugural Ball that ensued put me and my family on a whole new level of state leaders. This next phase of my Nevada tenure would now be played out under the hot spotlight of public scrutiny. The Department lent itself to controversy by nature; escapes from the mental health facilities, high profile resignations, theft of food from state hospitals, fraudulent contracts with bogus companies in the Welfare Department and highly publicized actions on hospital certificates of need were everyday occurrences. The truth is, I loved the action. With this as a backdrop, the legislature had an off year, and I was planning to settle in and devote my time to listening and learning and providing the Governor and his chief of staff, Chris Schaller, my advice and counsel.

I was completely unprepared when, after only two months on the job, the biggest controversy I had yet encountered began to unfold. I answered the red phone (reserved for a direct line to List) with a curt, "DiSibio here," and heard the governor respond, "Ralph, what's this about a fire at Beatty?" I didn't say what I was thinking, but instead said, "I'll get right back to you on that." As I hung up the phone, I called for my executive secretary and asked her, "Lynn, what's a Beatty?" She nonchalantly called back, "Oh, that's a nuclear site near Las Vegas; John Carr is responsible for it." "Did you say nuclear, you mean like in bomb, nuclear?" She replied in the affirmative, and I told her to get Dr. Carr, my head of the Department of Health, to my office ASAP. Within minutes, I was getting briefed on the situation.

Beatty, it turned out, was a tiny berg 60 miles from Las Vegas. A private company had a license from the state to dispose of low-level nuclear waste in a shallow land burial dump in the desert there. Carr told me that a predawn fire had erupted in a truck that was waiting for the facility to open, and the ensuing smoke and debris had been handled. He thought that no one was injured, urine samples had been taken to ensure that there had not been any exposure to radiation and, all in all, he said, it was no big deal. I admonished him for not having informed me immediately, told him I would decide on how big a deal it was and demanded updates on the half hour. I called the governor back, briefed him, and told him that I was taking action to shut down the Beatty facility, pending a full investigation. I then commandeered the state plane and directed the state fire chief to join me on the 400-mile trip to the scene. I intended to take personal charge.

I was lucky to have made the right decisions. There was an enormous headline in the Las Vegas Sun, "HUGE NUCLEAR CLOUD BLANKETS PORTION OF THE CITY," followed by a story that reported that no injuries had resulted and that the Governor had dispatched his top cabinet official, who would head up a full probe, to the scene. Along with many other controversies and duties too numerous to mention, this event would consume me for the remaining time I was to spend in Nevada.

After three days of conducting interviews and studying reports, I was ready to brief the governor. It turns out, I told him, that Nevada was one of only three states that accepted commercially-generated low-level radioactive waste. The wastes were, in part, made up of the residuals from contaminated water in nuclear plants, as well as slightly contaminated clothing, rags, rope and paper from those plants, and a variety of medical nuclear waste, which included radiation therapy materials, cancer research residue, carcasses of animals used in experimentation and contaminated needles. In addition to Nevada, Washington and South Carolina were the recipients of the nation's waste. I had further learned that the regulations promulgated by the NRC (the Nuclear Regulatory Commission) were being regularly violated, while the NRC turned a blind eye toward the violators. Finally, I said, the violations had the potential to endanger the health of our citizens through radiation exposure.

The governor asked me for my recommendations, and I outlined them. We should set up a meeting with the governors of the other two states to provide them a briefing. We should demand a meeting with Joseph Hendry, the powerful chairman of the NRC, setting forth enforcement demands which, if not implemented, would result in the closing of the three sites, a move that could impact national energy production and bring cancer research to a halt. He liked the course I had charted and could see how it might bring him some national attention in the bargain. I began to execute my plan.

Following my meeting with Governors Dixie Lee Ray and Richard Riley, of Washington and South Carolina, respectively, I was dispatched to Washington, D.C. to meet with a wary Joseph Hendry. It was my first trip to our nation's capital since assuming my new job, and I showed signs of still having the Camden kid in me, when I called brother-in-law Vito to tell him I would be in D.C. for this meeting and invited him to join me. All he would have to do, I said, was dress up and takes notes, occasionally whispering in my ear as if he was giving me assistance. He was intrigued, and we both loved the idea.

Vito and I were ushered into the large conference room where Chairman Hendry sat surrounded by several staffers, his ubiquitous pipe cupped in his hand. After I announced the purpose of my visit as a representative from the three governors, I handed over a formal letter of demands to the Chairman. He thoughtfully sucked on the pipe, while he read the communication. Vito, to look learned, leaned over and whispered, "I think I'll light up a Marlboro; if he can smoke, so can we." I remained stoic, as I whispered back, "Don't you dare." He nodded soberly and made some scribbles on his note pad. After brief comments, the Chairman said he would take the letter under advisement and he would get back to us. I told him that I knew he was aware of our sense of urgency and that I would keep Beatty closed until I got a response; the other sites would take no action for at least five days. I thanked him for agreeing to the meeting and left. Vito and I went to have a beer and a great laugh at a memorable experience.

Eventually, we did close the sites, because the NRC did not comply with our demands. President Carter threatened to use Federal sites for the waste, and we, in turn, threatened to use our state police to stop the shipments at our borders. All in all, it was quite a series of events. The President caved, agreeing to our demand for an Executive Order that called for a national task force to make recommendations for new and tougher regulations. I was appointed to serve on the task force, and a new era in nuclear waste policy commenced.

In the meantime, I was holding a national conference in Lake Tahoe on the issue. I invited representatives of every interested or impacted group to gather to discuss the issues and make suggestions for improvements. It was at this Lake Tahoe event that

I met my next guardian angel, Barry Koh. Dr. Barry Koh, a graduate of Cornell, who had previously had a long and distinguished career with Westinghouse, was at this time the President of Hittman Nuclear and Development Company located in Columbia, Maryland. Barry and I hit it off from the beginning, and we remain close friends; a bond that had its origin in nuclear waste was buttressed by the mutual respect that developed. The conference at which we met was an event that helped to make the use of nuclear materials for peaceful purposes safe, but it was only the beginning.

My family was adjusting well to life in Nevada. Janis was growing closer to state senator/lawyer Jim Kosinski and his lovely wife, Judy, of social psychology fame. We had met them at the Inaugural and took an almost instant liking to one another. Jim had followed my rise in government from both sides of the legislative table, and Judy was also a state employee. A new legislative session was looming, and we would see even more of our new friends as the year progressed. Jan's religion was becoming an increasingly important part of her life, and she was finding her way out of my long shadow and feeling sunshine of her own. Dean was making a name for himself in wrestling, while Doreen was making friends and influencing people. Back home, Mom and Elaine were doing well, and the Zeccolas were rolling along.

I continued to be the governor's point man on the nuclear issue, and we were making great headway. Ed Helminski was the point man for the Carter administration and the National Governor's Association. Together, we worked out strong language that would clean up the industry. Senator Laxalt was a powerful man who was instrumental in passage of the new provisions that became the law of the land; the Nuclear Waste Policy Act of 1980 was landmark legislation, and my wording about state compacts and "consultation and concurrence" was the crux of the newly enacted law. Barry Koh and I continued the relationship that had begun with our work on this same issue, meeting every time I returned to D.C. He began a subtle campaign to recruit me into the commercial world, but, at least for the moment, I had no interest, since I was still riding high on my successes in Nevada.

It is not easy to condense the 33 months of relentless challenges we met and lived through during our stay. Every day of my 24-month stint as a Cabinet official was as stimulating and exciting as any in my work life, and to reconstruct them would probably test credibility. Suffice it to say that each of the seven divisions I was responsible for sorely tested my leadership ability. I have chosen two particular trials to include here, because they are the ones that offered the greatest opportunities for personal growth. My involvement had some part in the development of the nation's nuclear policy, and that had an impact on the country; but the second major challenge that I faced had a deep personal impact on me and my family. The resultant attacks were not professional, but personal.

Early in my Nevada tenure, while I was the state Superintendent, I went to a conference on Padre Island in Texas. The state paid for my trip, and the conference organizers gave me expense money, which I used to bring Janis and the kids down for a little fun in the sun. It would be a reward, I thought, for all their support. As far as I was concerned, that was the end of it. But more than a year after I had begun my cabinet post, where I was ruffling some feathers, someone called the Nevada Attorney General, Dick Bryan, to accuse me of taking a double dip in the expenses that the state had provided. They said I should not have accepted state money if the sponsoring organization was giving me expense money. Attorney General Bryan, about to challenge List for the governor's seat, launched a full investigation.

I was just returning from Harvard University, where I had completed a program for advanced executive management, when I got wind of the investigation that was getting underway. The headlines, a testament to my high profile, read, "STATE'S TOP CABINET OFFICIAL UNDER THEFT PROBE." The story, that went on to describe me as the sometimes brash confidante of the governor, did not detail the nature of the probe, beyond saying only that it involved the inappropriate use of state money. The fact that I had fired several employees in LV's mental health agency for stealing made the accusation all the more titillating. Considering the facts, the whole affair might have been amusing, except that the investigation lasted several months and was marked by damaging innuendo and ill-intended backbiting. One of the Mariani girls had been on a trip to Las Vegas and saw the headline. That resulted in a phone call from Aunt Marie, who wanted to know how I was doing. She told me that this was the nature of politics and advised me to keep my chin up. At least I knew that the "tell a Monarca" system was alive and well.

From this point on, the job became much less fun. I went to the governor, as any loyal appointee would, and privately offered my resignation to save him the continued embarrassment. To his credit, List said he would not accept it and that I should continue to do the fine job I was doing. I remained resolute in public, but inside I was devastated. Everything I had worked for and that my family had sacrificed for was in jeopardy. And I knew that I wasn't completely blameless. I had pushed the envelope when I accepted the money, even though my motivation was pure. The harmless Vito episode came to mind, and I realized that what had been funny then could also have been an embarrassment to me and to the state. I vowed never to let such events be repeated if I escaped with my reputation intact. If it cost me my job, I would once again be faced with the prospect of being the subject of sympathy. I had not concerned myself with the sympathy issue since graduating college, but here it was again.

Much good came from the journey through the dark tunnel of uncertainty. Friends emerged from every corner; the church, past employees, present employees, legislators and other government officials gave me notes, letters, flowers and hugs. But, no one persevered more in their support than the Kosinskis, and Janis and I will leave this earth before their loyalty, friendship and guidance are forgotten. In the end, the newspaper headline read, in bold red letters, "DISIBIO EXONERATED." I was grateful and relieved and would soldier on, 100 percent engaged in my job. Still, my skepticism about politics and the press had been heightened, and it seemed that my star, which had been ascending at a rocket clip, had steadied its pace.

I remained at my post for a full year after my vindication, before I considering leaving. I continued to dedicate myself to achieving the vision the governor and I had shared for the Department. I faced all manner of professional tests during that year and won most. Most people viewed the expenses episode as simply the nature of partisan politics, but not me. I viewed it as a moment in my life when I went to the edge of a building, and looking over the edge, I saw Camden below; if I had fallen, it would have been back into my past. My zeal for the challenges I faced everyday, continued to drive me, but I knew that my enthusiasm had been somewhat diminished. It was in that context that Barry Koh got me to listen to his recruitment song with renewed interest.

Barry had a plan—he felt as though he needed to make a statement in the nuclear industry if Hittman was going to be a competitive force—and I was part of his plan. If he could land the top regulator in the country and bring him to Hittman, then he could claim the regulator as the differentiator. He was a hunter of sorts, and I was a prey. And so it came to be that Barry brought me to meet the irrepressible Fred Hittman, a veritable legend in the industry. I was impressed with them both, and soon we reached an agreement on salary ($55,000 per year), title (Vice President for Government Affairs) and assistance with relocation costs.

Throughout the constant turmoil of the Nevada experience, Dean and Doreen continued to make friends and generally be as resilient as could be. Janis was ready to head back toward New Jersey; while she had been cultivating new roots in the desert sand, in terms of community, the church and friends, the probes into my conduct and character and the unrelenting disquiet of my job had taken a toll. Dean was a junior in high school and he implored us to allow him to stay with friends until the close of the school year. Since it was already February, we agreed. Doreen was excited about getting nearer to her old friends and relatives again but still had second thoughts about leaving the Silver State.

The announcement of my acceptance of a job in the nuclear industry was the subject of the last major headlines about me in the newspapers around Nevada, and there were a number of retrospectives on my tenure, in which I was described variously as tumultuous, dynamic, ground-breaking and controversial. The sun was setting on my 20 years of public service and rising on my career in private commerce and industry, a phase of my life that would span the next 25 years. I was running scared.

24
Hittman's Hitman

**Make mine Hittman
...extra dry**

*I hit my creative stride at Hittman. The poster, which adver-
tised our liquid-free disposal technology, was a real highlight and
graced many of the customers' hallway walls.*

*Barry Koh gave me a lot of latitude, and I enjoyed it. I only
had to worry about customers, and not reporters or politicians.*

Hittman's Hitman

"I got a major assignment with Westinghouse. I was to head up a multi-million dollar effort to win the newly announced contract to construct and manage the nation's first new nuclear waste site."

I HAD GAMBLED IN NEVADA and was able to leave a winner, although it may not have looked that way. I had left a prestigious position with national acclaim and the responsibility for 4,000 employees and a budget totaling hundreds of millions of dollars. I had two secretaries and a personal assistant, and I worked out of a massive office with a private conference room and a wrap-around desk, surroundings suited for a prince. At Hittman, things were different. I had no employees directly reporting to me, no budget of my own, shared a secretary with Barry and had a 9 by 9 office with furniture of gun-metal gray. So, how was I a winner? I was a winner because in my new position, I was exposed to brighter people than me and was challenged every day to understand a complex business; I had no exposure to politicians, and, more importantly, no one knew me when I was in public. I had died and gone to anonymity heaven.

On the home front, I was not faring as well. Dean was writing often and seemed to be adjusting well to his temporary home back in Nevada. Doreen, however, had entered the mysterious early teens when forces from the nether side enter the brains of young girls and paint ugly pictures of their mothers. These phenomena create their own brand of havoc and result in all manner of odd behavior. I could run complex businesses and agencies, facing down issues that would challenge the Pope, but I couldn't make much headway with this little beauty.

While Dean followed directions pretty well, Doreen was someone who looked upon the Ten Commandments as the Ten Suggestions. In Maryland, we began having trouble with her tendency to fib and her unwillingness to own up to her indiscretions. Of course, I thought I could handle this. As I had done in the past, I sent her to my home office to fetch my fraternity paddle. I announced threateningly, "If you don't tell me the name of the girl who scratched your eye, I am going to take you to school in the morning and whack your fanny in front of your class." I was confident she would cave under the pressure, but *no-o-o-o-o*, she stood stoically silent, so I sent her to bed to contemplate her impending punishment. Still, I felt certain she would capitulate by morning. When morning rolled around, she was as determined and unyielding as ever.

Together we got into my car and drove to school, passing the school bus as we pulled into the parking lot. With the paddle prominently displayed on the dashboard during the short ride, I talked nonstop about how she could avoid the embarrassment she was about to endure; and...still nothing. I marched her ahead of me, starting by then to pray that she would give in or that some adult would intervene. I marched to the front desk and, wielding the paddle, requested that I see a guidance counselor.

In truth, it was me that needed some guidance at this point. In private, I confessed my dilemma to the counselor, and she came to my rescue. She called Doreen in to visit her alone, and, finally, I could see Doreen crying. The counselor called me in and explained that Doreen had told her the name of the girl on the condition no punishment would befall the perpetrator, her best friend. I harrumphed and declared victory by announcing that, "I know you will handle this," and turning to Doreen, I said, "I will see you for dinner, young lady." Never had I felt such relief at being saved from myself. With that, I escaped with my pride more or less intact and didn't mention the incident again for several weeks. This is just one illustration of what makes Doreen such a loyal friend—you can trust her with your life.

Dean and Doreen were both great kids then, and they are even better adults now. Surely they are better at parenting then I even tried to be as, once again, I had dragged them across the country to satisfy my ambitions. While I am sure that even a stable life with Ozzy and Harriet parents would not have suppressed the normal teenage rebellions, it didn't help to have me leading the band. Lest I leave the wrong impression, I think I can take credit for being a loving, compassionate father, who provided well and set strong examples of loyalty, family ties, friendship and strength of character; but I could have done better in the sensitivity field. Of course, I had come from the North Camden "walk it off" school of psychology, where sensitivity was not a subject.

Janis, meanwhile, was not impervious to my insensitivity. Having been ripped from her freshly-planted roots of church and new friends in Carson City, she was again left to set up another home, albeit a grand one, on Dancing Sunbeam Court in Columbia, Maryland. We were arguing more, and the escalation of conflict surely impacted Doreen and eventually Dean. I had sowed the seeds of an existence that put me at the center of everyone's attention where I got everyone's adulation. As Janis grew tired of her secondary role, she fought to extricate herself and looked outside the home for satisfaction and esteem. I was blind to her emotional needs, because I was building a new career as a captain of industry. In my behavior, I was often wrong but never in doubt.

Barry Koh had a vision of making Hittman a force in the nuclear waste disposal business, and he was relying on me to help. I was brought into the small organization at a lofty level, and I was treated with due respect by men of superior intellect and expertise. Chuck Mallory was such a man. He was possessed of a remarkably creative mind, one of the most brilliant engineers I ever encountered. I eventually found out that even men of his talent needed men of vision and drive to be part of a successful team. Succeeding in business is all about team, and Hittman fielded a good one.

Our first big opportunity came by way of the State of Kentucky. They were seeking a company to manage a defunct disposal site with huge technical challenges due to the influx of ground water and rain into the trenches that now held millions of tons of nuclear waste. Some of the waste was in the form of sludge and liquids that were contaminating the land surrounding the site. A difficult situation, to be sure, but we were up to the task. In a weighty brainstorming session, we decided that the key would have to be whatever we could do to differentiate ourselves from the competition. The practice of digging a hole in the ground, dumping in the nuclear waste and then covering the hole with dirt had led to the problem, and now the state was spending millions every year to keep water away from the waste. Past contractors had caused the problem, but no solution had yet been offered.

Our team made an innovative proposal. We decided to remove the waste and place it in engineered vaults that would preclude water intrusion. The cost would be initially great, but over time, the "life cycle cost" (a concept we practically invented) would be less, and our system would certainly be more protective of the environment. We were up against stiff competition, including the incumbent, Dames and Moore, that had the advantage of real time site knowledge. But, like Cassius Clay in his victory in Lewiston,

Maine against Sonny Liston, we "shocked the world" when Hittman Nuclear and Development became the new contractor for the State of Kentucky. We took one giant step toward fulfilling Barry's vision; we were a force to be reckoned with. The contract represented the largest of its type in Hittman's history, and, as the project director, I had solidified my reputation as a creative and successful leader.

Fred Hittman was thrilled and attended the signing of the contract in Frankfort the following month. With Barry, Chuck, Fred and I in the car, Fred went on a rant about the stupidity of America in not exploiting nuclear power. He was building to a crescendo with a flourish, "Air pollution is no issue with nuclear," he shouted. "You see Mt. St. Helens?" he asked (referring to a recently erupted volcano in Washington State). He went on at an even higher pitch, "Mt. St. Helens spewed more pollution on the earth, in minutes, than mankind has produced since we have inhabited the earth. When God pollutes, he doesn't screw around!" We all still roar at the thought of the bright red-faced Fred, spitting out the last phrase. We all miss the late Mr. Hittman, and it was marvelous to have been part of making him so proud.

Hittman, the company, meanwhile was getting more and more attention in the industry. We expanded the notion of "The Hittman Concept" of engineered disposal and posited that it could be an acceptable methodology for a new site. I devised a radical marketing concept to dramatize the notion. We designed a simple but elegant brochure, outlining the concept, along with quotes from various national leaders on environmental issues, and sent it to every nuclear power plant president and state environmental agency.

The brochure was less innovative than the shipping method. I had procured newly-manufactured three-pound cans, the kind that are normally used to package coffee, and painted them steel gray. I had "THE HITTMAN CONCEPT" painted on the cans in huge letters. Then, I sealed the brochures inside the cans and labeled the top of the can with the name and address of the recipient, and off they went. They became the talk of the industry.

Not only was the shipping can unique, and even attractive, but it had other, unintended consequences as well. When the cans arrived at some of their destinations, the clerks thought the word HITTMAN had underworld implications and called for security to open the metal package. At nuclear plants that received them, the guards looked warily at the gray cans, then immediately put them through the x-ray machines to check for explosives. So, the whole thing created a stir. It was also gratifying later to enter executive offices and spot our cans on book shelves, where they were being kept as mementos. The entire effort had been kept secret, even from Barry and Fred, and I had sent them the first cans to test the shock value; they were elated. It was all great fun and a very effective campaign. We made another splash when we created a poster touting our method of shipping waste without any liquid residue. It pictured a piece of concrete that resembled a 55-gallon drum. On top of the drum were a martini glass and a lemon twist, and the caption read, "Make mine Hittman: Extra Dry." If nothing else, we were creative.

Barry called me into his office toward the end of my first year and announced, "It's time to approach Westinghouse." Westinghouse was the major player in the nuclear business, and Barry had been in their employ before running Hittman. We had developed the Hittman Concept but had nowhere near the financial backing to actually implement such an ambitious scheme. Westinghouse, on the other hand, had money to burn, and Barry wanted some of that Westinghouse money.

Soon after Barry's announcement, I made the first of many trips to Pittsburgh's Westinghouse headquarters, where we entered a richly decorated conference room, full of a dozen or so management and executive types, all looking very Westinghouse-like. We had a little slide show to present, along with our proposition—to allow them to be our partner in the development of a new radioactive waste repository, based entirely on the Hittman Concept. All they had to do was pay for it and stay out of our way. They were less than enthusiastic, allowing as to how the concept was far too expensive a solution for a simple problem and that utilities would never pay for it. We told them that they didn't get it: the customer wasn't the utilities, it was the public, and the public didn't care what the utilities had to pay, so long as the public felt secure. We two upstarts were telling the great minds of Westinghouse that they didn't know the customer. We left with cool, but civil, goodbyes. Less than a year later, Westinghouse purchased Hittman, and Pittsburgh loomed in my future.

Things at home were as cool as our Westinghouse farewells. Dean was entering his last year of high school, while Doreen was still a handful for her mother. Janis was taking classes to explore the possibility of a degree, and I suspected that she was reaching out to more sensitive beings in her quest for enhanced self esteem. It was, of course, no wonder, since I was caught up in my latest quest for success and did little in the way of providing her emotional sustenance. So, she was seeking it elsewhere.

Dean had attracted a terrific group of new friends, including Jimmy DeCarlo, whose dad played on the Johnny Unitas championship Baltimore Colts teams. Jimmy was a standout on the lacrosse team, and Dean was becoming proficient as a wrestler. Dean was applying to colleges at the time, and Frostburg was among those on his list. Since Doreen was still a challenge, Janis and I decided that she needed a change of scene, and Mt. DeSales Catholic girls' school was on our list. To say that Doreen was not crazy about the idea is to suggest that the slaves were not crazy about slavery. After the tears, tantrums, and displays of ill temper, however, we finally convinced her to give it a try. As it turned out, Mt. DeSales became the wellspring of lifelong and loyal friendships that still endure for our wonderful daughter. Frostburg would also be in her future, as it would be for Dean. In the meantime, the pool I had installed in the backyard was an attraction for all of their friends and brought us all together for a time.

Westinghouse bought Hittman in 1982, just a little more than a year after my coming on board. I had made a name for myself in the nuclear organization, and when Barry was made president of the newly-formed Hittman Associates, a general engineering operation, he put me in charge of it. I now ran the engineering organization, as well as heading up our disposal efforts. I was up to my eyeballs in alligators, as the saying goes, when the test of a new owner gave me more to concentrate on. I was too naïve to worry about losing my job in the transfer of ownership and was only concerned about no one getting in my way. Barry had spoiled me by giving me my head and watching me succeed, with little direction and much respect.

In addition to all of my existing challenges, Westinghouse presented more. True to Barry's prediction at the time of the acquisition, when he said, "You watch, Ralphie, before the year is out, you will be traveling internationally," I was now making regular trips to Japan, Korea and Taiwan. I was drinking from a fire hose but loving it. I was part of one of the largest and most respected corporations in the world, and I reveled in the respect by association.

Conditions in my marriage were not improving; in fact, they were deteriorating. Janis' outside activities exposed her to people from whom she was able to glean more than she could from me. There was a real potential of a transfer to Pittsburgh looming, which didn't help matters. In between the ever-increasing arguments, we had some serious talks and reached a mutual agreement for a "temporary" separation.

It was all very civil. Janis helped me find an apartment close by and even helped pick out furniture needed to supplement what I took from my former home. The parting was sad, and we both knew, inside, that temporary would become permanent and our marriage was over. Dean, in college at Frostburg, and Doreen, at DeSales, were both devastated by the turn of events. We tried diligently to ease the pain, but I am sure neither of us comprehended the depth of their feelings. Except for these efforts at family stability, I devoted all my energies to my career.

Most of the extended family was progressing normally. Mom and Elaine were doing well, even though Elaine's boys could be hard for her to handle. Tommy and she had split up some time before, because he had gotten into the habit of forgetting to pay taxes on the earnings he made as an independent contractor, and the strain on the marriage only exaggerated an already difficult union. Mom was an ongoing responsibility, which Elaine took on with grace and dedication. Cousin John had by now parlayed his expertise in real estate law into a corporate position of esteem, while Dr. Bob was developing a solid business in the medical field and had visions of a giant practice with hospital affiliations. Joe was engaged in various schemes to make a killing with "OPM"— other people's money. It was around this same time that Joe was placing bets for the underworld at the Atlantic City racetrack and dealing cards at night.

As the Garden State Race Track was ablaze with a massive fire, it was Joe who headed in the opposite direction of the fleeing patrons, because he was sure he could "liberate" some of the money that was certain to have been left behind by the panicked tellers. When that scheme failed, he sued the track for his feigned smoke inhalation that resulted in him being carried out on a stretcher, complete with oxygen mask, as shown in a picture that appeared on the front page of the Courier-Post. Ya gotta love Joe. Aunt Lydia and Uncle Joe moved south, where he was running a clothing manufacturing plant for Jonathan Logan. Everyone else was busy providing for their families in routine but pleasant ways.

Eventually, I got a major assignment with Westinghouse. I was to head up a multi-million dollar effort to win the newly-announced contract to construct and manage the nation's first new nuclear waste site. California was to host the facility and the competition, and I now had the responsibility, and also the massive resources of Westinghouse, to execute the plan. Once again, we were looking for a way to differentiate ourselves. The engineers at Westinghouse were not short on ideas, but the truth was that we had already discovered the ideal plan—and it was some form of The Hittman Concept. Chuck Mallory made the plan even more sophisticated by designing octagonal-shaped concrete containers to put into the engineered modules, creating a beehive effect. I dubbed this the world's first removable storage system. Until now, the knock on storing waste was that if something went wrong, as it had in Kentucky, there was no way to remove the waste; but this idea changed all that. Chuck patented the concept as the Surpak, and my name is on the patent. I thought, as I often say, "Is this a great country or what?"

We shocked the world once again when we won the competition, despite what would be an order of magnitude increase in the cost of our system. It turned out that Barry and I had been right: the customer was the public. The state couldn't dare choose a cheaper burial concept, while walking away from a more environmentally sound approach, albeit one that was described by some as over-engineered.

The decision was thus made that more protection is better than less, as long as the utilities were the ones that would eventually have to pay the bill, and I was off to California to negotiate the deal along with our new boss, Leo Duffy. Leo had been given the assignment to incorporate Hittman into the Circle Bar W, as Westinghouse was known, by Ted Stern, a high-level Westinghouse executive who had orchestrated the acquisition. Both of these men would play significant roles in my future. But Barry and Leo clashed from the outset. Barry was not enamored of Leo's slapdash style, and Leo did not appreciate Dr. Koh's erudition. The two were as destined for divorce as Janis and I.

I was practically living in Pittsburgh during the intense proposal effort that led to the win in California. Months of work by scores of talented people, had helped to elevate my star in Westinghouse, and now I was to be a key player in negotiating the contract with the state. I was supremely confident that we would reach easy agreement on the terms and conditions of the contract, and I was somewhat surprised at the number of representatives we had sent. In addition to Leo himself, there was me, Steve Winston, some scribes and two attorneys. I remember thinking, "How tough can this be?" After all, I had been writing contracts since I was sixteen when I bought the '48 Ford. One of he attorneys was Vince Campbell, and the other one Carol Knutson. My life was about to change once again.

I was right about the impending change but wrong about the success of the contract negotiations. Following many days of discussions, arguments, and compromises, Leo declared the negotiations at an end and we told California, "Thanks, but no thanks."

This did not, however, diminish my reputation for success. In classic Leo fashion, he spent a small fortune on a gala affair for all those who had engaged in the proposal effort. My contribution was particularly acclaimed, resulting in an offer to me to come to headquarters and become a member of Leo's staff. I was off to Pittsburgh.

If there were any doubts about where the marriage separation was headed, they were erased by the hundreds of miles now between us. Janis was seeing someone, in a casual and quiet way, and I was in search of a relationship. I had not been without one since Marie Ciri. I did not know how to behave like a single person and did not look forward to the prospect. It would take a couple more years before a final, and official, divorce decree ended my marriage, but that did not end my relationship with Jan. We were friends before we were married, and to this day we remain friends, with a shared respect for one another. We have an unbreakable bond, two wonderful kids who grew into fantastic adults. They are, as I have said, better spouses and better parents than we were, and we both are blessed to have them. We could find ways to blame the other if we really searched, but neither one of us would find solace in such a search. I know how I contributed to the dissolution of our marriage, and my own search ends there.

The female attorney with the thick black hair, Carol Knutson, became the target of my search for companionship in Pittsburgh. She was raised almost as an only child, although her half-brother Jim was around during her early childhood years. She lived in a run-down home with three cats and a collection of old furniture stained with cigarette smoke. I came to enjoy spending time there, adding to the smoke with my Marlboros and learning all about cats and Scrabble. I was enamored of her mind from the beginning, and the rest of her drew me in over time. Her sense of humor is only exceeded by her sense of the value of truth. She is unequaled in integrity and is possessed of many talents, including an extraordinary singing voice. She would become my second wife two years later.

By that time, I was rising quickly in the environs of Westinghouse headquarters. While on Leo's staff, I was noticed by Dick Turneau, who was on the staff of Leo's boss, Dr. Bill Jacobi. Bill became my boss as well after a time. I became the director of Westinghouse Ventures, responsible for "making deals" with various entrepreneurs interested in associating with Westinghouse. I enjoyed the freewheeling action and continued to take on all manner of assignments. Dick and I went on a deal-making trip to Italy, where I showed off my knowledge of all things Italian, and Dick showed me how to spend the corporation's money. Then, I was assigned to work on another massive proposal effort. The Energy Department was seeking a company to operate the enormous Hanford Site, where materials for A-bombs were produced, in Washington State. Westinghouse was going to compete, and I would contribute.

I was responsible for putting together the strategy for how Westinghouse would make a positive contribution to the communities that were impacted by the Hanford Site. While the operations portion of the contract was technically straightforward, my piece of the proposal required out-of-the-box thinking that I was hoping could separate us from the crowd. The technical part could, and should, be won because of the cadre of superior people we could throw at the project; no one could compete with the quality of our people. The community portion was being written on a fresh sheet of paper.

Eventually, we conceived of the concept of establishing a venture capital fund that would "invest" millions of dollars in small businesses and technologies to better allow for the region to decrease its dependence on the government contract. In addition, we proposed the establishment of a separate company, not associated with DOE, that would specialize in environmental engineering. The venture capital company would be headed by a bright, young Westinghouse executive with experience in government and business and knowledge of technology. I had written a want ad for me, and I hoped that I would be offered the job if we won. Doreen would soon be in college, and little else held me back.

While all this was going on, Dean had found his soulmate in Missy Mumma, clearly the best thing that had happened in his college career. Missy was a tiny, blue-eyed blonde with a sweet and charming disposition. Just after the New Year in 1987, they celebrated their nuptials in a grand ceremony followed by a magnificent reception. The previous evening, a nervous Carol Knutson sat by my side as I played host to the bridal party, including Janis, at a formal dinner party.

The details of every aspect of the affair were a testament to the organizational skills of the Mumma family. The Monarca and DiSibio families were in attendance, and everyone had a grand time. What a joy it was to witness the esteem in which Dean was held by family and friends. Tears still well in my eyes when I hear the song, "Lady in Red," because Dean and Missy danced to it at the end of the perfect evening. He had come a long way from the little cradle at 310 10th Street in North Wildwood, and at that moment I recalled a friend, Joseph Mango, referring to an infant Dean, saying, "Here is your immortality." How prophetic that seemed as I watched him now.

The competition in Washington concluded, and once again we shocked the world with the news that we had won. I flew out on the corporate jet with Mr. Stern to attend the first news conference on the win. The community was particularly interested in what I had to say about the community contribution plan. We were all a big hit, and Mr. Stern began counting the money that Westinghouse could make on the multi billion-dollar contract. I have never seen him prouder. The next morning, we met in the offices of Kelso Gillenwater, editor of the Tri-City Herald. After nearly an hour of questions for all of us, Kelso asked Ted, "What time does your plane leave?" Mr. Stern didn't blink or smile when he said, "Whenever I want it to." I knew that I had arrived, because I was getting on that plane, and we were winners. Hittman was no more, nor was my first marriage. I was about to get a new title, and I was running scared.

25
Pittsburgh Ping Pong

In Washington State, I had an enviable task: help business, help the community and designate the recipients of millions of dollars in Westinghouse grants.

In this picture, the Director of the Tri-City Industrial Development Council, Mike Schwenk, the Department of Energy Site Manager, Mike Lawrence, and I host a major conference on general economic development.

Pittsburgh Ping Pong

"In addition to running a successful venture capital management organization and serving on several community boards, I was about to launch a brand new business from scratch based on an original, untested idea.."

THE PROSPECT OF STARTING ANEW WAS REFRESHING. The last couple of years had been action-packed but also emotionally draining. Financially, things had stabilized when Dancing Sunbeam was sold and Janis I reached agreement on my child support obligations and alimony. I had purchased an old home in a quiet neighborhood near the Westinghouse Energy Center and had formed few friendships, beyond Carol and her closest friends, Jim Lieber and Margie Hammer. I looked upon the opportunity that was offered to me to go to Washington State as one that could provide a final break with all emotional ties excepting Carol. Carol had accepted a position as staff counsel for the executive team, and I was ready to take up the challenge of executing the plan I had proposed in our offer. I was about to become President of Westinghouse Tri-Cities Investment Management Company.

The Hanford Reservation, as it's called, is a 354-square mile section of desert in the southeastern part of the state of Washington located at the confluence of the Snake and Columbia rivers. In addition to being massive, the site is the home of hundreds of buildings including chemical processing facilities, five nuclear reactors, huge underground storage tanks, numbering in the hundreds, and, at the time I made my move there, about 19,000 employees. The remoteness of the location, some 25 miles from any city, was due to the security required by the nature of the work, which was the production of weapons-grade plutonium for use in atomic and hydrogen weapons. Security fences and elaborate systems were maintained by hundreds of heavily-armed guards, who had dogs, armored personnel carriers and a helicopter at their disposal. The Westinghouse team won the right to manage all of these operations.

My particular job, by contrast to all of this, was to establish a little office in the commercial section of town and give away money. Well, it was more complex than that, but not much. It wasn't long before I was inundated with requests for Westinghouse grants, so my first priority was to establish criteria for assistance. I put together a small local board of directors and, together, we issued some procedures. I hired a secretary and an assistant, whose job it would be to screen applicants, and set up a free workshop for would-be entrepreneurs. Before the first month was up, we had a system that was promising, and the process we established was working.

I spent time visiting the campuses of the branch university and junior college and established ties between them and Westinghouse headquarters in Pittsburgh. I also put together a system whereby excess company computers and equipment would be offered to schools before disposition or salvage. All in all, the first six months proved productive. The next phase was to cosign for bank loans for small businesses that we deemed worthy. I set aside $500,000, which would be used as a revolving fund for this effort. As the loans were paid back, the money went back into the fund to provide for a source of loans for other businesses. For the most exciting potential businesses, the ones that had some synergy with Westinghouse, I made investments in return for an equity position in the company for Westinghouse and took a seat on their boards. This approach enabled the recipients to get direct financial support, as well as access to business expertise.

The Westinghouse Investment Management Company was soon seen to be making considerable progress as a force for good in the community. As a result, I was fairly high profile and much sought-after, not too difficult to achieve since I was giving away $100,000 a month on average. I was not satisfied to let the system run itself and play a little golf with applicants, not me; I needed more action. I was elected to the board of directors of TRIDEC, the Tri-City Industrial Development Council, which represented Richland, Kennewick and Pasco, the three adjoining communities that made up the Tri-Cities, in promoting the economic well-being of the region. It wasn't long before I was recruited to head a major fundraising effort on the Council's behalf.

The effort entailed soliciting every major business entity and cajoling each into pledging money for a fund to be used to recruit new businesses into the area, as well as to redouble efforts to lobby the Department of Energy and Congress to earmark funds and projects for the Hanford Site. The task was a huge undertaking and great consumer of time. Through the effort, however, I became entrenched in the business community and made some new friends. The board of directors I put together was made up of the major players and went a long way toward our ultimate success. With the Westinghouse commitment of $250,000 leading the way, we managed to raise well over $4,000,000. This sum exceeded our goal of $3,000,000, and, given that the area had a population of only 150,000, represented a major success; and my positive reputation increased as a result. "You want to start a business? You want to raise money?" "See Ralph," was the answer. It was all very rewarding, but not too challenging.

Carol and I got married by a judge (I still wisecrack that I should have asked for a jury), only a month after we arrived. On June 6, 1987, we said our vows in front of our dear friends,

Jimmy Lieber and Margie Hammer, who had flown in from Pittsburgh for the modest ceremony. We all retired to our new home on the Canyon Lakes Golf Course, a spacious tri-level, with a back deck that enjoyed an unobstructed view of a western sun setting over the distant Cascades.

Carol was deeply engaged in legal work with her friend Karen Hoewing under the direction of the Westinghouse Hanford President, Dr. Bill Jacobi, who was heading the Westinghouse effort. The Westinghouse team had nothing to do with my little operation, which by its second year was in a steady, profitable and successful progression. I ostensibly was my own boss and could set my own schedule.

Back East, the beat went on. Elaine had discovered gold in a warmhearted Irishman by the name of Michael McDonough and was unconditionally loved. Doreen was making a fine transition into adulthood. Toward the end of the second year in the Northwest for me and Carol, we were blessed with the birth of Anthony that occurred while Dean and Missy were at Fort Carson in Colorado, where Dean was completing his Army hitch. I became the infant's first sitter, when I flew directly from my radial keratotomy surgery to Colorado Springs to mark the appearance of my first grandchild. This seemed like a good time to take it a bit slower and to enjoy the western culture and the new boat that we had purchased to cruise the meandering rivers. The rewards of my hard earned position were mine for the taking, but *no-o-o-o-o*, I craved more action; and I had an idea.

Ever since I gave Cousin Peggy Iannetta one of my business cards and she responded by saying, "I always wanted to have a card of my own," I recognized the perceived prestige of these items. I remember how proud my dad was of the business cards a paint company had given him with his name on it, and I, too, had been proud of my first business card as an assistant super-intendent. My idea was that everybody would like to have a card of his own. In addition, since mobility was becoming the norm, it seemed that addresses and phone numbers were changing with frequency. So, the old fashioned "calling card" seemed to be just the answer. Cards could be used for the purpose of personal num-bers, not just business ones, and homes could have binders with card slots instead of address books with old numbers scratched out and new ones scribbled in. This could be a new concept, and the key to making it work would be the newest technology craze: the personal computer.

Up to now, these cards were the business of printers with usually a week or more required to order, produce and deliver the result. If I could figure out how to computerize the product, I could deliver 100 cards almost instantly—while you waited. Where would you wait? Where everyone was buying stuff, of course: the Mall was my answer. I would not need a whole store, just a free-standing kiosk would allow me to do what had to be done. How tough could that be? I was soon to find out.

In addition to running a successful venture capital man-agement organization and serving on several community boards, I was about to launch a brand new business from scratch based on an original, untested idea. In all of the time I had to spare (none), I put together a business plan. For the two previous years, I had been reviewing plan after plan and critiquing them all, and now I did my own. On paper, the concept looked doable. I would have to design a kiosk to house a computer, a paper cutter and the necessary raw materials, as well as cash registers and credit card equipment, display case areas and the like. I would need to do research on malls around the country, since I would also have to find space and negotiate the terms and conditions of the leases. I planned to open in three parts of the country to attract investors. Now all I needed was the technology, original software and designs. Oh, yes, I almost forgot, I would need about $300,000. Even that didn't seem too tough.

Within four months, there were "YOU IN PRINT" kiosks opened in Florida, New Jersey and Washington, and I had all the action I could crave. After I had shared my business plan with my friends and offered equity positions for $25,000, Barry Koh, Vito Zeccola, Phil Lippincott, Jim Petersen, Jim Walton, Dominic Fermani, Dr. Tom Sykes, Ray Robinson, Kelso Gillenwater and Jeff Dryer were among those to invest and join the company as board members. Others came aboard to fill out the initial offering.

The business plan included trusted investors being responsible for the initial stores: Jim Walton in Washington, Vito in Jersey and Dr. Sykes in Florida. Trusted employees that included my sister Elaine, Joey Cini, Joey Zeccola and Laura Robinson, supported them. Ray Robinson and Kelso were responsible for development of the software, which worked flawlessly after some initial hiccups. A local design team did a magnificent job on the oak kiosk; all three were prefabricated in the Tri-Cities, and two were shipped to the locations in Florida and Jersey. Vito came out to see the erection of the one in the Tri-Cities Columbia Mall so he would be able to replicate it in Jersey. Linda Gillenwater, Kelso's wife and an artist, was responsible for design of the cards and other products, including note cards and stationery.

Essentially, we had invented the commercial version of instant desktop printing. We didn't intend it, but we were Kinko's before there was Kinko's. We were going to make a fortune! Soon we would open in scores of malls across the country and cripple the commercial printing business when it came to cards.

The business failed in five months. While we paid off every debtor, negotiated our way out of every lease and avoided having to declare bankruptcy, all of us lost our investments. Barry Koh bought the remaining equipment and the rights to the business and kept it alive for a few more months. The sad truth was, the business had failed. My idea failed. I had failed. But the good news was that I learned that failure did not result in being swallowed up into a black hole, and no one painted a large red F on your forehead. In fact, I learned much from the experience.

The failure was due to several factors. While we were ahead of the technology curve for a few months, it wasn't long before people were printing cards at home. Three months after we went out of business, there were ATM-like machines at turnpike rest stops that allowed a customer to print 100 cards without a clerk. They didn't need us.

We were also too ambitious in opening three locations virtually simultaneously, draining our cash prematurely. I did not anticipate the need to build a market over time. We were on the right track, because we were losing less money each week, but the money ran out before sales caught up. The blood, sweat and tears I poured into the concept, and the thrill of launching the business, were never regretted. For nine months, I had all the action I could desire. I turned an idea into reality, and little else can be more satisfying. The experience created a bond between me and Jim Walton that would last forever, and the loyalty and friendship of the rest of the partners has never declined. We lost the battle, but the war was fun. We were in the combat of business together, and we survived, bent but not bowed.

Carol remained disengaged from the You In Print effort but not immune from its impacts. She was against the idea from the outset, for fear of the eventual result, and she was right in predicting the degree of difficulty. I worked day and night and was obsessed with the effort. Since I still worked as diligently at my "real" job, she saw little of me. She had a demanding position of her own and, between the two of us, there were few leisure moments during our last nine months in Washington.

Dr. Jacobi was promoted to a position back in Pittsburgh, where he would head all of the Westinghouse government businesses, which were becoming significant. My efforts at making significant investments were returning rewards, and I had put in place a number of ongoing programs that ran without direct leadership. So I was able to leave, and Dr. Jacobi wanted me on his staff. He offered me the post of Director of Strategic Planning for his business unit along with a transfer back to Pittsburgh. Carol and I discussed the move and, although she had no promised position for herself, we were confident that she could secure one that would use her considerable talents. Pittsburgh was always attractive to both of us, and the corporation agreed to a substantial raise and to purchase our home. And off we went.

DiSibio left solid impact on Tri-Cities

Ralph DiSibio rushed off to new challenges at the same pace with which he attacked his Tri-Cities responsibilities. Whoosh! He was gone. What a loss, yet what a presence he has been.

DiSibio was president of Westinghouse Tri-Cities Investment Management Company, established to carry out Westinghouse Electric's commitment to aid in diversifying the Tri-Cities after it won the Department of Energy contract three years ago to manage the Hanford site.

It is important that the Herald acknowledge DiSibio's success and the faithfulness of the company he represented. We were fierce in our insistence that contractors sweeping into town to manage hundreds of millions of dollars worth of Hanford work should return something of substance to the community, to aid in its diversification and to reduce its dependence on the federal government.

The Herald campaigned vigorously to make community investment a mandatory part of the DOE contracts. We were concerned from experience how and elsewhere that voluntary programs were often superficial and little more than two or three most deserving candidates for empty public-relations gambits. We wasted teeth in the plans. DOE wanted it to be voluntary, however, and, as usual, DOE did it the way it wanted.

Yet Westinghouse seemed determined from the beginning to operate its voluntary, non-binding program as if it was a requirement. The results speak for themselves and Westinghouse can be proud of both the quality of its commitment and

the quality of its planning and execution.

Primarily, however, it can be proud of selecting DiSibio to represent it in managing its $35 million portfolio of community support activities. The peripatetic DiSibio was a whirlwind of community activism, bringing a can-do spirit and his rich professional and civic background to a wide range of important issues and initiatives.

If forced to choose between the benefits to the community of the investments DiSibio and his company made and those that came from his personal involvement in community affairs, I would be forced to choose the latter. His impact was extraordinary, far beyond the management of Westinghouse's dollars. He helped redefine community leadership here. Frankly, as implausible as it may appear since he was here only three years and is now gone, I believe he could easily have been one of the two or three most deserving candidates for Tri-Citian of the Year.

His leadership was felt in many ways. For example, it was DiSibio to whom Tri-City Industrial Development Council (TRIDEC) leadership turned to organize and lead the Renaissance fund-raising campaign when it became evident that dramatically expanded resources were necessary to deal with the economic crisis the community faced.

DiSibio

He was a major force in improving higher education, using personal talents and Westinghouse resources to work for expanded graduate programs for the new Washington State University campus here and to support Columbia Basin College. A Ph.D. educator who once served as head of Nevada's school system, he was passionate in his commitment to education. He wanted better tools for teachers — like one he knows 35 years ago who somehow saw in a desperately poor New Jersey street kid the makings of something special.

I remember the day at least three years ago when I first met Ralph. It was at the Red Lion in Pasco, when all the new and old Westinghouse and Boeing executives who would be managing the new contracts here met with several Tri-City Herald people. Westinghouse had suggested the meeting as a way of forcefully acknowledging its commitment to its voluntary community investment responsibility.

DiSibio and his team eclipsed the $1.7 million goal, raising an astonishing $2.5 million. TRIDEC turned to him again when a search was necessary for a replacement for Executive Vice President Mike Schwenk. His committee identified and helped recruit John Lindsay.

DiSibio and his team eclipsed the $1.7 million goal, raising an astonishing $2.5 million.

Ted Stern, Westinghouse Electric's executive vice president and head of its government operations, made it clear that day that Westinghouse was taking its role very seriously. Not just the site management role under the direction of Westinghouse executives Bill Jacobi and John Nolan. He also introduced DiSibio and said a separate company accountable to him would manage the community investment program. He pledged that DiSibio would have his authority and support and, by inference, his close attention. The weight of Stern's words, and the credibility his reputation lent to them, was not lost in the room.

Ted Stern and Ralph DiSibio raised high expectations that day. They made some big commitments. Not everything they tried was successful. They took some risks and risks don't always pay off. But they left us better than they found us and, sadly, most big companies and DOE administrations who have touched this community and site in the past 15 years cannot say that.

Our community has been hammered by broken promises, assurances breezily made and cynically withdrawn. In that mixed context, Westinghouse's performance is doubly gratifying.

So to Ted Stern: Thanks for sending Ralph DiSibio to the Tri-Cities. And if you run out of things for him to do back in Pittsburgh, send him back. We'll think of something.

☐ Kelso Gillenwater is publisher of the Herald.

Kelso Gillenwater ■■■

Parting was not easy. We had both made several good friends in this charming little area, where we were respected in the community, big fish in a little pond. The Tri-City Herald and Kelso Gillenwater highlighted the departure with a memorable article that I, not so humbly, include here, partially to memorialize our dear friend Kelso who died prematurely of heart failure.

We didn't take long to pick out a new home in Pittsburgh when we arrived in April of 1990. Three years in our new home in Washington had settled any issues about old fixer-uppers. We selected a new home on a steep lot on Trotwood Drive, only a few miles from the Energy Center where Dr. Jacobi was enthroned. I occupied an office next to his and near Phil Woods, another departed friend, who would be of inestimable assistance during my stay. Dick Turnau was now at the Westinghouse Defense Center in Baltimore, and Leo Duffy had parted company with Ted Stern and Westinghouse with bad blood all around. Few of the old crowd from prior days at Westinghouse were still around, but my new assignment required little support, excepting for that of Phil Woods. Carol was snatched up by the Westinghouse operation at the Bettis Atomic Power Laboratory outside of Pittsburgh, and they were glad to have each other. She had the additional task of settling us in at the new digs. There was much to be done in the pristine abode, including landscaping and window treatments.

Within the first two months, I had the initial draft of the strategic plan ready for "Dr. J's" review. He wanted me to provide a mock presentation that he and his staff would use to shower me with questions, as if I were defending my doctoral dissertation once again. On the appointed day, I stood before the mock board with confidence and began, "Ladies and gentlemen, the Government business provides Westinghouse a vast opp—." Before I completed the word "opportunity," Dr. J interrupted me in a disdainful and booming voice, "Vast, what the hell is vast? There is no such word in business; lucrative, risk-free, profitable, maybe, but not vast." He went on to admonish me, "Cut the crap out, and stick to the point. I don't want hyperbole; I want facts, just the facts." Welcome to the world of the Westinghouse Board of Directors.

My next drafts were far more precise and to the point. I developed a strong rationale for our business model and a strategic path forward for growth and eventual dominance. The formal presentation to the board was delivered superbly by Dr. J, and his boss, Mr. Stern of "whenever I want it to take off" fame, was pleased. I was making some points with the people at the very top of the corporate ladder, including Stern, who was now the second-in-command of the mega corporation and likely to head it up one day.

As July approached, the landscapers were still in the design stages, and some trees were planted in an effort to beat the heat of summer. Carol was doing a great job of arranging some furniture that we had moved from the Tri-Cities and had ordered custom drapes that were scheduled for delivery in six weeks. The United States intervened in a somewhat bizarre way to make sure that she never realized the fruits of her decorating labors.

Admiral James Watkins had been appointed as the Secretary of the Department of Energy. Of the old school in the Navy and a stickler for procedure and discipline, he had reorganized the Department into distinct areas of responsibility. The recent restructuring had recognized a new and expanding area that would require significant resources to get organized and under control; for the first time, the Department would pay attention to long-neglected environmental problems that it had created at many of its locations. Along with Rocky Flats in Colorado, both Hanford in Washington and Fernald in Ohio would cease the production of materials and be designated as "clean-up" sites, and the implications of these changes were huge for Westinghouse. The teams of experts deployed by Westinghouse to manage the production activities at these sites were ill-equipped to deal with the many complicated environmental issues that now confronted them. And, there was yet another shoe to drop—not at, but on, Westinghouse.

The Admiral was in search of an Assistant Secretary to head up this new challenge. When the phone rang at the home of Leo Duffy, he was not expecting to hear the voice of his old boss from Navy days, Admiral Watkins. Leo was being recruited to take over the huge, clean-up bureaucracy, with billions of dollars to dole out—the news could not have been worse for Westinghouse and Ted Stern.

I was not expecting to hear the voice of Ted Stern when I picked up the phone one evening, about a week after the Duffy/Watkins call. "Ralph, this is Ted Stern, I was wondering if you and Carol would like to join Liz and me for dinner at the Duquesne club tomorrow evening?" I almost said, "Is that you, Jimmy? Stop putting me on," But, instead, I stammered, "Sure, what time do you want us there."

Carol and I had an unsettling evening contemplating the events that might transpire. The President of the Westinghouse Hanford Company was Roger Nichols, and he had already contacted me a couple of days previous, inquiring as to whether I would like to come back to WHC and be on his staff. He knew I had somewhat of an environmental background and a great reputation in the community; but, most importantly, Leo Duffy liked and respected me. For the first time in my life, even I could not contemplate the eventuality of accepting his offer. I said, "Roger, I am flattered by the honor, but, as much as I would love the challenge, I couldn't ask Carol to quit her job and put the cats through the death-defying act of flying in the cargo section of a plane again. Thanks, but no thanks." Carol lauded my "sacrifice" and said, "They must be nuts if they think they're dragging me across the country again."

The Duquesne club was the most exclusive private eating club in Pittsburgh. The aged, wood-paneled walls and marble floors were complemented by the bone china and Waterford stemware on the tables. You wouldn't have been surprised to see Andrew Carnegie sharing a table with George Westinghouse, because this was dining heaven. The maitre de escorted us to the Sterns' table and, once there, although we wanted something stronger, Carol and I ordered white wine to match the drinks Ted and Liz had already started.

After very little small talk—one of the few things that challenges Ted—he got to the point. "Ralph, we have a serious problem at Hanford. Leo now controls our fate, and you're the only guy he doesn't have a grudge against. We need you to return." He paused to take a breath, and I started to speak, but he held his hand up, ending my thought, and continued, "I want you to go back and become the Executive Vice President, second-in-command, to Roger; of course, Carol will be appointed Deputy General Counsel. We'll handle all moving and house issues and anything else you both need. I'd like you to be out there next week, and Carol can join you when she is ready. I know this is a sacrifice, but the corporation needs you. What do I have to do to convince you to agree?"

I hesitated to pick up my wine glass. I wanted to give myself time to consider the words of my refusal and was hoping that Carol would revert to form, not parsing any words, and would say, "What are you, nuts?" Before I could finish my sip of wine, Carol began to speak, and I was seeing my career flash before my eyes. "Mr. Stern, there is no way I would even consider the offer...unless you agree to fly the girls (Trilogy, Brie and Deseret), our cats, on the corporate plane and agree to return them in the same way when our assignment is finished." She said this with a flourish and a finality that somehow she thought was a refusal. Ted didn't blink or even say, "The girls?" He simply said, "Done. Let's order."

The moving truck was pulling away towards Hanford as the home decorating truck was pulling in to deliver and install the drapes that Carol had ordered. I was already in the Tri-Cities, living in an apartment, while awaiting the completion of our new home that had been found by our friend, the irrepressible Jim Walton. Jim found and transacted a deal on a magnificent home on River-wood Drive just two miles from the office. It sat on a steep lot, at the entrance of a subdivision, and was the topic of conversation of all who passed it. It was a beautiful design, and inside it was even more dramatic. Carol would do a great job of decorating it with window treatments that would actually be installed this time.

It didn't take long for both of us to become fully engaged in the new challenges of the Hanford operations. Leo Duffy was in touch with me and warned me that our personal relationship would provide Westinghouse no slack, although he did say that he would give me fair warning before he took any serious action. Roger and I consorted to put together a new strategy for the site that required us to change out nearly the entire senior staff of 15 vice presidents and to bring in talent better suited to go in the new direction the site was headed. Instead of production, we needed to be concerned about leaking tanks and highly contaminated build-ings, reactors and chemical processing canyons. Carol was just as busy ensuring that legal risks were mitigated and the corporation was protected.

Even though I was fully engaged in the awesome challeng-es of the site, I managed to find time to regain my high profile in the community's efforts at growth and development. My old associates at TRIDEC didn't recognize that I had precious little time to de-vote and were relentless in calling to track me down for volunteer positions. Roger, meanwhile, was inundated with requests from both the Department of Energy and Westinghouse to do more and faster, better and cheaper. Besieged by constant complaints about Roger from Leo, the corporation adopted the Neville Chamberlain approach to Hitler: appeasement. Roger was replaced, and I would soon have a new boss. Jim Gallagher was the new head of Government Operations for Westinghouse, and he flew in to give Roger the news that he was being transferred and would be replaced by Tom Anderson. Tom was a long-time Westinghouse executive with a strong environmental, safety and health background who had recently been at another Westinghouse-managed site in Aiken, South Carolina.

I, of course, got the assignment of bringing Tom up to speed, and his Naval Academy education made him a quick study. We complemented one another in our styles, as well as in our areas of expertise. He reminded me of my relationship with Cousin John—we were opposite in many ways, but I became the stylish glove on his steady hand. We came to be forever bound by our mutual respect, derived from surviving combat together. And combat is, indeed, an apt description for what we faced over the next 18 months. There were constant barrages from Washington, D.C., and more than occasional second-guessing from Pittsburgh was the order of the day. Tony Massaro was our new leader at headquarters, and he took no prisoners. In the ensuing skirmishes, Tom and I watched each other's backs. Meantime, there were the constant challenges of the site, the local DOE offices, the state government with its many demand and the 24/7 nature of the job illustrated by the beepers we were required to don.

Tom and his wife, Carol, and my Carol and I were constant companions outside of work as well. The Andersons got along with our friends the Russells and the Waltons, and we all even got to play golf once in awhile. We were not just big fish in a pond, but whales in a small lake. The site dominated community life, and nearly one out of every two families had a member who worked for us. I was feeling like I was back in Nevada, where the job never left me. A simple visit to the grocery store was given over to several conversations about the site or working conditions or other work matters. It was relentless, but I must admit I loved it. I love the smell of challenge in the morning.

Then came 1993, a year from hell. Other then the delivery of Kayla, the long-awaited, beautiful girl to add to Dean and Missy's family, the rest was about to go downhill. January seemed relatively normal, in that Tom and I were pretty much in control of the difficulties all around. We had built a reputation for candor and professionalism, and even displayed moments of courage. Carol continued to make significant contributions to the legal team, now headed by her friend Karen Hoewing, and all was right with that world. In February, however, a frantic call from my sister ended any hopes of normalcy. Our mom had suffered a major stroke and had been rushed to the hospital in Marlton. I was on the next flight East and was devastated by her condition when I arrived. Elaine and I consoled one another, supported by numerous family members, as the doctors struggled to save her life and provide us with a prognosis. When it came, it was not good.

The next day, we were told that she would live, but the stroke would deprive her of speech and the ability to use her right side. Her mental capacity would be dramatically diminished, and she would have limited means to understand all but the simplest concepts. I couldn't get my head around it. I was crushed and Elaine was my twin in anguish. I had to do what I always did, take command and make decisions.

Elaine was insistent on taking Mom home with her and tending to her with the help of promised day nurses, but I would have none of it. I was determined to thwart any such plan that would have my sister sacrificing her future. Mom and Elaine had lived together for a number of earlier years, and that had proven to be both mutually beneficial and marked by tumult. Now, when both had flourished apart for several years, I could not see my way clear to support a decision that would have Elaine's life dominated by around-the-clock sacrifice. Elaine finally capitulated, and together we carved out the plan for Mom.

Now, almost 14 years later, Mom resides in the same nursing home we then selected. Visits, even from loyal family members, have become understandably few and far between, except for the almost daily visits from Elaine and the dear Patti Piech, who religiously comes by weekly to visit. I never leave the building after a visit when I do not weep at the condition of this strong woman. Once capable of delivering a right cross to a paratrooper, she is now relegated to pulling herself endlessly around the halls in her wheelchair with her one good arm, staring off into the distance, waiting for loyal Elaine to pick up the laundry and kiss her goodnight. God bless them both.

I was, mercifully, required to return to Washington and once again leave Elaine to hammer out the details, and she did a brilliant job. Unfortunately, all of the challenges I left behind at Hanford were waiting for me on my return. But, with Carol's acquiescence, I set about making some career-changing decisions. With my mother's condition, I could not remain 3000 miles away, separated by the distance and the three-hour time difference. I would have to find a position, inside the corporation hopefully, closer to New Jersey. I confided my predicament to Tom and to Jim

Gallagher, and they agreed to attempt to assist me in my quest. The prospects were not as robust as they had once been, because the corporation was now in the throes of massive reductions and potential major restructuring.

The year was further relegated to the waste bin of bad years when Kerry died within earshot of her physician-father, Dr. Bob. Also, we buried our beloved friend, Jack Ziegler. I vividly recall the look Phil Lipponcott and I exchanged as they wheeled Jack out of the church to the tune of "Stars and Stripes Forever." It was a sad look of recognition of the death of our own immortality.

Another guardian angel appeared at about this time. Joel Bennett was the Senior Vice President of the Parsons Corporation that was located in Pasadena, California. He and I had mutual interests in business and liked each other on a personal level. He began to woo me, with an eye toward recruiting me to Parsons, and his efforts culminated with my trip to the office of the CEO and Chairman of the Board, Len Pieroni. Mr. Pieroni and I hit it off immediately, and the mating dance continued. I wanted to remain with Westinghouse, but I had to have an emergency chute ready to open in the event of need.

Gallagher and Westinghouse were unable to offer a position and urged patience on my part. Having always been short on patience, in the fall of 1993, I accepted a position as Vice President of Government and International Affairs for the Parsons Corporation. The position was in Washington, D.C., and after a long discussion with an understanding Tom Anderson and a gala "retirement" send-off attended by a couple hundred staff and community leaders, I was off to our nation's capital. Carol continued to work at Hanford and naturally was left behind to handle the myriad moving details. I was running scared.

26

Life in the Big City

In addition to the challenges of Rocky Flats and international finance, the highlight of my five years in our nation's capital was the cousins' trip to Italy.

We drove to the town of Orvietto on an otherwise cloudy day to have a lunch fit for kings. John, Joe, Bob and I posed for a most memorable photograph against the backdrop of the famous town Cathedral.

Life in the Big City

"For several years, Cousin John and I had dreamed of a men-only trip to Italy with the Monarcas."

AFTER NEARLY A DOZEN YEARS WITHIN THE WARM CONFINES of mother Westinghouse, I was back to feeling my way along as a stranger in the strange land of a new corporate hierarchy. At Westinghouse, I had managed, with the help of a number of mentors, to rise to the highest level that had ever been reached by someone not an engineer or a lawyer or a financial type in the history of the corporation. I was one of the top 200 people in a company of 125,000 employees. Now, I was relegated to being the new executive kid on the block, needing the press clippings I had arrived with for validation. But, how tough could that be?

Carol came back to D.C. for a house-hunting trip and was shocked to see that the $360,000 we would get for our palatial property in Richland, Washington would not buy a basement condo on DuPont circle. In the end, we settled for a beautiful home in the Avenel golf course community near the Congressional Country Club, just 10 miles from the Kennedy Center. All of this for the mere sum of $660,000. Welcome to our nation's capital.

There were other benefits to be derived from being back East. I could visit Mom and Elaine, as well as the rest of my relatives, rekindling my bonds with Joe, John and Dr. Bob, among others. The two Uncle Mikes were always high on my list of people to see, and Aunt Louise was on that list as well because of her age. Dean and Missy had settled in Maryland, and my grandson was always thrilling, and I worried with Dean, as Kayla was offering significant challenges that were requiring major surgery and prompting a quest for a diagnosis. Doreen was at Frostburg, reprising her brother's college experience, soon talking about a young man, David Stovenour, who was stealing her heart. Carol took a couple of weeks off to settle the house and restart her career, this time at the Westinghouse Defense Center in Baltimore. The commute was a hassle, but at least Ted Stern had kept his commitment to fly the "girls" back via corporate jet, so they were able to get settled while she was working.

I had preceded her return by several weeks, taking up temporary residence at the St. James hotel, which allowed me to walk the 10 blocks down K Street to my office. My office was a spacious complex on the 8th floor of a building on 15th Street, N.W. From my expansive windows, I could see the Washington Post across the street and the Madison Hotel next door. Looking down the side of the Post building, I could make out The University Club, a private eating and men's club, to which I now belonged. I was Vice President of Government and International Affairs, and it was all quite heady.

On my first day, my new guardian angel, Joseph Volpe, the senior employee emeritus at Parson, greeted me. Forty years prior, he had been hired by Ralph Parsons himself, having been recruited from his position as General Counsel of the Atomic Energy Commission. At the AEC, Joe had counseled the likes of Edward Teller, J. Robert Oppenheimer and Harry Truman, and he was a legend in a city of legends. It would be Joe who would introduce me around town as the senior representative of the Parsons Corporation and would serve as my mentor during my entire tenure. I am still indebted.

Parsons had an impressive resume in the region. We had designed the highly-acclaimed Washington Metro system and now had the contracts to construct the new Ronald Reagan Airport and to expand both Dulles and BWI. As the company's senior representative, I would have to interface with major clients and ensure that they were satisfied with our performance.

I was also responsible for interacting with the many embassies of countries in which Parsons had ongoing contracts or was competing for additional work. "Embassy Row" became a haunt of mine, in addition to Capitol Hill where I provided testimony to Congress or attended conferences, fund-raisers and hearings. Jack Hargett, a member of my small staff, had direct responsibility for lobbying efforts, but I often met with the heads of various agencies and international financial institutions, like the World Bank. To most observers, the position was one to be envied; to me it offered little mental stimulation, since I was not fully accountable for any projects. I was used to keeping score for my own performance, through profit statements or statistical evaluations of financial success, and I did not feel like I could be satisfied for long, schmoozing with the high-rollers and heavy-hitters of D.C.

I count myself among the Americans who believe that even after decades of often-flawed performance, this is the greatest country man has ever created. Many scoff at the grandeur of the marble structures and monuments as the designs of a society that overindulges in such architecture while poverty surrounds it. I am not one of them. I think we should have more and grander structures, emblematic of our role as the greatest democratic nation on the planet. I never left my office without being cognizant of the history all around me, and I found working in the city to be a great experience. The multi-national cultures and rich ethnicity made Camden look like Salt Lake City, and the variety of restaurants and attractions could be rivaled only by New York City. The Kennedy Center was 10 miles from our new home, the Smithsonian museums were blocks from my office, and the White House was four blocks away on 16th Street.

When I was not being wined and dined, I was wining and dining others, using my considerable expense account. Tickets to great events were mine for the asking, and we often took advantage, with Cousin John and Peg joining us on occasion. We attended the Italian-American Gala, where 3000 sequined and gold-bedecked fellow Italian-Americans rubbed elbows with Sofia Lauren, Pavarotti, Al Pacino, Tony Bennett and Justice Scalia. It was very entertaining, exhilarating even, and I should have been satisfied. But *no-o-o-o-o*.

Parsons Corporation was about to launch a new initiative after Joel Bennett, then the senior VP in Pasadena, had convinced Len Perioni to go after the lucrative government contracting business. The Department of Energy was searching for new teams to provide innovative approaches to their cleanup challenges. Rocky Flats in Denver, Colorado was a top priority, and Parsons was preparing to compete for that job. Parsons would be the lead to put together a multi-million dollar proposal to manage the enormous site, an effort that would require us to team with several other corporations, identify key personnel who would take on high-level assignments and develop a winning strategy based on creative solutions to the challenges offered by Rocky Flats. The missing ingredient was a key executive to run the entire proposal effort and commit to executing the plan when the team won. I appeared on their radar screen.

My first year, under the tutelage of Joe Volpe, I was deemed a great success in the corporation. Joe was Godfather-like in introducing me, saying, "Ralph speaks for the corporation now; talk to him about the issue." He was generous in his plaudits when he reported my progress to the corporate leaders. "Never give Ralph a job you don't want done." This was high praise indeed from such an accomplished man. I had established many new and important relationships in all of my areas of responsibility and had uncovered several new opportunities for the company through inroads in Middle Eastern countries, membership in several organizations and many private briefings. My contacts within the international financial institutions bore fruit by way of uncovering new financing methods for our opportunities abroad. I also had close relationships with some key legislators and cabinet officials, and my first 15 months had been productive. Still, I was looking for more challenge. And Joel was about to provide the solution.

Carol, by now, had traded her job for one closer to home. Her commute to the United States Enrichment Corporation was less than five miles, and the position had not been easy to come by in a city that seems to have more lawyers than Utah has Mormons. But thanks to a friend, Bob Hanfling, she was successful. We managed to fly, with Mom Kridler, to Altus, Oklahoma to witness the marriage of Jim and Bunny's daughter, Linda, and this would turn out to be the last stretch of time that Carol's mom would be in robust health.

Our home in Washington, D.C. received more visitors then in Washington State. Cousins Michael and Joseph, Cousins John and Peg, Elaine and Michael, and, of course, my new grandson and his mom and dad came for visits. Dr. Bob, Sammy and Peppe came down for a golf outing at the Congressional Country Club in a huge white stretch limo (ya gotta love that Sammy), and we had a grand time. Cousin Joe visited with tales of the apple of his eye, Jesse, and his accomplishments. Joe also generously expressed pride in my achievements, a pride that was only exceeded by his pride in Jesse. Still I needed more action.

In addition to continuing to fulfill my duties in the Washington office, I was named to head up the Rocky Flats proposal effort for Parsons. The assignment would take more than nine months at a cost of $6,000,000. The project's main venue bounced around from D.C. to Denver to Pasadena, with months spent at each location. I chose Steve Marchetti and Nadia Dayem to be my senior operations executives and Holly Coghill as my executive assistant. Together with Paul Butler, who was running the guts of the proposal, we recruited major corporations—Boeing, Duke, Rust and others—to join in the effort. We put together an impressive team of senior leaders consisting of the major stars from all the participating corporations, then had to manage this ego-laden cadre. We combined efforts and put together an innovative strategy that would be difficult for the government to turn down as a solution to surmounting the obstacles presented at Rocky.

The team came together as a seamless force for excellence. The 12-hour days and six-day weeks we devoted to the effort, while living in close quarters, produced a family. After weeks of wrangling over organization charts and graphics, we began to think as one. We soon were able to anticipate each other's thoughts and approaches, and the disparate individuals with names like Ralph, Smokey, Holly, Nadia, Paul and Steve became one concept, "The Rocky Flats Solution." The best evidence of the closeness of the group came at the end of the effort, when Nadia and Paul prepared to become Mr. and Mrs. Butler, despite the fact that Paul already had a wife. I told you we were creative.

The team was about to have its first break, a respite that followed seven months of grueling, nonstop work that included the first submission and preceded the orals. The orals were two days of intensive presentations before an evaluation board, in which we were required to orally present highlights from the thousands of pages of the written proposal. This effort was the most important part of our work and required a month of preparation. I gave the team two weeks off to clear their heads, revisit neglected families and get ready for the home stretch. I was going to Italy.

For several years, Cousin John and I had dreamed of a men-only trip to Italy with the Monarcas. There had been an aborted effort two years before, when we tried to organize a dozen or more cousins, at best an unwieldy undertaking, much like herding cats. So for this journey, we toned down our ambitions and settled on a more manageable group—me, John, Dr. Bob and Joe. The timing fit in with the planned break in my schedule; Bob and John had flexible schedules; and Joe's availability was facilitated by the encouragement of his new wife, Sandy. All of the wives were supportive of the trip, and the plan was executed in November of 1994. The excursion remains one of the high points of my life; it only lasted eight days but it solidified a lifetime of brotherhood and love for one another. It was made more memorable, because not long after the trip Joe was dead and Bob was later to be crippled in the aftermath of a stroke that confined him to a wheelchair in a nursing home. Bob was in his 50s when he had the stroke, and Joe was barely 60 when he died.

From the outset, our travel was riddled with laughter and warmth. We commenced the trip at Dr. Bob's home in Cherry Hill, and Aunt Pat, Uncle Bob and Judy were there to witness as we piled into the van that had been rented by Dr. Bob and popped the cork on the Champagne bottle, all recorded on film for posterity. On the other end of the journey, when we arrived in Rome, Joe paid tribute to the Italian ground by kissing it with a flourish. We stayed at the Parco di Principa hotel, just off the Via Veneto. On the first day, Joe summed up the whole trip when he responded to our inquiries about how he liked it, "Anybody that don't like this is crazy."

We packed a month into the week that we were there. We had dinner at our cousins' apartment in Rome, where we borrowed their car so Dr. Bob could drive to Canale Monterano, where we were treated like returning kings. We walked for miles every day, consuming copious quantities of wine and pasta as we went. Joe often complained about the walking, because his health was just beginning to deteriorate, but he was a trooper. We spent after-dinner hours at sidewalk cafes, sipping anisette and delving into one another's views on family and life. We were a band of brothers before there was a Band of Brothers. Of course, we did the Vatican, the Trevi Fountain and the Via Condotti, but the biggest attraction was each other. We had a fantastic meal at a little trattoria in Orvieto, where we gorged on gnocchi and meats and dolce, and it was the Orvieto trip that provided the venue of the photo we all treasure as a commemoration of our bonds.

On the last day in Italy, Bob reprised the Canale Monterano visit, while Joe rested at the hotel. John and I walked for miles and lunched together at Gianni's Trattoria, were we shared the prediction, sadly prophetic, that we would never be able to replicate this time together. We returned to the States the same as when we went to Italy—the same, but different. Our greetings to one another at family gatherings thereafter would be a little warmer, enhanced by the experience that only the four of us had shared.

Reality hit me in the face on my return. Orals preparation, as rehearsed as any Broadway show, was to prove to be every bit as grueling as the written proposal. The entire team of 20 executives had to be prepared to present their areas of responsibility over two days to a skeptical board and respond to questions. I was to handle the opening, introductions and the summary and closing, and Mr. Pieroni and Joel Bennett had flown in from Pasadena to pledge corporate commitment. With the spotlight on us, the team performed

magnificently. In my summation, I felt like Clarence Darrow, pointing out the irrefutable evidence of our superiority. By the end of
my presentation, most of the audience, including the members of
our team, had tears in their eyes. I had told the board how much
we wanted to help the DOE to succeed in this effort, extolling each
member of our team as the best in the country. To a person, we
were convinced that we had made them an offer they wouldn't
refuse. We knew we had won.

Incredibly, they refused our offer, and we lost. Some weeks
later, we learned that CH2M Hill had edged us out by 10 points out
of 1000. We had beaten them on technical approach and executive
team but lost on price and the acceptance of risk. I was devastated,
literally brought to tears (again). I couldn't believe that the efforts
of these incomparable people over the last nine months were for
naught. I felt responsible for the failure, but worse for the impact
on the team members. The thousands of hours of stress and hard
work had taken a toll on us all, and we all reacted differently. Some
quit their jobs, some retired, and some went on extended leave. I
went back to work and had a heart attack five months later.

In the time leading up to my own health problems, Kayla
remained a medical mystery. Her initial neurosurgery was performed by the world-renowned Dr. Ben Carson at Johns Hopkins,
but that didn't uncover a definitive cause of her developmental issues. Continued investigation by her tenacious parents, however,
proved more fruitful. They finally learned that Kayla had a chro-
mosomal abnormality, essentially the result of a missing piece of
a chromosome missing; q-22 deletion is the official name for this
condition. The discovery and its implications would be the source
of significant challenges and life changes as the years unfolded.

We belonged to Lakewood Country Club at the time and
enjoyed occasional family brunches with the kids, while Anthony

got his first taste of golf with his dad and me. All else was fairly normal in my own home and my extended family. Much to my delight, Doreen and Dave had gotten engaged and were preparing to celebrate the union in Maryland the next year. Mom's condition had settled into a routine, as Elaine took up the challenged of whipping the nursing home staff into shape.

I was back to the challenges in Washington full-time and taking on new duties as a result of my promotion to Senior Vice President. I had also been named as President of the Parsons Development Company and had taken on responsibility for the investment strategy for potential major projects in power and oil and gas production abroad. Owing to our work in a joint venture with the Bechtel Corporation, I was dispatched to Saudi Arabia on several occasions to oversee our projects there, and in between my trips to the Middle East, I was spending time in the United Kingdom on similar issues.

My continuing responsibilities in Washington kept me more than occupied, but I took up the task of designing and constructing the rooms to finish the lower level of our house at Beman Woods Way. Toward the end of that effort, I was forced by Carol to heed the pains in my back and jaw by taking an emergency trip to the hospital, where we were informed that I was having a heart attack. The staff administered TPA—and then another drug when my pulse rate dropped to 30 beats per minute; and I eventually was stabilized. After a trip to Washington Hospital for the insertion of a stent, I was released to go home, and I was back to work in 10 days. A few months later I would be back in Washington Hospital Center when that stent was closed; it was reopened and another stent put in as well, and life went on.

With my own heart repaired, I was fully engaged in all my old and new duties alike in the heart of the nation and beginning to have a certain level of comfort with it all. Carol and I were contemplating a move into the city to more fully benefit from its urban flavor. Stability was on the horizon for the first time in several years, and anyone in my position would have been satisfied; but *no-o-o-o-o.*

Doreen and David were married in a ceremony at St. Peter's Basilica in Baltimore, followed by a grand reception at Ft. Mead, thanks to Capt. Dean Disibio's affiliation with the Army. It was a wonderful affair that Doreen and her mother designed. I still weep when I hear any rendition of "The Way You Look Tonight," the song Doreen chose for her dance with me. When Doreen approached me, with some trepidation, about the financial arrangements, I tried to put her at ease. I asked her to think about how much she would need to have the kind of wedding she wanted. I said that when she was ready with a figure, we would discuss it. She followed my instructions and visited me to share her conclusion.

She was still nervous about the number of people she was planning to have and was hesitant about asking for enough money. She had carefully figured the cost, aided in this effort no doubt by having been in what seemed like countless weddings of her friends and her own woman's sense of these things. She told me the number. I thought she had been gentle with me, and I added an additional $2000 to the check I handed her. She protested, insisting she did not need it all yet. I said, with as much firmness as I could muster, "Dor, I want you to have it all now, and then I don't want to hear the details about the cost of flowers or bands or anything else. I just want you to spend it in any way that you and your mother want; if you choose to elope, you can still keep the money. I just want to avoid any arguments between stepmothers, mothers-in-law or whatever. Have a great time spending it, but, as my father once said, "My name is Bess, leave me out of this mess." "I love ya, honey," I said, "but these are dangerous times for fathers and other men." We still laugh about the conversation.

Carol and I decided to move slowly toward retirement and were in search of some place near the ocean. We honed in on Rehoboth Beach, Delaware, where I bought a lot in the relatively new Kings Creek Country Club development two miles from the beach. We selected a house plan that had been the 1994 Time-Life House of the Year, and 10 months later we made settlement on our getaway/retirement home at #1 Black Walnut Court.

The call from Bill Hall, President of Parsons Power & Petrochemicals was as surprising as the call from Ted Stern eight years earlier. "Ralph, I have a problem in the Power organization, and I'd like you to come down to Houston to chat about it," was Bill's cut-to-the-chase opening comment. We set a date, and I found myself in his offices the following week. I assumed he wanted to seek my assistance in exploring international opportunities. But before I could speculate too much, he once again cut to the chase. "Ralph, would you consider running the Reading operation for me? I would make you the President of the Power division, and we could negotiate other issues if you have an interest." Once again, someone had selected me to turn an organization around. I needed to think about it and chat with Carol.

Things in the corporation had been changing. In a tragic turn of events, Len Pieroni had lost his life a couple of years earlier when he and a couple dozen other executives accompanied Secretary of Commerce Ron Brown on a goodwill mission to the Balkans; the plane crashed in Croatia with no survivors. Ironically, it was me, as the Washington representative of Parsons, that was asked to go on the trip, but I was in the hospital with stent replacement surgery, so Len had decided to go himself. Joel Bennett had resigned when he was passed over as Len's replacement, and I was set adrift with no one in Pasadena to watch over my future. I needed to assess my situation—and it was right about then that Bill called.

Parsons Power headquarters was located in Reading, Pennsylvania, about 45 minutes from Philadelphia. It was headquartered there because the 700 engineers were the remnants of Gilbert Associates of utility engineering fame, whose most important clients had been the regional utilities. When Parsons acquired Gilbert, they merged the firm with their other power unit, CT Main of Boston. Reading remained the headquarters, with the Boston operation serving as a satellite office. The Reading office had a good engineering reputation and had the potential to expand and capture a share of the business in a growing international energy market. Hall felt there was something I could bring to this effort that others had lacked, and I had enough confidence to believe him.

I called Carol from Houston and explained the situation, and, essentially, she said she would do whatever I wanted to do. Once again it was all about my career and my desires. The only good news was that Carol was not enamored of the position she had taken with USEC; she had no respect for the leadership and would not miss anything about the organization, except for some of her colleagues. I was in Reading a week later, leaving Carol to tidy up the loose ends.

Dean and Missy had made a courageous decision for Missy to postpone her career and move the family closer to Philadelphia, where Kayla was integrated into a special experimental group that would track her unusual malady. They settled in Marlton, and Dean took a new position, continuing to move up the corporate sales executive chain, while Missy was engaged in the complexities of managing Kayla's progress. Dave and Doreen were looking to purchase their first home in Finksburg, Maryland. David was teaching school in the Baltimore school system, and Doreen was working with the expanding Chevy Chase banking organization as a line teller.

For the most part, the rest of the extended family was doing reasonably well. Mom was an ongoing responsibility, which Elaine took on as routine and without complaint. Her relationship with Michael McDonough had blossomed delightfully, and I was warmed by the happiness he brought into her life. Cousin Joe had died in 1996, so my boyhood idol was no more. And other deaths and births continued to fill in the details of the cycle of life, but no other odd tragedies befell the family. I set up temporary living at a townhome near the Reading office, waiting for Carol to identify a home that she wanted. I hit the ground running—running scared—in the Reading office and wasted no time putting my stamp on the organization.

27
Power Is What Power Does

Here I am with the irrepressible Tankosic in Zagreb, Croatia. We spent many days and nights in the great intrigues of Eastern European negotiations.

When I was not his companion, Carol was, as she tried to put into writing the convoluted contract clauses we conjured up.

Power Is What Power Does

"The immutable truth is that if you inspire the right people by setting out a vision that they can share, they will always go beyond their own perceived talents."

THE POWER BUSINESS IN 1998 WAS ON THE VERGE of a major resurgence, and I was determined to see Parsons Power become a player. We had all the elements for success: a strong reputation for integrity, a corps of excellent engineers, processes and procedures that made us efficient and effective and a work ethic hardened in the hills of blue-collar Pennsylvania. The corporate leaders in Pasadena and Houston thought I could exhibit the leadership necessary to allow the Power unit to recognize its potential.

In addition to me, the company had recently recruited Bob Wood and Rod Regan to head up hard-money construction and business development, respectively. With the addition of Bob Alder to head our engineering services efforts, I formed a team of executives hungry for achievement, and I empowered them to submit proposals containing innovative approaches that we could use to win jobs and execute them profitably. We were good at what we did, and before long we had huge contracts in Texas, in Zagreb, Croatia and in Medellin, Columbia. We had our hands full and we had the undivided attention of the corporate fathers and competitors. In the three years I was to head up Power in Reading, our team set records for sales and profits. I loved the people in our division and took great satisfaction in our wins. I was negotiating alliances with partners all over North America and in Europe and establishing unique supply chains throughout Asia. Generally, I was breaking a lot of new ground.

The senior staff was superbly competent, and my job was to set the vision and get out of their way. The driver of our success in Croatia was Djurica Tankosic, among the most creative business development people I have ever encountered. A big component of his innovativeness was his street smarts, exemplified by an incident that occurred when we were scheduled to meet at the Four Seasons Hotel in Milan, Italy, where I had arrived for my stay. Djurica was driving to Milan from Zagreb and was to meet me for drinks. He called me as he was crossing the Italian border to let me know he was on time, and I informed him that he was going to find it impossible to reach the hotel, which sat in the center of a veritable maze of tiny streets surrounded by larger buildings. He replied in his usual way, his heavy accent infused with confidence, "Boss, never worry about Tankosic, I will be on time." The phone clicked in my ear.

When I exited the elevator at 6 o'clock, I saw my friend sipping a Campari and soda. After we embraced, touching cheeks in our delight to see one another, I challenged him, "So my friend, lie to me; tell me you didn't get lost." Djurica grinned his trademark grin and then gave me a lesson in creative thought. "Boss, it was easy. When I got into the city, I followed the many signs to the train station. I went to the taxi stand and asked the first driver if he knew how to get to the Four Seasons." Djurica paused for a sip of the drink and for effect. "Boss, I asked the driver how much would he charge me to get to that hotel. He said it would cost 4000 lira." I stopped Djurica there and said, "See, I knew you couldn't find it." His grin grew larger, "No, no, boss. I gave him 5000 lira and told him to go ahead and I would follow him. My car is outside. Problem solved, boss." He finished the last with a flourish as I shook my head in awe and ordered a Campari for myself. Ya gotta love Tankosic.

Reading, Pennsylvania was a dichotomy. The rolling hills surrounding the office and the beauty of the countryside belied the Camden-like atmosphere of the inner city. The gentle Amish in their black horse-drawn carriages to the northwest were in sharp contrast to the low-rider old Chevies in the decaying city. In our spare time, we visited the ubiquitous vegetable stands and rekindled our interest in motorcycle riding after we both purchased new street bikes. Aunt Lydia, Aunt Marie, Elaine and other family members visited, and Carol's mom took up residence in a nearby senior citizen high rise, a move that would not turn out to be a good idea.

Mom Kridler was spiraling into senility, the effects of the malady coming on at a much faster pace then either of us could have predicted. We should have had a clue when she showed signs of trouble during a dinner visit to our Reading home. Mom was sitting in the living room next to a wooden table that is made to look like a fully-attired butler holding a tray, and her orange juice sat atop the tray. Hearing her mother chatting away in the room where she sat alone, Carol went in and said, "Mom, who are you talking to?" Startled by the interruption, Mom said, "Why, to this young man," pointing to the table. Carol gently said, "You know, I always thought he was made out of wood." Unflustered, Mom turned and said, "That may well be, but he carries on a mighty fine conversation." Ya gotta love her. Shortly thereafter, we finally made the decision to put her in a nursing facility, where she would get 24/7 care.

I was extremely busy building a business and expanding the reach of Parsons Power by establishing a satellite office in Houston. As the growth in the energy needs of the nation made it very difficult to do anything but succeed, I was riding a bow wave of business opportunity, and I intended to make the most of it. In addition to our Zagreb success, we were building plants in several states and looking for more work worldwide. We competed for a contract to build a gas-fired power plant in the heart in Columbia, South America, right in the middle of the illegal drug trafficking region of Medellin, where the drug cartel was in control. I wasn't worried; I was from Camden. Whenever I arrived in Bogotá I was met at the airport exit by three heavily-armed bodyguards, who stuck to me like glue throughout my stay. We were all escorted, in armored limos, to and from meetings and negotiation sessions. A guard was stationed outside my hotel room while I slept. Those were exhilarating times, as we worked in association with the brave people who went into the jungle on the Magdalena River to bring power to the people.

The immutable truth is that if you inspire the right people by setting out a vision that they can share, they will always go beyond their own perceived talents. As a testament to this maxim, the Reading and Houston offices were booming with business because of people like Wood and Tankosic. The more difficult challenge was always to make as much profit as possible once we won a job, and this was never a slam dunk. In fact, I was always in awe of what we did for a living. Just imagine the degree of difficulty in succeeding at what we were attempting to do. Once a utility or a venture capital group would determine that a region was ripe for more power, it would purchase some land and ask for bids to build a power plant. We would respond by estimating what we would charge to design, build and start up a plant from scratch, all in a specific timeframe. We would essentially bet that we could deliver the plant for a fixed price, usually in the range of 170 million dollars or more, and in a specific time, usually around 18 months, and that it would produce a specific amount of power, typically 150-200 megawatts. If we succeeded, we made a good deal of money; if we didn't, we would be hit with damages and loss of profits that could cost us millions.

Of course, in order to do put together a proposal like this, we would have to estimate the cost of engineering, design, construction, labor, permits, equipment, roads, transformer lines, generators, turbines and a million pieces of material. We would have to order, on a worldwide basis, often from several countries, all of the pieces of major equipment and schedule the deliveries to coincide with a detailed construction schedule. We had to anticipate weather, tides and river flow to ensure delivery and erection, and then we would pray that, when it was all put together, it would start up when we "turned the key." And, of course, after it started up, it would have to produce the promised amount of energy at a steady state. So it's no wonder that I was in awe of what we did.

We were so good at it that Parsons Corporation decided to sell us, along with the oil and gas business that Hall ran, and once again, I found myself in limbo with respect to my future. The executives of the two units to be divested, including me, were enticed to remain at the helm in return for a considerable bonus that would be paid when we were sold. The corporation wanted to try and keep us around to give presentations to potential buyers and to maintain the stability of a nervous work force. The exhilaration of succeeding in the global power business was about to fade, as we geared up for the sale. We became far more conservative in our bidding approaches and much more risk-averse, so as not to frighten off potential buyers with our contracts.

There were many suitors for the successful power business, less enthusiasm for the oil and gas part of the company business. But we worked as a team, putting together a very effective pitch that had me, Hall and others describing the intricacies of our businesses and answering detailed questions. The presentations were based in Houston, and I was spending more time at headquarters there. The most interested party was the newly formed Washington Group that had been created when Morrison Knudsen of Boise, Idaho purchased the Westinghouse Government Services division and combined the two operations. The Westinghouse unit, as coincidence would have it, was the same one that Dr. Jacobi and Jim Gallagher had run for the old corporation.

Washington Group's interest in Parsons was motivated by its search for the missing pieces that would fill out the Washington Group resume. Dennis Washington was the self-made billionaire at the head of the company, with a vision he was determined to bring to reality. Parsons Power and Parsons Oil and Gas were on his hit list. When we gave our presentation to a team of Washington Group executives that included Lou Pardi, Tom Zarges and Steve Hanks, we were unaware that they also had Raytheon Engineers and Constructors on their list of potential acquisitions.

The presentation was flawless and, more importantly, we liked one another. There was little doubt in my mind that the Washington Group interest in the purchase of the Parsons units was real. Lou Pardi and I had a previous association through a joint venture we had run together, and we had gained mutual respect for one another during that shared experience. I valued his executive judgment, and he had a true understanding of the things that my Power Unit had achieved over the last couple of years. We both concluded that in short order there would be a deal that would put the two of us in the same organization, a notion we relished. As fate would have it, a part of our prediction would come true but in a most convoluted fashion.

While the year-long corporate divestiture strategy dragged on, I still had a difficult business to run. Carol had taken a run at the real estate business when her search for legal employment was stymied by our distance from a major population center, and the Parsons Power unit recruited her to do some complex legal work, which eventually had her handling the Croatia contract. While we both made business trips to the region, we never went there at the same time.

By the time that my work was interrupted by major surgery in 1999, my ardor for the challenges of the work had not diminished. But, of necessity, I took some time off to pay another visit to the Washington Medical Center and have Dr. Pfister open up my chest, take out my heart and use the arteries from my chest and the veins from my leg that he had removed to bypass six clogged coronary arteries—a more complex procedure than the one that had cost my father his life, but a less experimental one. I was back to work in five weeks.

I don't mean to make light of the trauma of such a procedure, but these things happen. It was more traumatic for my loving family than for me. I went through considerable pain, but I was never in doubt as to the eventual outcome. They, on the other hand, imagined all manner of negative results, like death and other surgical mishaps. I will say that it is at times like those that you take stock of your blessings and the bountiful life you've lived. I did just that and felt completely fulfilled. The kids had turned out even better than I had any right to hope for, and I had grandchildren to give me immortality. I was more distressed at Doreen's miscarriage that occurred while I was hospitalized than I was at my own condition. The outpouring of love from my family, friends and associates warmed my mended heart. One week after surgery, my sense of humor was proven intact when I joined the Parson's weekly international call and interrupted a surprised Bill Hall by wanly speaking, "This is DiSibio, I want to thank the board of directors for the get well card they decided to send...by a vote of six to three." I hung the phone up as a roar of laughter erupted.

I had kept Carol in the loop as the acquisition mating dance continued. The first year in the new millennium, 2000, was drawing to a close, and I was actively considering retirement if I did not like the results of any change of ownership. I was confident that any new owner would need me for awhile and I would have ample opportunity to plan for the future. I estimated that by the end of 2001, I would be wrapping up my career and could stop running scared. Not for the first time, I failed in my prediction.

The Washington Group made a decision to pass on the Parsons units, choosing instead to make a deal for the purchase of the Raytheon Engineers and Construction organization. I was disappointed, because I was tiring of trying to keep morale up in an organization of people who didn't know what the future held for them. For the first time in my professional career, I was looking for stability, and it would not be just around the next corner.

The Washington Group deal with Raytheon was proving to be a deal made in hell. The commitments made by Raytheon concerning an accounting settlement were delayed for months, and the cash drain on Washington Group generated rumors of impending bankruptcy. It was difficult to understand how such a good organization could have been deluded into believing in the smoke and mirrors that it now appeared had been presented to them. I had continued to keep in touch with Lou Pardi and a new executive by the name of Charlie Oliver, who had come out of retirement to help Steve Hanks right the listing Washington Group ship. They were in need of a few good men, and it had recently looked for a brief time like I would be in their employ.

Two months before the beginning of 2001, I had been flown to Boise to entertain an offer by Steve Hanks to join his company. I had agreed to accept the offer and returned to Reading the next day to inform Bill Hall. I told him that despite the potential bonus, I was resigning to join the Washington Group. He urged me to wait until I heard from the President and Chairman of Parsons, Jim Mc-Nulty, who called me within 10 minutes. Jim implored me to remain because of an imminent presentation to the Shaw Group, another company that had expressed an interest in the acquisition of our units. "Ralph," he said, "if you were to leave now, our chances of selling the unit without you would devalue the company and maybe even prevent the deal." I told him that if I had known about the circumstances, I would not have accepted the offer, and I promised to call Hanks to see if he would agree to permit me to renege on my acceptance. Hanks was cool, but cordial, as he expressed his understanding of my reluctance to punish a corporation that had, essentially, been good to me. We concluded by saying that we would revisit the situation if circumstances permitted.

Hall and I made a presentation to a bombastic Jim Barnhard, the multi-millionaire President and founder of the Shaw Group. He was a piece of work, with his constant ramblings about his successes, and I remember thinking, "This guy could commit suicide by jumping off his own ego; I could never work for him." The deal went through the due diligence process and several rounds of negotiations, which continued over a number of months. Barnhard concluded the process by offering an insulting price, and McNulty dismissed him and the offer. I had wasted months of time, to no avail, and still had a business to run.

A month later, I called Hanks and offered my services. By then, the corporate writing was on the wall; it was clear to the industry that Washington Group would have to seek protection under the bankruptcy laws. When Steve asked me if I was sure I wanted to join a crippled company that might not survive, I said, "I love the smell of challenge in the morning."

28
Going Home Again

As Washington Group International came out of bankruptcy, we gained much respect. We hosted seminars at a retreat in Canada, where we arrived by seaplane. At the conclusion of the trip, enriched by the experience, we waved farewell to a remarkable staff.

Pres and Jerri Ann Rahe, Cynthia Stinger, Carol and I, Gail Papp and Senator Lindsey Graham.

Going Home Again

"In a career that, by any standard, had more than its share of "once in a lifetime" opportunities, this one was the very embodiment of the phrase."

I RETURNED TO A NEW JERSEY ADDRESS, for the first time since 1978, when I entered my office in the Princeton headquarters of the Washington Group Power business unit. I had been named Vice-President of the Power group by Tom Zarges, with the blessings of Charlie Oliver and Steve Hanks. Once again, I was the new kid on the block, with a lofty title and a commensurate salary package to ease the transition. One question remained for me, the former successful President of Parsons Power, concerning my motivation: What possessed me to join a faltering corporation? "Do you have a death wish or what?" was a frequent inquiry. A good question, since we went into bankruptcy a month after I joined the corporation.

I once again took up residence in a small, company-provided apartment, while Carol remained in our home in Reading, which now had a "for sale" sign in the front yard. We did have a game plan: I would find a small home in the Princeton area; she would sell the Reading home and eventually move to the home we had built in Delaware in 1997; and she could join me in Princeton on weekends. We were now in a position that would allow her to retire soon and devote major time to Mom Kridler, who needed more attention. We had begun exploring nursing homes in the Rehoboth Beach area and, within a year or two, we thought, would both be there enjoying retirement. So much for game plans.

As I was wont to do, I threw myself into my new challenges at work. The effort was made easier by the gentle leadership of Tom Zarges and the upbeat style of my peer, Lou Pardi. I wasn't in the company for a month when I was made part of the team that was dispatched to the New York offices of Steve Cooper, the Chapter 11 "workout maven" who would lead our company out of the black hole of bankruptcy and whose efforts on behalf of Washington Group would be a precursor to his work as the funeral director for the Enron fiasco. In New York, I was stunned by the openness of the leaders of the corporation in searching for the path that would be best for everyone. We all were concerned about the workforce, the shareholders, the vendors, our creditors and, mostly, about keeping the venerable companies that had been merged to make up the Washington Group intact.

We were now fully submerged in Chapter 11, subject to a law that required us to come up with a plan that would be acceptable to a judge assigned to our case for our emergence from bankruptcy. The team designed a plan which minimized the negative impact on most parties, excepting the shareholders who lost their investment in the company. All groups suffered some pain, and we designed an incentive package that we hoped would entice senior leaders to stay at their posts and see the process through. These were delicate times, requiring courage and stamina, and the team was up to the task. Sharks were in the water, trying to rip off pieces of the corporation or swallow us whole by buying us intact, but on the cheap. All of the top executives, including me, were getting recruitment calls from the industrial ghouls, all of whom were trying to deal the company a death knell by stripping it of its leadership lifeblood. We went into Chapter 11 in May of 2000 and came back out by the end of the year, much to the amazement of the financial and industrial onlookers.

The dark months spent in bankruptcy required Herculean efforts on the part of every leader in the corporation. We had the unenviable task of convincing many constituents to stick with us; the workforce, the suppliers, old customers, landlords, and partners all had to be handheld, as we made our way into the light. None of the challenges was more formidable than maintaining the confidence of our present customers and convincing others to give us new work.

We undertook a major effort at Power that was replicated in the other business units of the corporation. Tom Zarges instituted a massive employee communication campaign, highlighted by weekly all-employee meetings abounding with senior leaders who were in attendance to answer, without benefit of any rehearsal, questions from the audience. Lou Pardi visited every current customer to pledge our commitment to effectively complete our contracts. I visited all potential clients, to describe our plan for coming out of bankruptcy and to lay the foundation for putting trust in Washington Group in the future. I enlisted SNC Lavalin, a major Canadian Corporation, to back all of our bids with their financial strength, to provide assurance to our clients that they would be protected. We cut every piece of fat from our budgets and reorganized our units to reflect the lean and mean picture we were painting. Slowly, we regained the confidence that we had shaken so seriously with Chapter 11, as the entire corporation became the poster child for emergence from bankruptcy. Our schedules were horrendous, but we willingly accepted the small sacrifice, because we believed in what we were doing.

Tom, Lou and I and many other senior people in Princeton were recruited from other parts of the country, and we lived in temporary quarters. This condition had the vice of its virtue; one unplanned consequence was that the group lived together 24/7.

Our work never left us. Over pizza or steak or breakfast, we were together, talking about our challenges and motivating each other. It was like being back in the fraternity house, and Lou was Bluto of Animal House fame. It was grueling, but it was fun.

Other lives proceeded apace. There was little fun to be had by Carol; when the house sold in Reading, she was relegated to her own temporary quarters, a nearby apartment, with our two cats, Deseret, one of the girls who had flown on the corporate jet, and Seka, adopted from Elaine. Carol's services were still required at Parsons, and she would not be able to "retire" for at least several months. Kayla was in the program at Philadelphia Children's Hospital, and Dean was getting more responsibility in his career, while Missy was taking a leading role in running the house, and Anthony was maturing beautifully. Doreen and Dave were blossoming as newlyweds and putting together a lovely home in Finksburg; Dave was pursuing a Master's Degree, and Doreen was happy in her new position with Duratek in Columbia; and they were both praying that the new pregnancy would come to term. Elaine was caring diligently for Mom and moving toward fulfilling a life-long dream that she was pursuing tenaciously, of living in a model community with a view of the lake. Michael deftly provided for her emotional needs. Elaine's grandmotherly duties were accepted with love and pride as all three of the oldest sons had children of their own while Jeffrey remained in sunny Southern California.

The Washington Group was seen as a success as it came out on the other side of Chapter 11, and I learned first-hand what dedicated leaders can do on the strength of a shared vision. The story of the corporation could probably best be described by a full-blown Harvard Case Study or by a professionally written business book; and the lessons to be learned could benefit anyone who is engaged in a business enterprise. We were leaving bankruptcy behind by the fall of 2001, and the senior leaders were justly rewarded with financial packages that included stock options. Our prospects in Power were substantial, and the future looked bright for the business and for me. I could now plan on working for a couple more years, then claiming victory with retirement. Finally, I could see the light at the end of the career tunnel. Stability was at hand, and all I had to do was keep my head down and be astute in avoiding new challenges. But, *no-o-o-o-o.*

I was not expecting to hear the voice of Charlie Oliver when he called to invite me to dinner in Philadelphia in late October, shortly after we started on the path of leaving the bankruptcy behind. It was unusual, in fact, since Zarges was my direct boss. I met with Charlie over a fine Italian dinner, and I ended up being completely stunned by the message he delivered, although I had heard a similar refrain before. "Ralph, we have a problem in Government Services." Charlie went on to explain the problem. He said that our partner in the government business in the UK, British Nuclear Fuels, was dissatisfied with the president of that division and wanted new leadership; in addition the corporate leaders felt that an infusion of new leadership could reenergize the once preeminent force in the Department of Energy challenge. Charlie wanted me to consider becoming the new president. The conversation came out of the blue, and it set me off to begin an all too familiar pattern of breaking the news of a new career offer and a move to a new location to a harried spouse.

In a career that, by any standard, had more than its share of "once in a lifetime" opportunities, this one was the very embodiment of the phrase. I was being offered the chance to lead the very organization that Ted Stern, Dr. Bill Jacobi and Jim Gallagher had built and led. I had joined Westinghouse as a mid-level manager, who had become part of the company by way of the Hittman acquisition, and I now had the chance to be at the top. Horatio Alger would envy me this chance to grab the brass ring and live the elusive American Dream. Carol recognized the significance and, after much initial trepidation, she acquiesced to my acceptance of the offer. She was a trooper.

The position required three immediate actions: a quick trip to England to get concurrence from our partner, official approval of the board of directors of the unit I would be heading and an introduction to the senior staff in Aiken, South Carolina, where Government Services was headquartered. These three tasks were accomplished within 10 days of Charlie's request over dinner. After a meeting in England, we returned to Denver, where the board was scheduled to confer, then took an immediate flight to Aiken for me to have my first meeting as the new president. Shortly after this, I was in my new temporary living quarters. My head was still spinning as I lay it on the pillow. I had come full circle, and I was the antithesis of the Thomas Wolfe book, "You Can't Go Home Again." Wolfe was wrong, and I did go home again. I was "the man" at the Westinghouse units that I joined almost 20 years before as a novice.

Headlines in many newspapers and journals trumpeted the corporate change. I was off and running scared once again, but this time with a clear vision of what I wanted in the new organization. I was blessed with a great senior staff, with Chris Verenes as chief of staff. I knew Chris was my kind of guy when I called him in confidence from Denver to ask him to prepare for my arrival without revealing my new assignment. His cell number ended in three zeros, making it highly prized, and in an attempt to break the tension of this delicate first call, I said, "Wow, Chris, that is a great number you have." He did not skip a beat before he replied, "If you like it, boss, you can have it." Ya gotta love Chris. Once I arrived, my goal was simple: restore the business unit to its former glory as the dominant corporate entity in the government services business. The vision was clear and simple, but the task was going to require every ounce of energy of every leader in this part of the business.

The holidays of Thanksgiving, Christmas and New Year were just a blur, as I dedicated every waking hour to the tasks facing me. This was not difficult, since I was again alone and almost within walking distance of my second home, the office in Aiken. Carol was still in Delaware, where Mom Kridler was unexpectedly deteriorating and, indeed, lost her battle with cancer and a cerebral hemorrhage in the first month of the new year. Carol was at her side, as she had been for weeks. To make matters even worse, Deseret had just reached the end of her own life a couple of months before. Even in light of these events, Carol was coming down to Aiken to survey the homes I had scouted out with Aunt Sally, our real estate agent and soon-to-be dear friend. We were finalizing our choice on Yellow Pine Road when an emergency phone call from David, Doreen's husband, rocked my world. Doreen had been rushed to the hospital, with preeclampsia, a life-threatening condition connected with her pregnancy. We caught the next flight north.

Doreen had been stabilized, and she delivered a 2-pound, 4-ounce baby boy, whose prospects for survival were slim. The next several days were tense, as Andrew Joseph Stovenour clung to life with tenacity. He refused to give in to the many difficulties that confronted him. Somehow, the little fighter survived and went on to offer his own challenges over the next several months. I confess that my relief over the survival of my beloved daughter was so deep that it nearly overshadowed my joy at Andrew's successful fight for life. Satisfied that all was well and in David's capable hands, I returned to Aiken.

The next two years were as action-packed as any in my career, as I occupied the loftiest and most universally respected position in our industry. The Washington Group reorganized around six major business units, and I headed the one which I helped to name, Energy and Environment. The name signified our primary customer and our areas of expertise. I could use this chapter to detail the many successes we were fortunate enough to achieve during my tenure, but the exercise would only feed my ego rather than giving any benefit to the reader. The basis for our success is, however, significant, proving as it did that the lessons I learned with Barry Koh at Hittman had served me well. Everything I designed and executed had one complex, yet simple, focal point: Know your customer. In addition to the Department of Energy, I knew that the leadership team, the workforce and even our competitors were also customers. They all had to buy what we were selling, and I was diligent in keeping my eye on the real prize: the customer, not profit. If you pay attention to the customer, profit will follow.

I paid attention to three areas: motivating the senior staff to higher levels of performance by shaking up the organization, reestablishing credibility with our major customer, the DOE, and striking fear into the heart of competitors by winning some noteworthy competitions. The senior staff stepped up to the plate, exceeding my expectations, if not their own; our competitors began to seek alliances with us, as we won new work; and the customer responded to our commitment to excellence that we backed up with improved performance. When visiting DOE, I stole a line from Jim Little, one of my executives: "WGI stands for *We Get It*." The customer loved it.

I formed a troika model of leadership, with Pres Rahe watching over business development strategy, the proposal strategy supported by Dave Pethick, and the Operations part of the business covered by my old friend, Steve Marchetti. My back was always ably covered by Chris Verenes. These men performed with such alacrity and skill that I was freed up to concentrate on developing a strategic business plan. I was laser-like in my obsession with the care and feeding of the customer, on developing strategic alliances that would ensure our growth and market dominance, and a succession plan that would guarantee staff development. The last phase would be done under the leadership of Jennifer Large and Steve Muller.

I sent all senior staff and directors within the DOE a wooden box that had our new mantra inscribed on the top along with my signature. The message was clear and announced our expectations for ourselves: "No spin! No surprises! Instant and massive response!" I wanted everyone to know that we would be honest about problems, accept responsibility without excuses and use every available resource to respond to the concerns of our workforce, our partners and our clients. I am happy to report that the people of the freshly-named Energy and Environment business unit made the vision a reality. Our reputation was restored, the unit made record profits, and we were positioned for sustained growth.

In my last mission, I had the opportunity to incorporate all of the lessons I had been taught by family, friends and guardian angels. I had been taught to listen on the streets of Camden. Joe's Meat Market taught me to be responsive to the varied needs of people. My family, including Mom and Dad, taught me the value of a work ethic. My sister taught me loyalty and tenacity. My spouses taught me that I was flawed. The New York Shipyard and Campbell Soup taught me how leadership sets the tone of any organization. Wildwood taught me professionalism. Gloucester City taught me the strength of empowerment. Northern Burlington taught me the power of leadership. Nevada taught me humility. Hittman taught me about business. Westinghouse taught me about corporate life. Hanford taught me the value of compromise. The Washington, D.C. office of Parsons taught me the value of diversity. Parsons Power taught me the power of a team. Washington Group Power taught me the power of dedication. Energy &Environment taught me that the application of lessons learned leads to success. My work there was done.

Afterword

This picture represents the family that, in addition to my mother and sister has supported me unconditionally. They lived with my flaws and endured them. I hope they have the good fortune of receiving the unconditional love they have provided me.

Standing left to right: Dean, David, Anthony, the author

Kneeling left to right: Doreen, Carol, Kayla, Missy

Sitting left to right: Mary Frances, Andrew Joseph

Afterword

"Even a casual observer, one who only skims the pages of this memoir, must conclude that I have had 'a full life.' "

I BEGAN THIS PROJECT WITH AN INQUIRY: How did I get here? Through this effort, I hope I have answered that question. I got here, two and a half years into retirement, through personal effort, but always building on the foundation of my forbearers and the support of family and friends. Guardian angels appeared at opportune times to augment that support. I mentioned Thomas Wolfe and his book entitled "You Can't Go Home Again" in the previous chapter. I can not help but recall another Thomas Wolfe novel, "A Man in Full," that comes to mind when I reflect on my life. Even a casual observer, one who only skims the pages of this memoir, must conclude that I have had "a full life." And I am thankful for it.

Since my retirement in April of '04, the lives of the people who were part of this memoir have continued.

THE KIDS: It is hard to imagine two offspring who could have been buffeted about by the moves, twist, turns and emotional upheaval of the life I have outlined with less outward appearance of trauma. While I am sure there are scars that they have hidden, I am just as certain that they have been strengthened by the challenges thrust upon them. To know them is to describe them as loving, caring, sensitive, warm and thoughtful people. They, like me, are the sum total of the many influences on their lives; I am thankful that they did not assume some of my most unlikable traits and am hopeful that some of what they are is as a result of my contribution. In any case, I admit bias when I say that I take enormous pride when I am presented as their father, my favorite introduction. It has only been in the last several years that I have not responded with a modest, "So far, so good" declaration, when people tell me how wonderfully these adults have turned out. They are complete in every way now, and I am in awe of them. In some ways, they will be judged on how my grandchildren turn out, and I hope they are as fortunate as I was in that regard. So far, so good.

Dean is a highly successful sales executive with Johnson Diversey of Johnson Wax and Windex fame. He is a regional vice president with responsibilities that extend from Boston to Baltimore. He missed additional promotions to be activated into the United Stated Army Reserve, but the 18-month assignment will end soon, and Lt. Colonel DiSibio will go back to the world of business. My grandson, Anthony, is poised to enter his first year of university life, likely at West Virginia University, where he has already been accepted. He is talented both academically and athletically. He has the devastating good looks of his late great-grandfather, Anthony James DiSibio, my dad. Kayla has developed into a musical talent worthy of consideration by Broadway, with charm and a smile that never fail to light up every room she enters. She will start high school soon. These two youngsters will no doubt carry on the traditions of hard work and family loyalty that preceded them. Missy, who has resumed teaching in the Marlton School System for a lucky principal, keeps the whole family stable.

Doreen has developed into someone deserving of the Mother of the Year Award. To do so, she postponed a promising career in human resources. She not only nurtured a fragile Andrew Joseph back to robust health but also delivered a gorgeous baby girl, Mary Frances, who is rapidly becoming a diminutive Doreen. Andrew now has a teenager's vocabulary in a four-year-old's body.

Under Dave and Dor's direction and care, these two might become the first brother and sister astronauts. Doreen and her long-suffering husband moved into a new home in Finksburg out of the fray of passing traffic and perfect for the four of them. David, an excellent person who is tremendously patient, is a rising star in the Baltimore school system, where he has risen to an assistant principal level. Doreen and he are lucky to have one other.

Mom continues to endlessly roam around the halls of the Kresson View Nursing Home. She has shocked everyone with her positive countenance in the face of all her adversity and her feeble attempts to cheer others up as she strives to make her visitors feel less guilty. Somewhere behind her blank stare, I know she still takes pride in Elaine's dogged protection and my occasional visits. Her most consistent and loyal visitors are Patti Piech and her own beloved daughter.

Elaine has willed her dreams to come true. She is mortgage-free, in a house in Southhampton that sports the renovations of her design on a lake in Southhampton. The guards in the gated community wave to her in recognition, as she smiles at her good fortune every time she comes home. She has found a loving companion in Michael. Her sons are in good health and making their way in this world. Except for Jeffery (as far as we know), they have all provided Elaine with healthy grandchildren that number 11 at last count. Elaine is as diligent in defending her grandchildren as she was her sons, and is blind to my many faults as well. She will soon retire from her job as a security officer in the Gloucester City School System, where she served with distinction.

Pooky Binder married for the second time and made a very good and legitimate living as a union leader, working as a rigger in the conference and entertainment exhibit set-up business. He is retired in Orlando, Florida.

Tom Harris died of complications from a heart condition without reaching settlement with the Internal Revenue Service. His debt is now uncollectible.

Michael McDonough has continued to be a wonderful part of the family as he shares love with Elaine. He is stoically gallant as he fights lung cancer and its effects. His thoughtfulness is exceeded only by his sincerity.

Aunt Lydia is the last of the Monarcas, excepting my mom. She is beginning to fail physically, but her mental powers and her attitude are intact. Although she lost her soul mate, Uncle Joe, years ago, her son Joey is nearby to attend to her wellbeing, and she is the recognized matriarch of a great family. Mel and her grandchildren are in the South and in frequent contact. Aunt Lydia herself has constant contact with the Marianis who provide comfort and support. Cousin Phyllis, Cousin Peggy and John, Cousin Tom and Elaine are regular visitors as well. She fights the ravages of old age valiantly.

Uncle Mike DiSibio, as cantankerous as ever, has a Lucky Strike as his constant companion. His recent accommodations with his sons have allowed him to finally enjoy the rewards of having been a good provider, if not a good example, over the years. He is the last surviving DiSibio of his generation. One wonders, if the Japanese and cigarettes didn't get him, what will?

Janis Zeccola is nearing retirement from her position as a social worker in Maryland. She attained her MSW and teaches part-time in the college system. She basks in her own sunshine. She recently purchased her dream home in a retirement community, 20 minutes from Doreen. Carol and I still engage affably with her at family affairs.

Vito Zeccola is retired from a career as an educational administrator in Gloucester City. He lives with his sweet wife, Dorothy, in Cape May Point, New Jersey, where they enjoy grandchildren and my nephews, Danny and Joey, and niece MaryKay. We are still like brothers, and to quote him, "We are lucky there is a statute of limitations."

Cousin John enjoys semi-retirement as a real estate law maven. He and Peggy take pleasure in extensive travel and nearly constant interaction with their six grandchildren. Their retirement community fits their lifestyle perfectly. I communicate with them often and see them somewhat regularly.

Cousin Bob is wheelchair-bound and is becoming less obstreperous each time Sammy and others visit. Judy and the kids are all doing well and enjoying life. Judy loves her grandchildren and is settled in a retirement community discovered by John and Peg.

Cousin Joe has been gone for 10 years. The apple of his eye, Jesse, is hugely successful as a financial advisor with Wachovia. He has taken his father's place as the leader of his brother and sisters, to whom he provides guidance and support. Joe would be proud.

Cousin Phyllis has her hands full with her grandchildren and the other friends and family members to whom she gives support. Over the last several years, she followed her own career path as Frank eased out of the barber business. They remain that unlikely cute couple from the 50s.

Tommy is in Pittsburgh with his lovely wife, Corby. He just celebrated his 60th birthday and the wedding of his daughter Tara, one of his four children. As loyal a guy as you can find in the family, he should retire soon as an executive with Sunoco. He will have grandchildren to cherish.

Cousin Jimmy is a successful chiropractor in Maine, where he is the beneficiary of the charm and stability of his lovely wife, Jeri, and four children. He is proud of his youngsters' accomplishments and has two grandchildren to celebrate as well.

Cousin Michele died a few years ago, after years of many maladies. She did find happiness with her husband Jim.

Cousin Joey is working hard in the transportation business, continuing to search for a computer opportunity, while providing support to his mom, Aunt Lydia.

Cousin Melvin continues his successful marriage to Brooks. Their children, Melissa and Mason have children of their own, who, bring joy to Aunt Lydia.

Then there is the Mariani clan: Donna and Sammy with Samantha and Dante; Teresa and Richard with Gina, Debra and Richard; Debbie and Walter with Albert, Camile, and Walter; Emelia and Michael with Jayme and Michael; Dominic and Glenda with Giavana; Emidio and Katrina with Natalie and Emidio. The clan lost their matriarch, Maria, in 2006, and she is deeply grieved by one and all.

The Marianis have had all of the progressions of every special family: kids are growing and eventually graduating, weddings are being planned and careers are being built. Major contractors, business leaders, chiropractors, court stenographers, salesmen, politicians, budding civic leaders, potential U.S. senators and educators are all represented in this group. Most importantly, they continue to provide a model to all of us as a loving, caring and close family.

Cousin Michael DiSibio is a master plumber and nearing a well-deserved retirement. His son, Michael, and daughter, Nicole, bring him great pride and joy. He is still in his decades-long marriage to the sweet Ginny, who enjoys a career as a caregiver in the nursing home where my mother resides.

Cousin Joseph DiSibio is approaching retirement as a superb educator and coach at Gloucester City High School, where both he and I are on plaques in the hall. His superb wife, Marie, is in the business world, and sons Joseph and Mark are succeeding as master electrician and recent college graduate, respectively.

Joe Mazzarella lost his son early in life and his wife Carmella when she was in her 50s, and he now lives alone in Pennsauken. I am lucky to see Joe at wakes on occasion, and I still get reports from Cousin Frankie, who cuts his hair and passes along my regards.

Godfather Pippy was found stuffed in a plastic bag in the trunk of his Oldsmobile in 1973, after suffering the effects, in various parts of his body, of five bullets fired at close range from a large caliber handgun. Foul play was suspected.

Dukie Kirk retired from the Camden City Fire Department.

Skippy Flamini joined the Marine Corps, with parental permission, when he turned 17.

Benny Jones went to Trenton State Prison for 2nd degree murder committed during an armed robbery.

James Loving acquired a Beverly Hills post office box and, with a hot band, became a rock semi-star in the South Jersey area. Then, he left California to be an expatriate living in Cambodia, where he still contributes articles to various entertainment media in the U.S.

Ray Granfield retired from the Delaware University System after touching many young people; he now lives with his wife in Seaford, Delaware. We recently chatted.

Patti Whittick Piech retired after a distinguished educational career and lives with her husband, retired IBM executive Joe Piech in Cinnaminson, New Jersey. They greatly enjoy their two daughters and four grandchildren. Patti remains Elaine's closest friend and confidante.

Natale Girgenti retired as an educator after decades and lives alone in Sewell, New Jersey, where he continues to fend off the advances of women seeking long-term relationships. He is thrilled by his granddaughter, Carley, and visits son Stevie and his wife often to spend time with this little beauty despite his fear of flying; he also makes visits to Oregon to call on his dynamic daughter Dina and her husband, Tatts. We have missed spending New Year's Eve together only three times in the last 20 years. We remain like brothers.

Don Allen retired as an educator and author in Denver several years ago and resides in the same house he purchased with his darling Toot more than 30 years ago. They still enjoy the company of each other and their offspring, Josh and Molly. I eagerly await his book of poems.

Frank Caterini is retired from the Wildwood School system after more than three decades. He works part-time and serves proudly as president of the Wildwood Country Club where he achieved Club Champion status. He loves his children, educator Natalie and musician Johnny. We also continue to be like brothers.

Jim Lieber and Margie Hammer continue to practice law in Pittsburgh. Jim has distinguished himself as an author and practitioner before the U.S. Supreme Court, and Margie has a deserved reputation as a fierce combatant in the divorce courts. They reside in a large empty nest, which is frequently visited by their three especially talented daughters, Sara, Molly and Annie. They remain our dear and loyal friends.

Jim and Bunny Kridler reside in Altus, Oklahoma in blissful retirement from government service. Daughter Linda and grandchildren Desarae and Nichole are thankfully close by. Jim is battling the effects of diabetes and a recent complication, which has affected his eyesight.

Jay Craven died of cancer at age 42; tragically, his son also died an early death.

Joe Mango went on disability from Cape May High School before dying of heart disease in his early 50s.

Jim Kelly and his brother Joey succumbed to cancer much too early. Jim was in the middle of an exemplary career as a teacher and championship baseball coach when he met his untimely end.

Diane Lusk is an openly lesbian entrepreneur and retired Gloucester teacher, leading the comfortable, but exciting, life of an unattached single. We communicate often.

Ron Pritchett retired after many years as the principal of Gloucester High School.

Kathy Malan retired as an educator in Gloucester and is married for the second time. Her sons from her first marriage bring her great joy.

Paul Gibbs is a retired Gloucester biology teacher and happy in his art work avocation.

Ron Verdicchio retired from the Ridgewood School District and is an assistant professor at Fairleigh Dickenson University in

North Jersey, where he lives with his wife and daughter. We are still in touch.

Lorenzo Fontana stayed in contact for many years and played guide to several of my relatives who visited Rome. We lost touch in the late 70s.

Frank the Fruitman died from a massive heart attack in 1974. Air conditioning was not implicated as a probable cause. Rose inherited the bags of money he left behind in a safe deposit box.

Eileen Sheedy succumbed to cancer before retirement from Northern Burlington.

Lorraine Gower served as the executive assistant to other superintendents before retiring to be with her husband, retired Northern Burlington teacher Fred Gower.

Chris Schaller died of alcoholism soon after leaving state government in Nevada.

Governor List lobbied for the nuclear industry in favor of the Yucca Mountain site for disposal of high-level nuclear waste. He continues to practice law in the state of Nevada.

Jim and Judy Kosinski are still in close touch with Janis. They are both retired, Jim from law and state government, and Judy from living the well-earned good life in between residences in San Francisco and Reno.

Fred Hittman succumbed to cancer in his 70s, leaving an enviable legacy.

Chuck Mallory is still thinking up new ideas in retirement.

Barry Koh and his delightful wife Susan are enjoying their newly constructed home overlooking the water on the Eastern

Shore of Maryland. The boat tied to their dock provides great fun to children and grandchildren alike. We still socialize with them and always enjoy their company.

Dr. Jacobi is long-retired and living in Hilton Head with his great wife Maureen. We visited them two years ago, along with Tom Anderson, and had a grand time.

Dick Turnau retired to Ford's colony Virginia, having enjoyed as much as possible of all advantages available to any Westinghouse employee.

Leo Duffy is retired and living with his long-suffering wife, Marlene, and spending time with their many children and even more grandchildren at their headquarters in West Chester, Pennsylvania. We saw him last year at the Snowbird resort in Utah on the occasion of a nuclear industry reunion hosted by Ed Helminski and attended by the Kohs.

Ed Helminski went from the Carter White House to the National Governors' Association and eventually started his own publication, the Radioactive Waste Exchange. He lives in Washington, D.C. with his wife, Carol, and travels to the several conferences he holds every year.

Ted Stern is semi-retired. He maintains a rigorous lifestyle as a business consultant and board member, while finally spending time with Liz, his retired educator wife. We remain in touch.

Jim Gallagher retired from Westinghouse Government Services but, as a part-time consultant, continues to extract the benefits befitting a former president of the organization.

Roger Nichols, retired in Jacksonville with his bride Louise, continues to enjoy the game of golf at which he excels.

Tom Anderson is retired on Calawassie Island in South Carolina with his engaging wife Carol. They are loving life in their beautiful home and enjoy the time they spend with their two sons, who both have well-chosen spouses. The grandkids bring them much deserved joy. We are fortunate to be able to see them from time to time.

The fun-loving Jim and Betty Walton, to the initial surprise of all, left the Tri-Cities and have retired in Jackson Hole, Wyoming. They have great times with their sons and grandchildren. We communicate often and see them occasionally.

Bud Russell and his wife Janet still keep up careers in the Tri-Cities. He still sometimes inquires, "How tough can this be?"

Kelso Gillenwater died young from a heart condition complicated by an eating disorder. His loss deprived us of his monumental talent and his incomparable friendship.

Phil Wood also died as a young man, with much left to contribute to his wife and his daughter and his friends.

Joel Bennett left Parsons and retired after a considerable career with Parsons Brinkerhoff. Fortunate to have survived a bout with lymphoma, he recently retired to spend more time with his enchanting wife, Sera, who has a thriving practice as an architect. We still meet when we can.

Although Len Pieroni lost his life on the ill-fated Ron Brown goodwill mission to the Balkans when the government plane crashed in bad weather, I still think of him often as a very special figure.

Holly Coghill continues her career as a superb designer of major proposals. Her proposal work is only exceeded by her performance as a mother to two beautiful girls and a wife to husband Joe. Our paths continue to cross.

Paul and Nadia Butler are as busy as ever with a booming business in homeland security run by Nadia, while Paul, who continues to play a role in the business, also pursues his avocation as a tri-athlete. They reside in South Carolina and grow orchids on a farmette. We dine with them regularly.

Joe Volpe left this earth at the turn of the century leaving his lovely bride a widow. His funeral was attended by hundreds of Washington dignitaries, along with his many friends and acquaintances.

Bill Hall is still the President of what is now Worley Parsons located in Houston, and we chat on rare occasion.

Bob Wood has just, at my urging, joined the Washington Group as a Vice President.

Rod Regan has his own consulting business in Houston, where he lives with wife Suzan.

Bob Alder is working as an executive in Kansas City and his bride Elisabeth, good friend of Carol, commutes between there and their home in Florida.

Steve Hanks is the Chief Executive Officer of Washington Group International. Under his leadership, the corporation exited bankruptcy at $15.30 a share and is now at $60.00 a share, quite an achievement by any financial standard.

Charlie Oliver retired for a second time and lives comfortably on his multi-acre ranch in a most scenic portion of Montana.

Tom Zarges is now the head of Operations for Washington Group in the Office of the Chairman in Boise, Idaho.

Lou Pardi, who lives in Princeton with his wife Dolly, is the successful President of the Power Business Unit for Washington Group and a would-be comedian extraordinaire.

Steve Marchetti is the President of Washington Group Services located in Cleveland, but he can often be found elsewhere. He finds it easy to quit smoking; he has done it 12 times. When he is in town, we sometimes get together with him and his wife, Annette.

Pres Rahe replaced me as President of Energy and Environment and exceeded the records I had set. He's a regular golf companion of Carol and me, and we both enjoy the company of Pres and his wife Jerry Ann. He keeps the makers of Nicorette in business.

Dave Pethick is the Senior Vice President of Business Development for the E&E unit, and we sometimes get to spend time with Dave and wife Pam. His recovery from a rare disease was remarkable.

Jennifer Large fights off offers from other major corporations and has taken on significant human resources responsibilities for Washington Group. She was the co-recipient of the Presidents Award for Employee Development. When not in the office or traveling on business, she helps out at the SideTrack, the bar and restaurant owned by her husband Chuck.

Steve Muller heads up Employee Development for the Washington Group and recently received the prestigious President's Award for his remarkable service. He continues to aid me in my writing avocation by inspiring me and designing my books. Mostly, he enriches the lives of the people he touches, including Carol and me who wine, dine and converse with him regularly.

Chris Verenes left the corporation shortly after my retirement to accept the presidency of the Security Federal Bank. He spends what free time he has with his wife, Carol, who recently retired from her job as a transportation coordinator. They delight in their two children, Bradley and Natalie. We bank with Chris and bank on his friendship.

Aunt Sally continues to work as a realtor and is still going strong despite a couple of rounds of shoulder surgery this past year. She has become an extremely close friend, almost another member of the family, and to be a member of Sally's family is to have an association with many people. We have been introduced by Sally to many special people who we now count among our friends, including Bill and Sandy Tucker, K.D. Justyn, Mark and Vicki Meyer, Tom and Susan Hallman and You Bet Patterson.

So, too, has my life continued. By design, I work about six days a month. It is fearless work, in that I cannot fail in my present endeavors. My fear of failure is at last fully and finally retired. Unfortunately, my flaws are intact. I am compelled to answer a ringing phone, I lack patience, I create stress when none is thrust upon me, and I am still often wrong but never in doubt.

Carol continues to endure me, and we have finally settled on a retirement path. When we left Yellow Pine Road, we purchased a large home in the Kings Creek Country Club in Rehoboth Beach, Delaware, where we had sold our original retirement home. We intended to live in Delaware for nine months a year, and we purchased a small home in the Woodside Plantation in Aiken, South Carolina for the remaining three winter months. After the first year, that plan was altered when we decided we needed something bigger in order to spend a little more time in Aiken.

We built a 3,000 square foot home to solve the four month problem. After we moved into the new house, we decided to stay in Aiken for nine or 10 months a year and sell the "primary" home in Delaware. We are now building our "retirement" home while living in our 3,000 square foot home in Aiken and selling the home in Delaware. That is the "final" plan we have settled upon. At least that was the plan when Carol left for work this morning. She has been recruited back into the legal department of the E&E unit to bail them out of a temporary overload. The assignment was supposed to last a few weeks. That was over six months ago. In her limited spare time, she assumed the monumental task—working in tandem with Stephen Muller—of editing this manuscript. The task was made more difficult by the shortcomings of the author's first draft. After receiving threats of a fate akin to that of Godfather Pippy's, I have promised them I would not start another literary venture, at least for now. Stay tuned for the continuing saga from post-retirement DiSibioland.

Appendices

What I've Done

December 2006

While my most rewarding personal experiences are inter-twined with my loves–my extended family, my mates, my children, my grandchildren and my friends—I have been blessed with rich experiences over my 65 plus years of life.

Some interesting things I've done:

- Traveled to 32 countries
- Climbed the pyramids in Egypt
- Rode a camel in the Egyptian desert
- Strolled the Roman Coliseum
- Climbed the Eiffel Tower and the dome of the Vatican
- Toured scores of museums including the Louvre, Vatican, van Gogh, Salvador Dali, the Victoria and Alexander, the British Museum, the Stockholm City Museum, the New York Museum of Modern Art, and many of the Smithsonian museums
- Viewed the world from the top of the Swiss Alps
- Toured a game park in South Africa
- Toured a remote nuclear disposal site in Korea
- Dove on a fully armed atomic sub (Alabama) in the Puget Sound
- Owned scores of cars including a '58 Vette and an '80 DeLorean
- Witnessed the first moon landing while at graduate school in Italy

- Saw many celebrities, including Sinatra, Dean (Martin), Sammy (Davis), Tony Bennett, Bette Midler, James Taylor, The Smothers Brothers, the Supremes, Little Anthony, Fats Domino, Dennis Miller, Allen King, Pavarotti and Andrea Boccelli
- Attended a performance of Aida with Leontyne Price in an ancient amphitheater in Verona, Italy
- Jumped from an airplane at 11,000 feet
- Owned watercraft from 16 feet to 46 feet in length, docked in waters from Tahoe to Charleston
- Golfed Cypress Point, Pebble Beach and Pine Valley
- Played golf on five continents
- Held membership in eleven private country clubs
- Attended the Masters Tournament on several occasions, witnessing Mickelson's victory in 2004 and Tiger's in 2005. In 2005, attended with son Dean and grandson Anthony, and we appeared in a Sports Illustrated photo
- Attended the Ryder Cup in the United Kingdom at the Belfry
- Shook the hands of three U.S. Presidents
- Entertained a Saudi prince in my home
- Enjoyed an Arabian feast with the prince in the Saudi desert
- Was published in several professional journals
- Gambled in Las Vegas, Atlantic City, Switzerland, Italy, England, Palm Springs, Spain, Rio and Costa Rica
- Ate fish eyes in Korea and drank snake's blood in Taiwan
- Lived in Washington (twice), Nevada, Colorado, Maryland (twice), South Carolina, Pennsylvania (twice), Delaware (twice) and New Jersey
- Went to JFK's funeral with Frank
- Attended undergraduate and graduate school part- and full-time from 1959 to 1974 while pursuing BA, MA and Ed.D degrees and attended special programs at Harvard and Johns Hopkins Center for International Relations in Bologna, Italy
- Had one heart attack in 1995 and a sextuple bypass in 1999

- Appeared on television news and interview programs more then 30 times over my career
- Owned and operated all manner of vehicles, including golf carts, motorcycles, mopeds, every type of car, and every class of boat, from runabouts to yachts
- Performed numerous impromptu animal rescues
- Participated in organized sports programs in baseball, softball, football, fencing, tennis, gymnastics, bowling, bocce, billiards, darts and deep sea and fly fishing
- Coached high school state champions in baseball (1971); inducted into Gloucester City sports hall of fame in 2006
- Produced and directed four plays with high school participants
- Traveled the underground transportation systems in London, Tokyo, Seoul, Paris, San Francisco, New York, Boston and Washington, D.C.
- Visited Nazi concentration camp in Poland
- Made a confession in the Vatican with Natale
- Had an audience with Pope Paul II with Joe, John, and Bob
- Saw scores of sports greats, teams, games and venues, including Wilt Chamberlain, Mickey Mantle, Roger Maris, Tiger, Arnie, Jack, the Shark, Freddy, Gentle Ben, Mohammed Ali, Joe Frazier, Ted Williams, Willie Mays, Stan Musial, Bernie Parent, Bobbie Clark, the Whiz Kids, the Philadelphia Athletics, Julius Erving, Shibe Park, Yankee Stadium, Dodger Stadium, Candlestick Park, Three Rivers Stadium, Joe Theisman, John Riggins, Temple, Penn, St. Joe's and Villanova basketball games
- Took the Chunnel train from London to Paris, the bullet train from Osaka to Tokyo, and the ICE train from DC to NY. I rode the caboose on the Jersey Seashore Line with Uncle Phil
- Was granted a United States patent for nuclear waste disposal technology
- Co-authored the Low Level Waste Policy Act of 1981, which became the law of the land

- Authored "Reel Lessons in Leadership" in 2005 and sold in excess of 2000 copies (published by the Paladin Group LLC)

Career highlights

- Mort's Deli in Philadelphia 1955
- Joe's Meat Market 1955-59
- Joe Cini's clothing manufacturing (sweatshop) 1959-62
- New York Shipbuilding Corp. (USS Kittyhawk, NS Savannah) 1960
- Campbell Soup Co. 1961-62
- Wood Conversion Company 1963
- Wildwood High School 1963-66
- Johnny's Bar and Riptide Nightclub 1963-66
- Gloucester City School System 1966-75 (Teacher-Assistant Superintendent)
- Voorhees Swim Club 1967-69
- Woodstream Swim Club 1970-72
- Northern Burlington Regional Schools 1975-78 (Superintendent)
- Nevada State Superintendent of Public Instruction 1978
- Director of Human Resources of Nevada 1978-1981
- Hittman Nuclear 1981-1983
- Westinghouse Electric Corporation 1981-93
- Created "You In Print" business in three major malls 1989-90
- Parsons Corporation 1993-2001
- Washington Group International 2001-2004 (consultant 2004-2007)
- Developed and presented leadership course to corporate executives
- Presented "Reel Lessons in Leadership" seminar to Department of the Navy in 2006
- Presented "Reel Lessons" seminar to Western Regional Board of Boy Scouts of America in Las Vegas in 2006
- PaR Systems board member 2004-
- Post-retirement consultant for AREVA and Perot systems
- Established the Paladin Group LLC in 2005 ("Have Solutions, Will Travel")
- Elected to the board of Quanta Services 2006 (NYSE)
- Spent Thanksgiving Day 2006 with my son, watching my grandson compete in a junior golf tournament in Myrtle Beach
- Authored and published my memoir as a Christmas present in 2006

...So far, so good

Things I've Learned

1. Good humor trumps good looks.
2. Success is born out of fear.
3. You can only control you.
4. Families are roots, friends are branches, the rest are leaves.
5. Most people only want to hear about themselves.
6. When injured or facing adversity, "walk it off."
7. Curiosity trumps knowledge, wisdom trumps curiosity.
8. God created man so women would have a project. Really, she did.
9. Loyalty given is loyalty gotten.
10. Being a "people person" is not a talent.
11. Gossip is jealousy verbalized.
12. Wanting to be alone is worse than being alone.
13. God has a sense of humor; thus, politicians
14. Anger management is an oxymoron; only the reaction is managed.
15. Convenience trumps ecological concerns, as evidenced by disposable diapers and the plastic bag aisle at Safeway.
16. Even disliked parents are missed when they are gone.
17. Unguided empowerment equals anarchy.
18. Great leaders are great followers.
19. Contentment: no greater asset.
20. Charisma is a gift that cannot be purchased.
21. Men like men a lot more than women like women.

22. Humor is the way to a man's heart.
23. Displays of vulnerability are the way to a woman's heart.
24. Social security is an oxymoron.
25. Surrender wealth before reputation; you can regain wealth.
26. Invest in relationships; the returns are ensured for life.
27. Trust is relinquishing control without a plan.
28. Passion is unbridled joy.
29. Compassion is empathy displayed.
30. Insight is discovering what others already know.
31. Grandchildren: responsibility once removed.
32. Bigotry requires arrogance.
33. When there is a leadership vacuum, leaders fill it.
34. Competence begets confidence.
35. Customer service is an anachronism.
36. Always give, but never take credit.
37. Wealth does not compensate for bad manners.
38. Slippery slope: habit - addiction - obsession.
39. Integrity: doing the right thing when no one will ever know.
40. Doing the right thing trumps doing things right.
41. Doing the right things right=success.

An Oral History

Louise Vitagliano talks with Jesse Vitagliano
April 29, 1991

Q: Why did your parents leave Italy in 1912, and did they ever intend to return?

A: No, they never intended to go back. My mother had a sister who was married and came to America. They were very close and she wanted to be with her. She left a little town in Italy called Canale Montorano; a province of Rome. She only had the one sister but she also had two brothers. Once her sister arrived, she told my mother how things were so much better here in America.

Q: Why did your Aunt come to America?

A: One of the men in the village in Italy came to America, saved some money and came back looking for a wife. He married my mother's sister. They sent money back to Italy for my mother, father, sister Anna and I to come to America.

Q: What sort of work did your mother and father do in Italy?

A: My mother did not work. The men worked in the fields, whatever work was available. They worked in the olive groves—farm work.

Q: Did you ever know your grandparents?

A: I did not know them to see them, but my mother used to write letters and she would hold my hand to sign my name. My father didn't know how to read or write; he only knew how to sign his name. My mother was very talented. She knew how to read and write—and she would write to my father's people in Italy.

Q: Why do you think so many Italians left Italy?

A: People talked about how great it was in America. The streets were paved in gold; there was so much work, and one by one people came. Once here, everyone helped each other.

Q: Did mostly men come to America first?

A: Yes, my mother's brother was here. He was here before the two sisters. People who had it much more difficult in the south of Italy may have come earlier. Many men came to America first. When I went back to visit Italy, some years later, there were women waiting at the docks to see if their husbands were on the ships. The women were crying, asking if we knew their husbands because they had never returned. This was in 1957, Jess. I was at the dock waiting to greet my cousin because he had been working in Canada. The people would look at me and ask me questions because they knew I was an American because of the way I was dressed.

Q: When you arrived to Ellis Island, did you go directly to western Pennsylvania?

A: I am not sure if we came through Ellis Island or Boston because I know we somehow ended up in Boston. When we arrived they locked us in a small room because there was no one to meet us when we arrived. My mother only had some hard bread for us to eat and we were hungry. When we came over on the boat, we were deep in the low side of the boat; there was very little light and nothing to eat. There was another Italian family that was with us was going all the way to California. They had even less than we did so my mother shared everything she had, the bread and some tonic water called "fernete." It is like liquor that you could get at a drug store or liquor store. The tonic kept you going. My mother had all this stuff tied up in a cloth like the one you see on TV with the hobos. My mother gave everything we had away. Anyway, when we were on the train we all had tags pinned on us which said "Mistake." The conductor would point to the tag and say "mistake." Our parents thought the conductor was saying "Beefsteak" and that the tag meant we were finally going to eat a beefsteak and they got all excited; the "mistake" meant we were on the wrong train. The conductor was yelling at us to sit down. This was when we were locked in the station house. That night my father and another man snuck out through a window to look for food for us.

Q: Were others from Canale Montorano in the place you were going to in Pennsylvania?

A: Yes. There were people there, like my aunt. Others came at different times.

Q: When you arrived in Pennsylvania did you your Dad start in the coal mines?

A: Yes, he started in the coal mines right away. He was there three months, there was a cave-in, and every bone in his body was crushed. He was taken to the hospital in a wagon all the way to Phillipsburg, Pa (near Altoona).

Q: Please tell me more about your father working in the coal mines.

A: After the cave-in, he went back to work. While he was out of work, we had no money and my mother could not speak much, if any, English. The people at the hospital would make fun of her.

In addition, there was only one store in the little town we lived. In the store, she would go and she had to point at things she wanted. Again, she could not speak the language and she had no money (there was no welfare, no workman's compensation.) Other Italian people from the town would help. Here was my Mother with a husband in the hospital and two babies at home. Once a lady was making fun of her in the store, and she took her basket and hit this American lady in the head with her basket (laughter).

Q: What other ways were you and other Italians made fun of? When you went to school, was it all Italian kids?

A: No. There were other children of many nationalities—Polish, French, American. We always went home for lunch and they were jealous because we went home and had a hot lunch whereas the others ate cold sandwiches.

Q: Did your family own the home you lived in while in Pennsylvania?

A: No. We rented.

Q: Did the owners of the coal mine dictate where or how you lived, like in company houses?

A: Yes, there were company houses but we managed some way not to live in a company house; everyone else did though.

My father had bad rheumatism from being underground. His body did not take good to the coal mines. One lady—Mrs. Mountz, owned the coal mines, she was a millionaire. She had a beautiful home and servants. She owned the company store and she sold everything; you had to buy everything from her. The next thing you know, for some reason, there would be a strike, no work. She would close the mines and then there was no money and then you had to buy things from the store on the book, on credit—and then when the mines opened you had to pay back; no more money. It went on and on—the men eventually rebelled; went on strike, and then she brought in strikebreakers from Philadelphia (militia); there were shootings and people were killed. If my sister and I were boys, we would have been in the coal mines with my father to help earn for the family.

A girl from our town in Janesville went off with one of the strike-breakers to Philadelphia and she came back and told us how beautiful Camden was. My mother and father knew another family who also moved out to Camden, and they wrote letters to my parents saying there was lots of work. My father, sister and I went to visit to see what type of work there was. I was 15 and my sister was 13. Aunt Anna and I got a job at John R. Evans—a leather factory. We came to Camden to get established and to get jobs. My father went to work for Public Service, digging ditches for electricity, for gas; this was in 1924. We came in May and in June or July my mother came with the other kids. Aunt Pat was very sick, they did not expect her to live.

My mother used to get a newspaper in Italian called the "Progresso," and this is where I first heard of Sacco and Vanzetti.

Q: What was your mother like?

A: She helped all the families in the town. There was rarely a doctor—if anything serious happened while in Pennsylvania the doctor would take two to three days to arrive. In the meantime, my mother was the midwife; she would help the sick; she would make mustard plasters. She would stay up all night and make the parents of sick children go to bed to give them a rest. I use to get mad. I would say, "Gosh sake, why do you run and help others?" She would yell at me that I didn't understand. She was also the undertaker; she would dress the dead, comb their hair, and put them in the coffin. She also helped mend troubled relationships between other people. When she died in 1942 people from all over, including from Pennsylvania rode the train all night to be at the funeral.

Q: When your mother died, was Uncle Mikey in the war at the time?

A: He was in California. My mother had a stroke and she lived for 7 days. Uncle Mikey was on leave and couldn't be contacted. She was dead when he got home. When he came home, he got married the next month in Bridgeton. Only the Morronis were present; none of us went because our mother had just died. He got married all alone and we *should* have went.

Q: When you left school in the 6th or maybe the 7th grade—why did you leave school?

I don't know Jess; I just didn't want to go to school anymore.

[Gram's phone rings loudly and the taped interview ends.]

Printed in the United States
128403LV00002BA/3/A

9 780977 927326